WHAT MATTERS MOST

WHAT MATTERS MOST

Conversations on the Art of Living

Edited by Anthony Morgan

agenda
publishing

For Michael Bavidge, the philosopher

First published in 2023 by Agenda Publishing

Agenda Publishing Limited
PO Box 185
Newcastle upon Tyne
NE20 2DH

www.agendapub.com

ISBN 978-1-78821-623-4 (hardcover)
ISBN 978-1-78821-624-1 (paperback)

British Library Cataloguing-in-Publication Data
A catalogue record for this book is
available from the British Library

Typeset in Nocturne by Patty Rennie

Printed and bound in the UK by TJ Books

Contents

Preface

The Egyptian philosopher Plotinus (205–270 CE) insisted that philosophy should be concerned with nothing less than το τιμιώτατον (pronounced "to timiotaton"), generally translated as *what matters most*. Writing in the twentieth century, the Russian existentialist Lev Shestov considers this to be "the best and only complete definition of philosophy".[1] I'm pretty sure, however, that neither Plotinus nor Shestov would consider this volume to be το τιμιώτατον. After all, it does not follow their lead in seeking the transcendent, prophetic or mystical through the philosophical. Come to think of it, they may not consider it a work of philosophy *at all*.

Is living an art? Then it requires knowledge and effort.[2] "The art of living" has been captured by retreat centres, wellness escapes, therapy rooms. It brings to mind virtue, happiness, peace, mindfulness, freedom. This volume, by contrast, seeks the art of living in the midst of all the spectacular messiness generated by an aggressive, violent, anxiety-ridden, acquisitive, cruel and lustful species. The conversations that follow are rooted in those questions that matter most to us as citizens of increasingly fractious societies and inhabitants of an increasingly fractured planet: How do we cultivate the art of living under oppression when this oppression may be permanent? (Part I); How do we cultivate the art of living together when the cocoon-like embrace of our echo chamber feels so attractive? (Part II); How do we cultivate the art of living with technology in the face of prophecies of a forthcoming AI apocalypse? (Part III); and How do we cultivate the art of living through crisis when the climate catastrophe has served to shatter any illusion of solidarity or a common world? (Part IV).

---

1. See his 1932 essay collection, *In Job's Balances*.
2. I am paraphrasing Erich Fromm's book, *The Art of Loving* (New York: Harper, 1956).

In autumn 2020, *The Philosopher* launched its first series of free "digital dialogues" after our in-person events in the UK were cancelled due to the pandemic. These events have proven surprisingly successful, with over 12,000 attendees from 109 countries tuning in to date. This attests to an ongoing (ineradicable?) public desire to participate in rich philosophical explorations of important contemporary questions. Most of the conversations that follow are edited transcripts of these events.[3]

I am enormously grateful to Zara Bain, Frances Darling, and the team at Academic Audio Transcription for their help with transcribing and editing these chapters. Jeremy Bendik-Keymer offered a number of important editorial interventions, including some thoughts on how this collection should be structured, while alicehank winham highlighted a number of areas where my own contributions to this volume could be improved. Kathrine Cuccuru, Emil Kunna and Alexandre Leskanich all chipped in with crucial editorial support when my energies were flagging in the final stages of getting this volume together. An anonymous referee made numerous suggestions across numerous domains – all of them useful. Steven Gerrard at Agenda Publishing has been extremely supportive as this book has taken shape. I am excited at the prospect of building a long-term relationship between Agenda and *The Philosopher*. Nick Halliday (of Halliday Books) has designed consistently brilliant covers for *The Philosopher* these past five years for a fraction of what he should be paid. I am delighted that he agreed to design the cover for this volume and remain overwhelmed by Nick's generosity these past years. I feel a huge debt of gratitude to all those who participated in the events, agreed to be part of this volume, and took the time to edit their contributions. Your work is amazing and I am proud to have been able to collaborate with you all. I also offer thanks to the thousands of people who have attended the events these past couple of years. As long as you keep coming, we will keep running them! Finally, none of this would have been possible without the immense generosity and commitment of Michael Bavidge, Joanna Ciafone, William Eckersley and the editorial board members at *The Philosopher*.

Anthony Morgan
New Haven, CT

---

3. For more information on *The Philosopher* and the events series, visit: https://thephilosopher1923.org.

PART I

LIVING UNDER OPPRESSION

We begin with those who bear the greatest burdens of our current reality – those who remain violated, exploited, marginalized and powerless – and the systems of oppression – patriarchy, white supremacy, capitalism (to invoke the unholy trinity) – that generate and sustain these burdens.

Gender theorist Paisley Currah argues that prison abolition, the adoption of free universal healthcare, and a large-scale assault on income inequality "would make the *most* difference to the *most* trans people".[1] To riff on Simone de Beauvoir, no oppressed population can be free until *all* oppressed populations are free.[2] As I write, however, feminists remain divided over the status of trans people, while white working-class Americans continue to accept the psychological "wages of whiteness"[3] rather than unify their interests with those of poor Black Americans.

After a long, overlooked history, the theory of intersectionality finally broke onto the global stage in the late 1980s.[4]

---

1. This quote is from Paisley Currah, *Sex Is as Sex Does: Governing Transgender Identity* (New York: NYU Press, 2022).
2. The quote I have in mind is: "The other's freedom alone is capable of necessitating my being. My essential need is therefore to be faced with free men" (from her 1944 essay, "Pyrrhus and Cineas").
3. This phrase is from W. E. B. Du Bois' 1935 book, *Black Reconstruction in America*.
4. For an account of this history, see Reiland Rabaka's 2022 essay, "Intersectionality" (published in the spring issue of *The Philosopher*).

Through emphasizing the intersections between different dimensions of oppression, it opened up the possibility of challenging the idea of a single axis of oppression, showing that all axes of oppression are inextricably linked. But how many axes are there, and how far do they reach not just into human life, but into animal and vegetal life?

In the midst of all this, certain oppressed populations continue to be overlooked. Psychiatric populations, for example, experience some of the most appalling and inhumane treatment imaginable, and yet Mad activism remains a movement that few activists engage with – or even know about.[5] How widely can the reach of human compassion and solidarity be extended?

"In oppression, the oppressor oppresses himself".[6] The most dangerous populations are those who are oppressed but fail to recognize their own oppression; reaffirming their identity at the expense of others is their legacy to the world.

To paraphrase Lewis R. Gordon, the biggest enemy of oppression is the realization of its irrelevance; the result is individual oppressors without the structures of oppression.[7] What, then, are the conditions of possibility for the irrelevance of oppression?

---

5. To find out more about Mad activism, you can subscribe to the mental health magazine, *Asylum*: https://asylummagazine.org/.
6. This quote is from Jean-Paul Sartre's posthumously published book, *Notebooks for an Ethics*. (Chicago, IL: University of Chicago Press, 1992).
7. The original quote, from Gordon's 2021 essay, "Racialization and Human Reality" (published in the summer issue of *The Philosopher*), is: "The enemy of racism . . . is the realization of its irrelevance. When racism is unable to permeate institutions – through organising their structures – it ceases to be anything more than individual aspirations. Put differently, the result is racists without racism".

1

The politics of gender and identity

Finn Mackay in conversation with Jana Bacevic

Can we find a way through and even around the messy "gender wars" currently raging on- and offline? A 2021 profile of Finn Mackay in *The Guardian* described them as "the writer hoping to help end the gender wars". However, in the days leading up to this conversation in early April 2022, the UK government reneged on their promise to ban conversion therapy for trans people and Finn acknowledges that the gender wars have significantly worsened in the time following the publication of their book, *Female Masculinities and the Gender Wars*, in 2021. In this conversation, Finn explores the histories of feminist exclusions; the deepening political antagonism towards the trans community; the performance of gender; and much more.

FINN MACKAY is a Senior Lecturer in Sociology at the University of the West of England. A longstanding feminist activist, Finn founded the London Feminist Network in 2004 and is a frequent media commentator on feminist and LGBTQI+ topics.

JANA BACEVIC is assistant professor at Durham University, UK, and member of the editorial board of *The Philosopher*. Her work is in social theory, philosophy of science, and political economy of knowledge production, with particular emphasis on the relationship between epistemological, moral and political elements.

Jana Bacevic (**JB**): Your recent work has drawn attention to the fact that the so-called "gender wars" have a longer intellectual history than most people realize. What are some of the key points in the history of this debate, especially when it comes to the UK and the US?

Finn Mackay (**FM**): There are many different lineages here, but I

will focus on the feminist history. I come from a political background of organizing in the women's liberation movement and
the women's peace movement. I have worked with radical feminists and radical feminist organizations, and I have learned a
lot from radical feminists and revolutionary feminists, who
themselves had been active in legacy building, protest and
legal campaigning back in the 1970s and 1980s. I have also been
involved in LGBT organizing and queer community-building
for a long time.

As a result, I have been especially saddened to see radical
feminism, a politics that I identified with and resonated with,
being used in name to beat other minoritized groups: trans,
transgender and queer people. There is a lot of misunderstand-
ing about what radical feminism is generally, and particularly
on this question. The fact is that the issue of inclusion within
feminism is much bigger than the question of trans inclusion
– feminism of all strands has grappled with, and continues to
grapple with, alienating and destructive elements of racism,
classism, and so on. But it is radical feminism that has come to
be seen as the foundational exclusionary feminist movement,
despite the fact that trans women were historically present
and involved in the legacy-building second wave of feminism.

One thing I find interesting is that people will only selectively pick points from radical feminist texts about gender.
They don't, for example, promote political lesbianism as a way
to undermine patriarchy or argue that in order to destabilize
patriarchy people should build women's communities. They
are not out there agitating that the beauty industry is a form of
violence against women or that compulsory heterosexuality is
an oppression of women or that all women should eschew femininity on political grounds or that the nuclear family should
be ended because it is a site of the recreation of power relationships. In short, people are only using the name of radical
feminism when they want to push an anti-trans argument.

JB: Do you see the current "gender wars" as a continuation of
or a break with the histories that you have just described?

FM: In the contemporary world, our media has taken to framing the so-called "gender wars" as a binary issue. You have to
pick a side and then stick to it. The media has always loved a cat
fight within feminism. It wants to set generation against generation. And I think that demeans the seriousness and validity of

feminism and the women's liberation movement as social justice movements with complex histories and methods and forms
of activism. It also demeans the huge human rights issues and
debates surrounding trans rights.

In the UK in 2015, the cross-party Women and Equalities
Select Committee organized to look at updating the Gender
Recognition Act (GRA) 2004. They presented their first report
the next year, proposing liberalization and reform so that it
would be easier and cheaper to get what's called a Gender
Recognition Certificate (GRC), the document showing that a
person has satisfied the criteria for legal recognition of their
acquired gender. In 2017, Theresa May was at a PinkNews
Awards dinner (an LGBT awards ceremony), and she made a
speech saying that being trans is not a mental illness, and that
the Conservative Party was going to move forward and liberalize the GRA. At the time, the Conservative Party seemed to be
using this as more fuel to be seen as progressive on top of the
role they played in securing equal marriage.

Looking back, either they were naive and thought that no
one would pay any attention or they just didn't care. Because in
2018 they put the reform of the Gender Recognition Act out to
public consultation. This is very interesting, because if something is a human rights law, it should be a matter of human
rights law. Why put that out to public consultation? I think if
we put many things out to public consultation now about anti-
racism, inclusion, refugee rights, and so on, you would get
quite a lot of hostile responses saying that things as they are
have already gone too far, and we shouldn't have any more. But
if something is a human right, it's a human right – and tough if
some people don't like it.

The public consultation then led to a fundamental mis-
reading around so-called "self-ID". It looked at ways that other
countries have done this through legal processes, for example
via a statutory declaration like you would have for a change of
name. But lots of groups then started mobilizing, as they were
afraid that we were going to find ourselves in a situation where
the category of "woman" was going to be erased. *Anyone* could
now be a woman. As the narrative went, all a man would have
to do is to go online and change his documentation and legal
sex-marker in order to enter an intimate space with women
and children for the purposes of sexual abuse and assault. And
then change his gender markers back again. Even if that is a
rather far-fetched and extreme scenario, it was feared that the

idea of self-ID would make women even more unsafe than they are already. The sad reality, of course, is that men who want to rape and abuse women and children are still most likely to do that in their families, in their own homes, in the homes of friends and relatives. They do not need to go through a legal process of living and identifying as a trans woman in order to rape and abuse. But there were a lot of concerns around this one section of the consultation, and many anti-trans-inclusion groups and campaigns against liberalizing the GRA started around that time. And ever since then, this debate has carried on vociferously in the UK.

JB: These days, it seems that *everyone* has a position on trans rights, even those who have been in no way impacted by the fight for trans rights, the GRA, and so on. What do you think is the source of this polarization, and what is it driven by?

FM: We're dealing with a backlash against a human rights movement that has only recently come to wider public attention. It was only in 2014 that *Time* magazine did its "Transgender Tipping Point" cover, and Caitlyn Jenner was on the cover of *Vanity Fair* the year after. The social justice movement for trans rights had been going on for decades, but it only emerged onto the public stage in the last decade. And as with any social justice movement, when it finally hits the mainstream you will always get a backlash. For many people, once they even become aware of a movement, they already think it has gone too far. They would rather they had never found out about it in the first place.

Another polarizing element is the spread of misinformation. To take a classic example from last year, there was coverage in the press about how health trusts in Brighton and Sussex were no longer going to refer to anyone as a "mother" or "pregnant woman", or talk about "breastfeeding" for new mothers. They were *only* going to be allowed to talk about "chest-feeders" and "birthing parents". And then, of course, the truth came out that the trust had in fact been working with a group to come up with some specific guidance for midwives and health professionals who were working with trans parents – some terms and definitions that trans parents might use and would like to be used. However, by that point the dominant line in most broadsheets and tabloids was something like, "It's all gone too far now. You can't even use the term 'breast-feeding' in Brighton".

This kind of thing creates the public idea, which the media does not do enough to correct, that services, words, and spaces are being taken away, when this is just not happening. In fact, what *is* happening is an ongoing situation where minority groups who may become parents, or are going through health-care, have historically received bad treatment, have not been given terms to describe themselves, or have had stigmatiz-ing terms put upon them. It is *those* minority groups that have been wrestling with having no spaces, no terms, no language, no recognition – not the majority. Rather than a battle for scarce resources, this is an *additive* model – more services, more spaces, more awareness. And that can only be a good thing. But it is understandable that people who believe the headlines are quite exercized about it, because it does sound like whole insti-tutions are being changed in order to accommodate the needs of less than one per cent of the population. That's not actually what is happening, but people believe that it is.

JB: There's definitely something to be said about anxiety over status and identity. The closer to the norm that people are, the more anxiety it seems to provoke in them to think about the fact that not only may there be people who do not fit these norms, but that they may also no longer be closeted (and may even use the same bathrooms as they will). Where do you think that sort of anxiety comes from, and how does it map onto the collective rights issue?

FM: In the UK context, we cannot overlook the politics of scarcity that we're living with, and which is being actively pro-moted and whipped up by the Conservative government to justify their own ideological cutbacks to community services, to the welfare state, and so on. This in turn serves to generate a zero-sum approach to essential services and public goods which will inevitably lead to worries about new groups coming in and questions about who they are taking services and money away from. This has always affected social justice movements.

More generally, in precarious and insecure times, people find ideas of fixity especially seductive: they hold on tightly to a rose-tinted idea of the nuclear family, to times when "we maybe didn't have much and we had to work hard, but at least a man was a man, a woman was a woman. Mums were mums, dads were dads, and children being raised at home". Of course, this whole idea was always a fiction. Family has always been a troubled and fractious site of human relationships and abuses of power. I think people know that. But it doesn't make the *idea* of it any less seductive. This fits in with a general resurgence across Europe and North America of pro-natalist sex- and gender-conservatism, and a call to a return to traditional values. Two weeks before Russian bombs started falling in Ukraine, Oliver Dowden, the chairman of the Conservative Party, went to the US to speak to the Heritage Foundation – an anti-abortion, anti-choice, anti-divorce, anti-LGBT organization. And he made a speech saying something along the lines of how it was no surprise that strong countries like Russia and China are threatening the West, because the West is too busy worrying about pronouns, pulling down our statues, disrespecting our own traditions and history. This echoes very similar things that Putin has said himself about the dangers of the "decadent West". So, there is a backlash coming from fundamentalist religious organizations, right-wing states, right-wing parties and nationalist parties.

Finally, a lot of the anger comes from the fact that the media tells us we're having this "gender revolution", that there are a lot of young queer people that don't want to be boxed in or use traditional sex/gender labels. And I think some women are mobilizing because there is still very little evidence of an actual revolution in power between women and men. The pandemic has exacerbated pre-existing inequalities even more: women are more likely to have taken time off work; to have reduced hours; to have lost their jobs; to be subject to pregnancy or maternity discrimination; to be taking on more childcare and more work in the home. I think some people feel, "Hang on. We haven't actually sorted out gender equality yet. How are we suddenly having this gender revolution, when there's no concrete change in power between these groups that we call women and men?"

JB: Obviously, debates around what gender is, what sex is, what a man is, what a woman is, and so on, have become very heated. Do you think that there's anything useful to draw on from these debates? Do you think there is a constructive way, or even a need, to rebuild the discussion around gender?

FM: Of course we should have these debates. In fact, ideas around gender abolition and a post-gender society are radical feminist ideas. But when I see some of the discourse about rolling back existing rights for trans people, I find that quite extreme. I see arguments online saying that we should repeal the whole Gender Recognition Act because being trans is a delusion and we shouldn't have laws that cater to people's delusions. When you see these arguments, you wonder why any trans rights organization would want to have a polite or "civilized" debate with people who want to take away their rights.

There is also an important debate to be had about how gender is a delusion *in itself*. Why don't people who are critical of gender go out to stag and hen parties in Newcastle, Bristol or Leeds on a Friday or Saturday night, and go up to (presumably non-trans) women who are dressed in a feminine, sexualized way, and (presumably non-trans) men who are dressed in a heterosexualized, masculinized way, and ask *them* why they are reinforcing and perpetuating gender stereotypes? We see this process in operation from birth onwards. I could go out now and get a baby t-shirt that says "Supermodel in training" for a girl and "Future man of steel" for a boy. The public likes to accuse trans or queer people of putting their identities in people's faces. But the very opposite is the case. The public are putting heterosexualized, normative sex and genders in people's faces *all the time*. They are training babies into these roles from the beginning.

Gender criticism, if it means anything, should start at home – people should critique their own gender and their own gender identity, because everyone is operating within this system. Why is it that only trans people on their journey through, and presentation of, gender, gender roles and gender identity, are seen as some weird freakish problem, and not everybody else – not the majority group, who are also "doing" gender and presenting gender?

I am worried that these culture wars may have to get very bad before they get better. We've just seen the Conservative government do this U-turn over trans conversion therapy. They are basically sending out the message that it is open season on trans people. And I think that is horrific and shocking. If I was to write my book *Female Masculinities and the Gender Wars* again, I would be a lot less hesitant in critiquing some individuals and organizations who have now come out and said, "Remove the GRA. Trans is an illness." It has certainly got a lot more extreme since the book was published in 2021. And let's not forget that in the US, using trans rights as a wedge issue was *openly* announced by right-wing evangelical groups. For example, the Family Research Council (FRC) ran its annual Values Voter Summit in Washington, DC back in 2017 at which speakers said that the LGBT movement had gone too far, but that they can use the "T" and separate that off to bring the whole movement down – because trans people are less palatable to the public. They refer to the movements for trans rights as a third wave of attack against the nuclear family. And they've succeeded in getting that to be part of the mainstream discourse. So I worry that we are at a bit of a fork in the road.

JB: I am interested in the fact that we hear so much more about trans women than trans men in this debate. Why is this?

FM: There is a sexism that goes on around debates about trans men and trans masculine identity. They get constructed as victims. We are finding contemporary reassertions of border wars from the 1990s that took place in lesbian communities around this idea of "butch flight". J. K. Rowling has famously written about this. It is basically this construct of trans men *actually* being young women or young lesbians who are in a flight from the feminine. They dislike sexual harassment, the male gaze, experiences of sexual harassment or assault, and so they flee from femaleness and femininity. This is also often given as a reason why there are higher numbers of young sexed-as-female people going through gender identity clinics. The idea is that these "victims" need to be "rescued". But I find this such a bizarre idea because *all* people who've been born into this world as a female person know and have experienced sexual harassment, the threat of sexual violence, and the male gaze. But only a *tiny minority* of women deal with that by wanting to become men, or to masculinize their bodies, or to identify as men. Is sexual objectification of girls and young women a bad thing, and does it happen? Yes. Are there endemic levels of male sexualized violence against women and children? Yes. And all of these things are important issues. But does this mean that there is no such thing as a trans man, because everyone's just in a flight from the feminine?

I also think the reason we don't see so much about trans men comes from a related place of sexism, due to those people having had histories of being sexed as female. As a result, they aren't seen as a threat in the same way. They aren't seen as powerful or as change-makers. So, instead, they are constructed as victims who just need rescuing. Trans women, by contrast, are represented as an innate threat.

Finally, there is also something to be said about the way trans men are in some way affirming the hierarchy of gendered expression (as, of course, everybody wants to be a man and no one wants to be a woman!), while trans women are disrupting it. And because of those hierarchies of gender, there's less tolerance for people who have had the luck of being born into the dominant group dressing as or presenting as or seeming to want to present themselves as being from the "inferior" group.

JB: You have pointed to many current and future tensions for society as it navigates sex and gender identity. Despite all that is going on, do you feel hopeful about the future?

FM: Yes, absolutely! It is clear that change is happening. There is a younger generation of people who don't want to be boxed in, don't like labels, are more likely to refer to themselves as not a label than any other label, know people that use some of these fifty-odd different gender terms and are quite comfortable with it. Change is coming, whether people like it or not. These categories that we have previously seen as fixed and unchanging are not seen in that way by younger people.

FURTHER RESOURCES

Daresha Kyi, "Mama Bears" (2022), www.mamabearsdoc.com.

Finn Mackay, *Female Masculinities and the Gender Wars: The Politics of Sex*. London: Bloomsbury, 2021.

Finn Mackay, "Queer". *The Philosopher* 110:3 (2022).

Kathryn Bond Stockton and Ezra Klein, "Gender is complicated for all of us. Let's talk about it". Ezra Klein Show podcast (2022).

2

Submission and Emancipation

Manon Garcia in conversation with Kate Kirkpatrick

Historically, philosophers, psychoanalysts, and even some radical feminists have conflated femininity and submission. This conversation coincided with the publication of Manon Garcia's book *We Are Not Born Submissive: How Patriarchy Shapes Women's Lives*. For Garcia, what we call femininity in our patriarchal societies is submission, but it does not have to be this way. Rather, the concept of submission serves to give meaning to what women have been experiencing under patriarchy, as well as the tools to politicize it. What emerges from this conversation is not only an inspiring call to women to resist, but also a lucid and accessible introduction to many of the most urgent questions in feminist philosophy.

MANON GARCIA is a junior professor of practical philosophy at Freie Universität in Berlin. Her primary research is in political philosophy, feminist philosophy, moral philosophy and philosophy of economics.

KATE KIRKPATRICK is Tutorial Fellow in Philosophy and Christian Ethics at Regent's Park College, Oxford. She is an associate fellow of the Higher Education Academy, and treasurer of the UK Sartre Society.

Kate Kirkpatrick (**KK**): Much of your work looks at the concept of submission from a feminist perspective. Why do you think this concept deserves philosophical analysis?

Manon Garcia (**MG**): What we call femininity in our patriarchal societies *is* submission. Yet, unlike feminist theorists like Catharine MacKinnon, I don't think that this *necessarily* has to be the case. There is the possibility of redefining femininity in a way that is not synonymous with submission, but I take it that femininity and submission are the same for now. In this sense, I consider submission to be a, if not *the*, central concept for feminist philosophy to be addressing.

I felt very early on that a major problem with concepts like "oppression", "domination" and "exploitation" is that they look at the power dynamic from the standpoint of the people who have the power. And this leads to a problem, especially in the case of women, which is that their situation comes to be associated with passivity. People come to think that male domination means that women are passive. But the reality is that even traditional women who live by the norms of patriarchy, and even *like* the norms of patriarchy, are active – they are doing a lot of things, they are not just waiting and doing nothing, as the passivity model implies. Part of what submission to patriarchy entails is dieting, working out, being sexy, being extremely caring, and so on. Because there are a lot of things that women do because of the gender norms of patriarchy, I think it is a form of injustice that is done to them if we only look at their experience as one of passivity. Concepts that adopt a top-down view on women's lives are very helpful in many ways, but there is a value in looking at these power dynamics from another, bottom-up perspective. And this is where the concept of submission is so useful.

I certainly don't mean to say that the kinds of behaviours I just identified as submissive are *wrong*. It is not wrong to work out, it is not wrong to be caring, and so on. But what I find interesting is that these sorts of behaviours have been used to identify a weakness or inferiority in women. Being caring is great, but problems arise if you are the only one to do the care work and if care work is not seen as real work. This is why I am trying to initially propose a *non-moralized* account of submission. My project is initially a descriptive one of analyzing behaviours that are submissive before turning to the normative work of evaluating what is wrong, what is an injustice.

Another important point to mention is that I was initially doing this work in France where submission is seen as what Muslim women do in contrast to "real" French women. I found this racist trope very concerning, so, to put it a bit bluntly, I wanted to show my peers that the fact that they eat boiled zucchini with no olive oil for dinner in order to be sexy and to be able to wear miniskirts does not necessarily make them any freer than a woman who wears the veil. This assumption that sexiness "à la française" is far freer than traditional forms of women's lives is very concerning to me, and I think that the concept of submission is useful to clarify that it is not just the "other" that is the dupe of patriarchy – we are *all* to some extent the dupe of patriarchy. And we will only find our way to emancipation after we become conscious of the oppression that we live through.

KK: In your work, you emphasize that submission is an ordinary experience – it's lived by everyone; everyone submits sometimes. But what distinguishes the submission of men from the submission of women and, perhaps, queer or non-binary people?

MG: What I am trying to do with my work on submission is to provide a concept that helps us understand what is going on for people who live under social domination – people of colour in the context of white supremacy, women in the context of patriarchy, workers in the context of capitalism. All of these people are submitting themselves in a way that is very different to those who do not experience social domination. For submission to be *real* submission, it cannot simply be reversed on a whim. Take the husband who talks about submitting to his wife when it comes to planning vacations, for example: this is not real submission as it does not happen against the background of social domination. We empty submission of any meaning when we erase its political dimension.

There is also the question of what it means to be free. Someone like Rousseau sees freedom as something we are born with, a natural quality that we have. When we operate with this model, it looks like submission is the attitude of someone who has their freedom but does not want it; they want to give it back. By contrast, I think that someone like Beauvoir approaches freedom as something you need to achieve, something you need to work on. From this perspective, submission is not a matter of renouncing something that you have always had so much as saying that you not embarking on a quest for freedom. And, of course, there are good reasons for everyone to adopt this stance: freedom is scary and it is easier to follow the rules of society and to do exactly what you're expected to do. In that regard, *both* men and women submit to social norms, but because social norms are gendered in ways that encourage men to be adventurous and to experiment and to strive for freedom, whereas women are asked to submit, there is a clear additional sense in which for women to submit to social norms is to be submissive. There are social norms and social institutions that make submission relatively cost-free for women and freedom relatively costly. Therefore, it's especially difficult for women to be free.

KK: One of the ways in which you consider submission from a woman's perspective is via the bodily aspect of submission, especially in terms of objectification. How do you view the female body in relation to submission?

MG: Being a woman or being a girl is seeing that the entire world has – or feels like they have – the right to comment on, or even to touch, your body. I was recently pregnant and was amazed at the extent to which people would comment on or touch my body. This is just one example of why women come to feel as if their body is something public, something that belongs to others before belonging to themselves. For many teenage girls, before their body can be something that they have pleasure with or something they desire with, it is seen by others, it is commented on by others, it is touched by others. I think almost every woman has the experience of being a body for other people before having a body for oneself. And this creates the grounds for feeling that you need to serve other people; that your body – and, by extension, yourself – is there for others before it is there for you. This experience creates a feeling of alienation with your body and with yourself that is probably what makes submission both so tempting and sometimes so pleasurable. Submission to the gaze of men is also *validation* by the gaze of men – and this is taken to be the kind of validation that is worth having. Instead of climbing walls or climbing rocks or climbing mountains, you're looked at.

KK: To continue on this theme of the body, do you feel that getting cosmetic surgery is a submissive act, a form of internalized sexism akin to mutilating oneself for the male gaze? Is there a way that these things can be done authentically?

MG: This raises the deeply philosophical question of whether you can know what agents are doing better than the agents themselves. If a woman says that she only undertakes these procedures for herself, rather than because it makes her sexy by social standards and this sexiness gives her a better standing in society, can we believe her or not? I think it's an impossible question! I consider my role to be just to make available a concept to understand what *can* be going on, but not to judge women – not to say that this woman has fake breasts for a good reason while this one has fake breasts for a bad reason. I don't even wish to say that doing something out of submission is a bad reason.

KK: Now that you have discussed some of the ways in which submission can be imprisoning, what do you think is the emancipatory potential of thinking about submission?

MG: I think there are two sides of the emancipatory part. One is what feminists call "consciousness-raising". I do think that finally having a word to describe something that you've been going through is extremely freeing. It can allow you to connect the dots in a way that gives meaning to what you have been experiencing, and then gives you the tools to politicize it. So many experiences that we may take to be just our idiosyncratic experiences are actually common to so many women, and while they may take different forms they have a common meaning and a common cause – patriarchy. So, I think that the concept of submission is powerful enough that we can see the world through this prism and become more finely attuned to the various injustices and harms that we experience.

The concept of submission also allows us to be sceptical of the idea that our liberation as women is an individual endeavour. There are prominent branches of feminism that emphasize the need to fight, to be strong. In post-Weinstein France, a lot of women were saying things like, "I just don't understand these young feminists who pretend that they are victims. They should fight and not whine about the fact that they were victims of sexual assault." Implicit in this attitude is the belief that it is just on you to not submit, and that if you don't submit you are therefore not a victim of patriarchy. What I am trying to show is that this is not true. And not only that it is untrue, but that such a view *harms* feminism, because it confuses the meaning of what it is to be a feminist. What it is to be a feminist is to fight against male domination as a structure and not just in your individual life. One of the effects of patriarchy on women's lives is to convince them that they should side with men, that they should side with the dominant – and this individualist model of feminism is a clear example of this effect.

There may be a part of emancipation that you can do on your own, but much deeper structural and social changes need to happen. One very interesting realization that has been widely discussed these past few years is the extent to which patriarchy shapes our sexual desires. A lot of women have fantasies that are not aligned with their political beliefs and their feminist beliefs. For me, this recognition of the psychic life of power and the extent to which submission is ingrained in us in our body, in our desires, highlights the limitations of any individualistic approaches to the problems of patriarchy. It is crucial to understand how deep it all goes in order to build a meaningful emancipatory activism.

KK: What do you make of the intersectional critique of the notion that there is such a thing as the "common oppression" of women qua women – independent of their sexual orientation, class, race, and so on?

MG: It is certainly the case that for a long time what it meant to say that there is a common oppression of women qua women was to think that this oppression took exactly the same forms for all women. But Black feminists, in particular, have made a compelling argument that this is clearly not the case. However, I do believe that women qua women *are* oppressed in a certain way by patriarchy, and that the concept of submission allows us to understand some parts of what this involves. To give you an example, I've been thinking a lot lately about the role of this imperative of submission in racism. In the context of America, for instance, you have a very specific anti-Asian women racism that is grounded in the idea that they are *too submissive*. By contrast, you have a very specific anti-Black women racism that is grounded in the idea that they are *not submissive enough* – they are too aggressive, too outspoken, and so on. And then you have the valorization of the kind of white, Republican women who are submissive in just the right way. So, I still think that what all these women have in common is that they are evaluated according to this standard of submission – and that this is a form of specifically patriarchal oppression.

KK: Do you think feminists should aim to abolish the kinds of submission that you think of as particularly feminine?

MG: If patriarchy were to lose its power, what is now seen as women's submission may still exist as forms of behaviours, but it would no longer be coded *as* submission. In that sense, I want submission to disappear. But that does not mean that I want women to become competitive bullies or to abandon their kids, or whatever. I just hope for a future in which they feel like they do not have to submit to men.

FURTHER RESOURCES

Clare Chambers, *Intact: A Defence of the Unmodified Body*. London: Allen Lane, 2022.

Kimberlé W. Crenshaw, "Demarginalizing the intersection of race and sex". *University of Chicago Legal Forum* 1:8 (1989). http://chicago unbound.uchicago.edu/uclf/vol1989/iss1/8.

Robin Dembroff, *Real Men on Top: How Patriarchy Weaponizes Gender*. Oxford: Oxford University Press, 2023.

Manon Garcia, *We Are Not Born Submissive: How Patriarchy Shapes Women's Lives*. Princeton, NJ: Princeton University Press, 2021.

Kate Kirkpatrick, *Becoming Beauvoir: A Life*. London: Bloomsbury, 2019.

Catharine MacKinnon, *Feminism Unmodified: Discourses on Life and Law*. Cambridge, MA: Harvard University Press, 1987.

3

Madness, identity and recognition

Mohammed Abouelleil Rashed with Helen Spandler

Within all the various identity-related social justice movements representing marginalized and oppressed populations, the "Mad activism" movement represents an interesting anomaly on the grounds that hardly anyone knows it exists. In his 2019 book, *Madness and the Demand for Recognition*, Mohammed Abouelleil Rashed emerged as one of the only philosophers who has engaged closely with Mad activism and the politics of madness more generally. His conversation with Helen Spandler critically engages with our serious cultural impoverishment when it comes to mental health; with philosophy's history of excluding madness; with the politics of recognition; with the role of reconciliation in mental health services; and much more.

MOHAMMED ABOUELLEIL RASHED is a visiting lecturer in the department of philosophy at King's College, London, as well as an associate specialist in community psychiatry at Camden and Northwest London NHS Foundation Trust. His main research is in philosophy of psychiatry where he has examined a number of topics including the boundaries of illness, definitions of concepts of mental disorder and distress, and the diagnostic process in psychiatry.

HELEN SPANDLER is Professor of Mental Health Studies at the University of Central Lancashire. Her research expertise is in critical approaches to mental health, including the theory, practice, policy, history and politics of mental healthcare. She is also the managing editor of *Asylum: The Magazine for Democratic Psychiatry*.

Helen Spandler (**HS**): Where did your involvement in Mad Pride and Mad politics come from? It is certainly not a common thing for psychiatrists, or indeed philosophers, to get their hands dirty with the Mad movement and Mad activism. I am interested in why it influenced you so much and has had such a profound influence on your work.

Mohammed Abouelleil Rashed (**MAR**): When I was beginning to engage with problems in the philosophy of psychiatry, one of the first topics that I came across is the issue of the definition of mental disorder. If there is a defining topic for that field of study, that would be it. I was fascinated by the fact that *culture* was an exclusionary criterion from being considered to have a mental disorder. The main diagnostic tool for psychiatrists, the Diagnostic and Statistical Manual (DSM), accepted that if a person presents with something that looks like a delusion or a hallucination, they should *not* be diagnosed as having a pathological condition if these experiences are understood to be part of their sub-cultural experience, i.e., if these experiences are accepted by people in their group. Being part of a group thus protects from judgements of psychopathology.

A well-known example of this phenomenon in the West was the removal of homosexuality from the DSM as a result of a vote by members of the American Psychiatry Association in 1973 (a vote that was brought about by political campaigning at the time). From there, I became interested in the question of where else this was happening in the field of psychiatry. Where are our current cultural blind-spots? And I immediately came across the Hearing Voices movement, which has been trying to create a similar cultural change in relation to the phenomenon of voice hearing. From there, it was just one further step to engaging with Mad Pride and with other attempts to create new mental health identities.

Once I saw that these arguments were being made, and once I began to understand the historical context behind these movements and how they arose from civil rights activism in the 1970s; once I began to read the first-person accounts of people's experiences within psychiatric services; once I came to understand the terrible shortcomings in our existing language of mental health, it was no longer possible for me to see the arguments being put forward by the Mad politics and Mad Pride movements as simply a set of ideas. I set out to try and find ways of bringing these ideas into conversation with the current and existing understandings of mental health which have to date excluded them. What I discovered is that there is a serious cultural impoverishment when it comes to mental health. There really are not many alternative ideas out there within the public domain. As a result, people engage with psychiatric services in states of extreme distress, and they have nothing to hold onto except these fragments of medical and psychological narratives that have trickled into the popular discourse. What I try to do in my role as a psychiatrist is to tell them that there are alternative frameworks and other ways of looking at it.

HS: Madness is such a marginalized, oppressed, excluded, and subjugated identity, both in terms of common-sense public understandings of it, as well as in terms of policy and practice. Legal scholars even talk about madness as a kind of "human rights exceptionalism": you have your human rights until you are deemed to be mad, at which point your human rights can be overtaken. In this sense, madness operates as an exception in terms of mental health law and policy. And this exclusion and oppression of mad people is deeply systemic and related to issues of epistemic injustice, marginalization, oppression, stigma, discrimination, and so on. Many people consider Mad Pride and Mad studies as one of the last bastions of the civil rights, or human rights, movement. My question, then, is: What do you think philosophy can offer to mad activism and the struggle for social justice? Do you think there is something specific about philosophy that helps us with this claim for social justice and legitimacy?

MAR: I think it is important to start out by acknowledging that philosophy is part of the problem. Madness is excluded from many of the conceptions that societies take as valuable: what it is to be a free person, what is valuable in terms of identity and sense of self, and so on. In this regard, philosophy has always been part of the problem, because philosophy has always excluded madness on various grounds. To take one clear example: philosophy excludes madness on epistemic grounds, i.e., it excludes madness as a possible source of knowledge about the self or about the world. Madness is seen as a departure from common sense, and therefore as having nothing to contribute to philosophical inquiry. Furthermore, philosophy has also excluded madness on normative grounds, as the mad person is seen to lack the capacities required for being a moral or political agent. Philosophy has to reckon with its significant contribution to the historical exclusion of madness.

But philosophy can also help towards a solution. And this comes precisely from using a philosophical approach and methodology in order to address questions like: What are the sources of this exclusion of madness? What are the cultural ideas that underlie and reinforce this exclusion? Take, for example, moral theory rooted in Kantian respect for autonomy. Madness is excluded from such a picture by virtue of the idea that the mad person is perceived to be irrational, and hence lacking autonomy. Or take recognition theory rooted in thinkers like Hegel and Axel Honneth, and the importance of recognition for developing an unimpaired and coherent sense of identity. You find that madness is excluded from recognition theory because the mad person is seen to have difficulties or problems with forming and maintaining a coherent identity over time. This kind of diagnosis of the intellectual and cultural roots of the exclusion of madness is something that we can arrive at by a certain methodology, by certain ways of thinking. But even more than just diagnosing the problem, we can use the same philosophical methodology and ways of thinking to formulate the solution.

HS: What kind of solution might philosophy offer to the identity-based exclusion you just described?

MAR: Identity matters because it is part of how we orient ourselves in our lives; our sense of who we are is something that gives a sense of purpose, sense of value, and there is also a sense in which we want this to continue into the future. It is important because it has a temporal dimension – it is not something that lasts a few seconds, or a few days, or a few months. And what we find is that certain psychiatric conditions involve radical personality change or very different motivational states or values. The result is that this sense of continuing over time that we have established as a crucial element of identity formation is disrupted, with the result that it is difficult to form and maintain a coherent sense of identity. But now that we have identified the question of identity as related to temporality and the ability to maintain a project over time (such as parenting or writing a book), we can begin to think about the values embedded in this. How much temporal duration is really sufficient for a valuable life? How much continuity do we actually need in order to establish identities that are worthy of moral status and social recognition? This is just one way in which philosophy can focus in on the issue that matters, which is, in this particular case, the importance of identity for the continuation of agency over time. And this in turn enables us to see how we can modify those value limits in a way that might legitimate a wider range of experiences and ways of life.

HS: I agree that philosophies of psychiatry and psychopathology have tended to reproduce the kinds of problems with marginalization and exclusion that you describe in philosophy more generally – precisely because madness is seen to be outside of what we consider to be human. So, either this conception is correct, or we need to challenge the very ways in which we currently define what it means to be human. This is a very radical proposal, but may be an essential one if we are really to take up ideas of social justice.

In my view, one of the best critiques of philosophy of psychiatry comes from Nev Jones, who argues that philosophy tends to always talk *about* madness, rather than from the experience of madness or mad experiential knowledge. Does your approach bypass this problem, and if so how?

MAR: I have a lot of respect for Nev Jones and agree with her critique of phenomenology as applied to the field of psychiatry. Part of the rationale for using phenomenology in psychiatry has been to overcome the alienation that is seen to result from the use of reductive or biological language. By looking to the lived experience of psychiatric patients, these philosophers are attempting to bring back much of the richness and intimacy that is lost in the reductive/biological accounts. The problem, however, as Nev points out, is that their use of first-person accounts functions almost like curiosities or exotic fragments of subjectivity at the hinterland of human experience, which they then overlay with various extremely complex and jargon-laden philosophies of continental Europe. This serves to reproduce the same alienation that they consider to be problematic within biological psychiatry. Perhaps, though, this is a kind of alienation that is more satisfying to a philosopher's sensibilities!

The philosophers who work within this tradition come across descriptions of human experience that seem very alien and inaccessible to them, and they see their goal as interpreting these experiences with a view to understanding them better. In one sense, of course, this is a noble undertaking as it tries to make sense of that which has typically been seen as senseless, and, as a result, to bring the mad person back inside the sphere of human experience from which they have traditionally been excluded. But what is the cost of coming up with an interpretation that makes sense to the philosopher? As I see it, it has the potential to *add* to the stigma already faced by this highly marginalized population, to contribute further to the alienation and powerlessness of the very people about whom these accounts have been written. There is a clear problem in coming up with all these interpretations of other people's experiences without involving them sufficiently in the end product.

As to how I avoid talking *about* madness, rather than from the experience of madness, I am not really trying to offer any interpretation, or any explanation, or any account of what hearing voices or delusions are really about and how to understand them, and so on. My approach involves registering the range of diverse ideas about what mental health means and could mean, and then finding ways of making room for these ideas within the existing frameworks and perceptions. I see my role as trying to mediate between different sets of views, and to be as fair-handed as possible. If it turns out that when we bring different views and traditions into conversation, certain conceptions of identity do not work for certain groups of people, then, as you noted, that conception needs to be critically engaged with and potentially revised.

HS: Your book refers to a *demand* for recognition. We have already touched on some of the ways that mad people fail to achieve recognition, but what can we do to support this demand?

MAR: One of the biggest questions in this area relates to how we can change the public conversation around mental health, how we can bring in alternative voices. This is going to be very difficult as views on mental health and madness have been so sedimented for so long. To date, most anti-stigma campaigns have focused on the sole notion of parity of esteem, i.e., on the idea that mental illness is to be considered the same as a physical illness. The analogy is intended, in part, to draw upon the positive aspects of ascriptions of physical illness; it is to say that, like physical illness, mental illness is not something to be ashamed of, it is not the person's fault, it is not a sign of weakness, and it can be treated. But this approach does not always work to reduce stigma, and, in some cases, it might actually make things worse. Furthermore, it reflects exactly the kind of medical view that Mad activism seeks to resist by introducing counter-narratives of psychological, emotional and experiential diversity. I think it is time to find a way of bringing up alternative narratives in the public domain and also in mainstream media.

HS: One of the most interesting ideas that emerged from your book is the link between recognition and reconciliation. I co-wrote a 2017 paper called "Exploring the case for truth and reconciliation in mental health services", and this is a topic that is very close to my heart. What is your take on the role of reconciliation in mental health services?

MAR: The main thing that moved me towards thinking about reconciliation was reflecting on what is really involved in achieving recognition. When you offer someone recognition, it has to be a *genuine* affirmation of their identity, of their way of life. It cannot be forced, but needs to be freely and genuinely offered. As we know from the state of race and interfaith relations in many communities, banning certain terms or criminalizing their use might not lead to genuine and mutual recognition. In fact, such political actions are perceived by some as an infringement on free speech and may have the opposite effect of breeding resentment. Reconciliation is a process of accepting each other, of making room for each other's mutual understandings. This idea, especially in the current climate of general polarization, sounds extremely far-fetched, but, like everything else, sometimes setting certain processes in motion might be the best that we can do.

Another key element in the reconciliation process is the enrichment of our cultural repertoire. I think of culture as a resource or "tool kit" that we can call upon to help us make sense of our lives and to solve different kinds of problems. A key limitation on people's ability to make sense of their experiences is an impoverished cultural repertoire. Think of the experience of finding oneself attracted to members of the same sex in a society where such an attraction can only be understood as a sin or a crime. This is an incredibly impoverished cultural repertoire that is extremely harmful to those who are trying to interpret their experiences of same-sex attraction. I would like to see Gay activism and Mad activism as broadening our cultural repertoire as it pertains to sexuality and madness, respectively.

I would also like Mad narratives to become "cultural adjustments" in the same way that ramps for wheelchairs, for example, are physical adjustments. Wheelchair ramps not only benefit those who are the immediate beneficiaries, but also those who will be future beneficiaries, and, importantly, *society in general*. In the latter case, physical adjustments such as wheelchair ramps sensitize the public to people's different needs and abilities. Similarly, diversifying the social meanings of madness beyond illness and pathology can improve acceptance of unusual experiences, and of psychological and behavioural difference more broadly. If the usual narratives of Mad identity are no longer dismissed as "incoherent" or "irrational", but rather taken seriously as, say, "dangerous gifts", "spiritual emergence", or "healing voices" I believe that society would be much the richer for this.

Looking back to philosophy itself, it is certainly the case in philosophy of psychiatry that people's interests and concerns vary across different generations. The kinds of concerns that were most pressing in the 1980s and 1990s feel very different to concerns of researchers from my generation and, especially, the younger generation who are much more progressive and open-minded. I am excited at the extent to which these younger philosophers are becoming much more aware of the political dimensions of their philosophical research: voice and representation, epistemic injustice, and recognition. I find this trend very encouraging, and it suggests that reconciliation may be possible – within philosophy at the very least.

FURTHER RESOURCES

Awais Aftab, "Phenomenology, power, polarization, and psychosis". An interview with Nev Jones in "Conversations in Critical Psychiatry" series. www.psychiatrictimes.com/series/critical-conversations-in-psychiatry.

Kristina Lepold, "Recognition", *The Philosopher* 110:3 (2022).

Mohammed Abouelleil Rashed, *Madness and the Demand for Recognition: A Philosophical Inquiry into Identity and Mental Health Activism.* Oxford: Oxford University Press, 2019.

Mohammed Abouelleil Rashed, "Madness". *The Philosopher* 110:3 (2022).

Helen Spandler and Mick McKeown, "Exploring the case for truth and reconciliation in mental health services". *Mental Health Review Journal* 22:2 (2017).

Asylum: The Radical Mental Health Magazine (since 1986). Influential magazine edited by Helen Spandler. www.asylummagazine.org.

4

Reimagining Black men

Tommy J. Curry in conversation with
David Livingstone Smith

The publication of Tommy J. Curry's 2017 book, *The Man-Not: Race, Class, Genre, and the Dilemmas of Black Manhood*, was foundational for establishing Black Male Studies as a distinct area of study within disciplines like philosophy, history and sociology. In this conversation, Curry launches a stinging attack on the philosophical tendency toward abstractions and generalizations regarding matters that have profound social consequences, highlighting how philosophy's lack of accountability to the demographic or sociological realities of Black males has left it dealing with caricatures of Black men uncritically inherited from racist nineteenth- and twentieth-century social science and ethnology.

TOMMY J. CURRY is Professor of Philosophy at the University of Edinburgh. He holds a personal Chair in Africana Philosophy and Black Male Studies. His research interests are nineteenth-century ethnology, critical race theory and Black Male Studies.

DAVID LIVINGSTONE SMITH is Professor of Philosophy at the University of New England. His current research is focused on dehumanization, race and propaganda.

David Livingstone Smith (**DLS**): A little while ago you said to me, "I'm finished with the idea that one can just wake up in the morning and study race". You said this in the context of discussing what you considered to be major methodological problems inherent in how philosophers go about writing on race. What are your worries in this area?

Tommy J. Curry (**TJC**): The problem is that philosophy doesn't take race to be a sophisticated field of study. We hire Black people to inform us about their experiences, but we don't expect them to contribute to innovations around method or debates concerning historiography in a way that we do with other scholars within the academy. The effect of this is that we end up using identity as a metric for how we ascertain whether statements being made are correct or not. So, to the extent that a Black philosopher says things that approximate the worldview of white liberals, that Black philosopher is accepted as being a rigorous and intelligent philosopher. Whereas to the extent that a Black philosopher raises questions related to disciplinarity, related to how we study and approach a problem, related to what constitutes evidence for the claims of certain fields, that Black philosopher is alienated.

I've written about this previously as a problem of under-specialization – only the most superficial ideas about race and racism get through into the philosophical literature. There are certain questions – such as whether there is a Black identity or whether there should be Black solidarity – that seem to crop up over and over in every generation. But if you try to reorient how we see the problem of racism in ways that work against our common conceptions, what are the kinds of concepts that philosophy has to deal with that problem? The reality is that it has none. Another way of saying this is that whereas other disciplines reward expertise, philosophy rewards the common-sensical, i.e. those views which do not offend white liberals, feminists, reformists, pragmatists, and so on.

For example, in my research on the multiple vulnerabilities that Black men and other racialized males in the US suffer, I make a clear case rooted in epidemiology and social science which suggests that when we look at things like sexual violence victimization or intimate partner violence and homicide, you're not going to get the kinds of causal relationships you see coming out of feminist theory. Feminist theory is still enthralled with the Duluth model, which argues that men perpetrate violence, domestic violence, child abuse, and so on, for power – *because of* masculinity. But you have to ask yourself a fundamentally different question when you see the data sets about Black men. You have to ask why Black men are reporting higher twelve-month prevalence of sexual violence than Black women, and the highest prevalence compared to all other groups of women over a twelve-month period. Why do Black men report higher levels of twelve-month prevalence in sexual victimization and made-to-penetrate violence? The data doesn't allow us to say the same things about Black men that we've been used to saying about white men in society, but we've been so trained to thinking in terms of the Duluth model that it has become the basis of how we see everything. These figures are not only ignored by philosophers but seen as antagonistic to feminist frameworks that see rape and sexual violence as a vulnerability specific to female positionality.

Furthermore, if we know that prevalence rates of same-sex domestic violence in the United States is similar, if not higher, than rates of other-sex domestic violence, why is it that these groups completely disappear from conversations of domestic violence and intimate partner homicide in philosophy? When you look at social work and psychology, scientists take up these questions with a certain amount of rigour, answering to empiricism and qualitative data. But in philosophy if you dare say that 30 years of data have *shown* that there are similar concerns in same-sex partnerships, it is immediately shut down as homophobic. The mere utterance that the facts of the world differ from popular conceptualizations of theory brings a certain kind of hostility. But when social scientific facts about group behaviour contradict philosophical abstractions about the very same group, there is no justification to prefer the less accurate abstraction.

Philosophers tend towards abstractions and generalizations regarding matters that have profound social consequences, rather than concrete studies of the phenomena under question. As a result, what we are dealing with in philosophy is not any kind of rigorous engagement with the demographic or sociological realities of Black males; rather, we are dealing with *caricatures* of Black men that have risen to the level of theory. If you try to question this by introducing evidence that contradicts these caricatures, it is considered to be offensive at numerous levels. It is considered anti-woman because it disagrees with feminism, it is considered anti-liberal and anti-democratic because it calls out the failures of the ideas of liberal democratic theory and pragmatism through highlighting the extent to which Black men remain victims of harsh forms of state violence. These are realities that nobody wants to dig up or address.

Some philosophers would no doubt maintain that this is why intersectionality is needed, yet these same philosophers would be unable to explain why the data I just discussed has not appeared in any of the intersectional writings in philosophy over the last decade. Rather than refuting the gross generalizations of certain groups, intersectional theories have aided in confirming negative stereotypes about Black male violence while disregarding other forms of violence.

DLS: A key thread running through your work is Black male vulnerability, which stands in stark contrast with the archetype of the Black male monster, the predator, the beast. It's shocking when you consider the metrics on how Black males suffer, especially in the United States, on all sorts of dimensions. If anything should be common sense, it is the degree to which Black males have been, and continue to be, trodden on and pathologized, but instead that remains contrary to common sense.

TJC: To draw on your work about the psychological processes that allows violence to take place, there is such a level of dehumanization here. There is no amount of empirical evidence that seems to be able to change the psychological make-up of many of the philosophers and scholars in the United States. When you look at group dynamics and what Black men actually believe about gender, family, women working outside the home, and so on, their values are extremely progressive. And yet that in itself is taken as an affront.

We know as philosophers and scholars that part of our jobs is understanding the humanity of those who are victimized by oppression, but if you're offended by something that's empirically substantiated but deviates from the caricature you have of Black men to sustain your view of gender inequality, then it is simply not possible to understand the suffering of Black men and boys. You need the monster, the Black male misogynist, and so on, to sustain the arguments for why you think women across all classes and races remain victimized and oppressed. The consequence of this is that Black men are being socialized in a world where they are told that the violence that we know empirically, quantitatively, epidemiologically, happens to them, over and over again for decades, doesn't have a name. And when Black men speak of that pain, it doesn't have a category in academic disciplines. As a result, Black men are forced into silence, because any time they speak about their vulnerability, it disrupts the acts of perpetration and violence that we have to assert that they perform in the world to sustain our other worldviews on gender and criminality.

This means that philosophy, because it doesn't appeal to evidence or history, remains trapped by a peculiar kind of categorical supremacy. Even though we know that Black men experience rates of domestic violence and sexual victimization comparable to their female counterparts, we have to define them as predators or rapists. Whereas, if the Black man was allowed to become a victim like white men, white women, or even Black women, then this idea of his toxic masculinity, his savageness, disappears and we have to view him as a human being affected by his environment, not fundamentally corrupted and conditioned by his nature.

DLS: What do you think this silencing and dwelling in a world which does not have room to acknowledge terror and suffering, the infliction of violence, and so on, does to Black men?

TJC: The consequences are horrible. Black men in the United States have the lowest life expectancy and the highest rates of downward mobility. Whereas white women make 77 cents to every dollar that white men make, and Black women 61, once you look at incarceration and the removal of Black men from society they make 51 cents per dollar, and their wages, when controlling for workers and non-workers, has not increased since segregation. And the psychological and physical burden of that – I could talk to you about weathering, about the premature decay of our telomeres, about John Henryism, all as a result of cumulative exposure to experiences of social, economic and political adversity – is heavy.

Within an academic context, despite the data, despite the facts, despite what we grew up with in our neighbourhoods and in society in general, Black men choose to turn away from the evidence and embrace the ideology that we think will gain us employment and respect among our white liberal peers. One of the most dangerous things for Black men is that they are told that in order to be recognized and accepted within disciplines, they have to be less adamant about their own humanity. One of the things that I admire about your work is its focus on dehumanization and the inhumanity that we are all conditioned in multiple ways to accept. What I am really interested in exploring within Black Male Studies is the kinds of caricatures that mobilize the everyday dehumanization that we see.

DLS: When philosophers talk about intuitions, they need to ask where those intuitions come from. When you start seriously interrogating where the intuitions about race and masculinity come from, it's all very deeply ideologically-laden. We have to look to history to understand that and to interrogate these intuitions rather than take them as pointing the way to an accurate understanding. Philosophy has freed itself in large measure, particularly outside philosophy of science, from bringing claims before the tribunal of evidence – and that's lethal. As a final question, I have heard you say that you consider part of your aim with Black Male Studies to be "reimagining" Black men. What might it mean to reimagine Black men, and how can this be done?

TJC: Black Male Studies tries to rearticulate and reimagine how actual categories like patriarchy and racism function. When you look at societies that are racialized – like Apartheid in South Africa and Jim Crow in the United States – you will find the same structures, propaganda and caricatures directed towards racialized men. What I'm really interested in is how it is that under the pretence of theoretical advance – intersectionality, deconstruction, psychoanalysis, and so on – we see no disruption to, and in fact simply continuity of, the ideas of Black men now and how they were thought to be in the nineteenth and twentieth century? If we have theoretically advanced on the questions of race and gender, why are there still the static and decadent assumptions about Black men that white social scientists and ethnologists believed in the 1800s and early 1900s? Reimagining means a break with those ideas and finding out what it is that is allowing us to reproduce these static and decadent ideas.

I am interested in thinking Black men anew – not as victims of thought or theory that confine them within theories driven by the kind of anti-Black misandry I'm talking about. Thought and theory are the products of certain disciplinary arrangements that have constructed Black, Jewish, Roma, Muslim, and other racialized men as being threats to western civilization. I don't think it's controversial to say that. If you pick any historical text from the past hundred years, it is going to have some caricature that says that these groups of men are trying to destroy the West. What kind of thinking allows us to come up with a different hypothesis or result? How can we look at these groups of men and come up with something that has not already been reiterated by racist ethnologists and sociologists?

Another key part of the process of reimagining is explaining all the problems that are said to exist because Black men are in some way deficient. If you think about the level of perpetration of something like sexual violence or rape, you're talking about less than 0.5 per cent of the total Black male adult population. Even if we assume that only half of perpetrators are convicted and we double – or even quadruple – the number of Black men that are convicted, it is still less than 1 per cent of the population. Seen in this light, we have race and gender theories that only accurately describe the behaviour of less than one per cent of the Black male population, and then utilize these theories to dictate what are thought to be the inherent capacities and the nature of the 99 per cent. There is no other group that exists as a subject or object of theory in the western academy that is subjected to this sort of conceptual violence. While Black men who come from poor environments with early exposure to violence and sexual violence still end up being profound, productive, positive citizens, those are never the models of how we think about Black men because we always think about them as the excess of white men's toxic masculinity. Whatever white men do, Black men do it worse – they do it more savagely to inflict greater harm and injury.

When I say reimagine, I'm talking about this process by which we utilize the overwhelming positive prevalence of Black men and boys as a basis to do good philosophy: to challenge ourselves not to simply reinvent or reiterate ontological foundations of masculinity as if that gives us a clear causal explanation for the kinds of deviance we find in the world. Reimagining is digging into the humanity of Black men to find a grounding of theory that allows them to be conceptualized not as brutes and beasts, but as humans who are always in the process of becoming and living.

FURTHER RESOURCES

Tommy J. Curry, *The Man-Not: Race, Class, Genre, and the Dilemmas of Black Manhood*. Philadelphia, PA: Temple University Press, 2017.

Tommy J. Curry, "Must there be an empirical basis for the theorization of racialized subjects in race-gender theory?" *Proceedings of the Aristotelian Society* 121:1 (2021). https://doi.org/10.1093/arisoc/aoaa021.

David Livingstone Smith, *On Inhumanity: Dehumanization and How to Resist It*. New York: Oxford University Press, 2020.
Other scholars working in this field include Timothy Golden, Amir Jaima, Adebayo Oluwayomi and Dalitso Ruwe.

5

Iris Marion Young and structural injustice

Maeve McKeown in conversation with Alasia Nuti

According to traditional theories of responsibility, we would not think that western consumers have any responsibility for the exploitation of sweatshop workers, as we are not connected to them in a way that moral philosophy has typically been able to understand. Iris Marion Young, however, wanted to make sense of the kind of responsibility that western activists felt when protesting global injustices. This led to her model of structural injustice and our responsibility for structural injustice. This conversation between two scholars of Young's work offers a clear overview of Young's diverse and influential philosophical output. McKeown and Nuti explore questions such as: are corporations to blame for their unjust practices? How do individuals assume responsibility for structural injustice without feeling completely powerless in the face of so many injustices? What is the relationship between activism and political theory?

MAEVE MCKEOWN is Assistant Professor in Political Theory at the interdisciplinary faculty Campus Fryslân, University of Groningen. Her current research focuses on individuals' responsibilities for global injustice.

ALASIA NUTI is a lecturer in the department of politics at the University of York. She works in contemporary political theory and gender studies, and has a strong interest in postcolonial theory and critical race theory.

Alasia Nuti (**AN**): Who was Iris Marion Young and why has she become this very important political philosopher. Also, when and how did you come across her work, and what do you find so appealing in her writings?

Maeve McKeown (**MM**): Iris Marion Young is the greatest! Anyone who is interested in philosophy, political theory, or feminism, needs to read her work. She was born in 1949 and died in 2006 at the age of 56, which was a big loss for the political theory community. She contributed to pretty much every area of contemporary political theory: in her early work she dealt with justice theory, democratic theory, feminist phenomenology, and Marxist feminism, and in her later work, structural injustice and global political issues. She seemed to enter a research area in political theory, say some amazing things, and then move onto another area! While she was certainly a big name in academia, especially after her 1990 book *Justice and the Politics of Difference*, it is only in the last 15 years that her work has taken on a life of its own to the extent that she has almost become part of the canon. There are many people who would consider themselves Iris Marion Young scholars; she has developed that kind of gravitas.

I came across her writings for the first time during my undergraduate degree. I studied politics and international relations at the University of Manchester. At the time, a lot of the degree was leaving me cold – I was not especially interested in the political science aspect and a lot of the theory was dead white men talking about things that didn't relate to my life in any meaningful way. I was interested in global issues, but found the political philosophy literature on global justice abstract and detached. It was mostly focused (as most justice theory in the last 60 years has been) on John Rawls, and it certainly did not speak to me as an activist. I had been involved in activism since joining the anti-sweatshop protests in Belfast when I was 15-years' old. To me, activism and protest were what global justice was about, and yet nobody in the philosophy literature was talking about that. When I read Young's 2006 essay, "Responsibility and global justice: a social connection model", I immediately realized that this was what I had been waiting for. She takes the anti-sweatshop movement as her starting point for addressing wider questions related to global justice, such as why people are protesting when they are far removed from sweatshop workers in other countries. According to traditional theories of responsibility, we would not think that western consumers have any responsibility for sweatshop workers, as we are not connected to them in a way that moral philosophy can understand. But Young wanted to make sense of the kind of responsibility that these protesters felt. This is what she was doing when she started thinking about structural injustice, and our responsibility for structural injustice. And this just lit a fire for me which has kept me engaging with her work ever since.

AN: In a sense, she anticipated a recent trend in political theory which is to understand activism *as* political theory. In other words, rather than just using cases of activism to enrich what she was saying theoretically or normatively, she really considered activism as a source for political theorizing. While this kind of approach is more common today (in no small part due to her pioneering work), at that time it was quite exceptional – at least in mainstream academia. Within activism, there has always been an understanding of injustice as being structural, but nonetheless the way in which Young formulated her concept of structural injustice was incredibly fresh and original. What was structural injustice for Iris Marion Young, and what does it mean for you?

MM: Part of Young's inspiration for thinking about structural injustice came from her engagement with sociology. There are four aspects to her structural injustice model and these all relate to socio-structural processes rather than being static – these are all things that are happening all the time.

The first aspect is what she calls "objective constraint". This is where the structures of society are constraining; they constrain your options for action. This can be related to the material infrastructure, for example, it is not easy to ride a bike if you live in a city where there are no bike lanes and there is a lot of traffic. So, the material infrastructure constrains your options for acting in that way. But in addition to these material constraints, our options for action can be constrained laws, by social norms around gender, race, or ability, by the ways that you look and present yourself, and so on. All of these things constrain what we can and cannot do in society. The second aspect is "social position". In society, we are all positioned in different ways within the social field. Some people are positioned at the top and have a lot of resources at their disposal and a lot of opportunities for action, while others are positioned so that they do not have many options for action. The third aspect is the idea that we reproduce structures through our actions – an idea that Young adapted from the British sociologist Anthony Giddens and his theory of structuration. Giddens argues that, for example, when I use the English language, I'm reproducing the English language. Whenever we participate in the social structure, we're both drawing upon that structure and reproducing it through our actions. The fourth aspect is what she calls "counter-finality" whereby the coming together of all these different processes results in unintended outcomes. It's a kind of "tragedy of the commons" situation. We're all doing our individual thing and it results in bad consequences. She gives homelessness as a domestic example of structural injustice, and sweatshop labour as a global example of structural injustice.

AN: If we consider the homelessness example, simple distribution of money, for example, seems to be a clear solution to resolve the structural injustice they suffer from. But in *Justice and the Politics of Difference*, Young argued that structural injustice is totally different from economic distributive justice. Why was she so critical of the distributive justice paradigm?

MM: Young was not saying that we should get rid of distributive justice; rather, she is saying that distributive justice is not enough. Part of the solution to homelessness *will* involve redistributing resources. But it is also intimately related to other forms of structure. She gives the example of a single mother of two who finds herself homeless through no fault of her own, just because she cannot find an affordable place to live that is near her place of work. While landlords may not be *actively* discriminating against her, they may be implicitly discriminating against her because she is a single mother. You can see numerous different factors at play here: there is the material infrastructure that is constraining the places where she can live; there are social norms that lead to discrimination against her; there is the housing market which is not properly regulated, allowing some investors to become extremely rich at the expense of vast swathes of people who cannot find any form of housing. All of these different structures need intervention if we are going to make a difference to homelessness in the long term. Redistributing resources is only looking at one part of the problem, and it does not make any meaningful intervention in the unjust structures.

AN: This discussion brings to mind Young's idea of the "five faces of oppression", which showed how people are oppressed even beyond distributive concerns. Her intuitions were partly rooted in her worries about treating certain things as resources that can be distributed. For example, when we think about power and rights, these are not things that can just be distributed across a population; rather, they are *relations* in which we are embedded.

MM: Absolutely. In *Justice and the Politics of Difference*, she argued that the distributive paradigm of justice leaves out at least three things: one is the division of labour: why are the top jobs occupied by white men? Why are some jobs feminized and associated with women? Why are some jobs associated with people of colour? Another factor is decision-making power: who gets to make the decisions about distributions of resources? And the third one is culture: why is white western culture dominant globally? Why are patriarchal norms and imagery dominant? Young certainly did not wish to get rid of distributive justice, but rather was encouraging us to pay attention to all the things that this distributive justice framework is not allowing us to think about, and that we really need to think about if we are to do justice theory properly.

AN: What do you think Young got wrong or overlooked in her account of structural injustice?

MM: A lot of people have taken this concept of structural injustice and applied it to many different cases of injustice in the world, trying to show how these injustices are built into social, economic and political structures. As a result, they are very difficult to change, and so Young argues that the responsibility for making the necessary changes does not fall to any particular agent; rather, there needs to be collective action. Where I think that Young went wrong was that by not wishing to identify individual agents, she did not take sufficient account of the responsibility of the more powerful agents within these structures. We may all be constrained by structures and structural injustice, but some agents are less constrained than others. To take the sweatshops example: a massive corporation like Inditex (which owns brands like Zara) is clearly in a position to make some changes within the global garment industry. The idea that it is so constrained that it cannot bear moral responsibility for the injustices of the sweatshop industry is a bit difficult to swallow. In my work, I argue that there are different kinds of structural injustice, depending on what role powerful agents play in reproducing the injustice.

In her posthumously published 2011 book *Responsibility for Justice*, Young argues that if we blame powerful agents, they will just get defensive and then they won't do anything. And she pretty much leaves it at that! But this conclusion is unsatisfactory because this is not what actually happens in the real world when it comes to corporate scandals. An example of this in the global garment industry was the Rana Plaza factory collapse in Bangladesh in 2013 in which over 1,000 people were killed. At that point, consumers came together to protest the treatment of the workers and their working conditions. Consumers pointed out that there was not just criminal responsibility here, but also moral responsibility on the part of the corporations that are using unsafe factories. As a result, the corporations came together and signed up to the Accord on Fire and Building Safety in Bangladesh. The Accord was very limited in scope – it was only about fire and building safety, it was not about workers' rights, rights to unionize, and so on – but it did make a difference. It led to significant changes in terms of fire and building safety in Bangladesh for the period in which it was in operation. This was clear evidence that blaming corporations *can* lead to change and that there are things corporations can do to improve a structural injustice like sweatshop labour. It also demonstrates that there is a huge amount more that they *could* be doing: they could be improving fire and building safety in other countries, not just in Bangladesh; they could be improving wages; they could be improving rights to unionize, and so on. There is a lot of room for manoeuvre that these powerful agents have within these structures that I think Young didn't adequately account for.

AN: When you consider some kinds of structural injustice, such as global inequality, gender inequality, racial inequality, or historical injustices like colonialism and slavery, thinking that no one is blameless really seems to go against our intuitions of injustice and responsibility. This is not to say that Young did not have an important point to make – namely, that even if some people are not to blame for a particular injustice, they may still have certain *responsibilities* in relation to that injustice. But perhaps dispensing with blame completely at the structural level was not the right move. We have already discussed some ideas connected to responsibility of structural injustice, but I am keen for you to clarify: what does it mean to be responsible for structural injustice?

MM: Young argues that there are two models of responsibility. The traditional model of responsibility in moral philosophy and law is what she calls the "liability model". On the liability model of responsibility, a person has to have directly caused harm with intent to cause harm and knowledge of the likely consequences of their actions. Young argues that in the context of structural injustice, this liability model doesn't make sense. When I buy a t-shirt from a shop, I don't intend to harm sweatshop workers; I'm not directly harming them. I don't actually know what the outcome of my action is going to be because the money from my purchase of the t-shirt might end up paying the shop workers in that particular shop; it might end up paying the rental cost of the building; it could go to all sorts of places. In short, I don't *know* that it is directly exploiting a worker in a sweatshop. In the face of the shortcomings of this model, Young argued that we need a different conception of responsibility, which she called the "social connection model". According to this, anyone who is connected to a structural injustice shares a political responsibility to collectively organize to struggle against it. The *political* responsibility entailed by the social connection model is very different to the *moral* responsibility entailed by the liability model. For a start, it does not involve blame. For Young, we are not to blame for structural injustice but we do share political responsibility to collectively organize to try and change it if we are connected to it in some way. That is how she tries to get around the limitations she sees in conventional theories of moral responsibility. But there is a big debate about whether or not that actually works!

AN: Young drew inspiration from Hannah Arendt's distinction between moral and political responsibility. Please can you say something about Arendt's framework and why Young found it so fruitful?

MM: When Arendt was making this distinction, she was thinking through responsibility for the Holocaust. She distinguished those senior officials in the Nazi party who organized and oversaw the Holocaust, and who are morally responsible and legally responsible for it, from ordinary German citizens whose responsibility did not make sense through the lens of moral and legal responsibility. Could an average German citizen, who probably knew about the concentration camps but did not know the extent of the killing, really be said to be guilty in the same way that someone like Adolf Eichmann was guilty? Arendt thought not, which is why she introduced the idea of *political* responsibility. For Arendt, this meant a responsibility to uphold the public political sphere in which the citizens were living. She thought that the German citizens of the time had failed to do that. They had abdicated their political responsibility, retreated into their own personal lives, and left the public political sphere to be taken over by the Nazis. For Arendt, political responsibility is collective responsibility for a political community, but this is distinct from the guilt which applies to individuals for their particular wrongful deeds. Guilt is a function of legal and moral responsibility; political responsibility is something distinct. Young adopts this distinction, albeit with significant revisions, to develop her own distinction between our general responsibilities to other people to whom we are connected within our daily lives, and this further political responsibility we have to everyone to whom we are connected through unjust structures.

AN: We have discussed the responsibilities of very powerful agents like corporations, but when we start thinking about the responsibility that ordinary people have to change unjust structures, there may be a feeling that we are embedded in so many unjust structures and that we contribute to these injustices simply by exercising our agency. This could easily leave us feeling completely powerless because there are just too many injustices! Did Young think about this issue? Did she try to come up with a solution for the "overwhelmed ordinary person"?

MM: It certainly does seem overwhelming! When you think about the prevalence of structural injustices in the world, it's not just sweatshop labour and homelessness – it's structural racism, structural sexism, the climate crisis. The list goes on. And the natural response may be, "If I'm responsible for all of this because I'm connected to all of it, what do I do!?" It can lead to complete overwhelm and existential dread. In the face of this, Young tried to come up with what she calls "parameters of reasoning" for thinking about how to take up political responsibility. The first parameter she came up with was "power":

how much power do you have in relation to a structural injustice? She says that the power you have determines what kind of structural injustice you should be working on. So, if you have some sort of power in relation to a particular structural injustice, you should focus your energies on that injustice. The second parameter of reasoning is "privilege": if you are benefiting from an injustice, that's the injustice that you should focus on. The third is "interest": how interested are you in a particular injustice? Getting involved in anti-sweatshop activism was something I was passionate about; that can be a way to get involved in collective action. But, for Young, interest is also about whether you are a *victim* of structural injustice. This is one of the controversial aspects of her theory, because she says that everyone connected to a structural injustice shares responsibility to change it – including the victims. And the fourth parameter of reasoning is "collective ability": if you are already a member of a collective, you can focus your energies through your collective. If you are part of a university, for example, you can campaign to make sure that all the clothing that has the university logo on it is fair-trade; you can campaign for divestment from fossil fuels; you can campaign about zero-hours contracts and outsourcing work to companies that aren't treating their workers properly. We can use our position within a collective to try and do something about structural injustice.

This formulation has been criticized by many political philosophers for being too vague. There is an obsession in analytic, liberal, political philosophy with assigning specific duties to specific agents, which tells them *exactly* what they have to do. But Young is saying: this is way more complicated than that; it is *so* complex. Every person is positioned completely differently in relation to different structural injustices, and because of this we need to be able to think about it for ourselves. She preferred the "parameters of reasoning" model because she considered it a framework that can help you think about these issues and then do what you think is the right thing to do. But this is never going to be a neat process. Activism is about trial and error, and some of it will not be effective; some of it may even be counterproductive. In fact, one of the main reasons that she wanted to include the victims in political responsibility was so that activists, especially people in the Global North who might be far removed from some of these injustices, don't go around doing counterproductive things. By listening to the victims and taking their perspective into account, everyone can use that when thinking about how to act on their political responsibility for structural injustice.

FURTHER RESOURCES

Maeve McKeown, *With Power Comes Responsibility: The Politics of Structural Injustice*. London: Bloomsbury, 2023.

Maeve McKeown, "Responsibility". *The Philosopher* 110:2 (2022).

Iris Marion Young, *Justice and the Politics of Difference*. Princeton, NJ: Princeton University Press, 1990.

Robin Zheng, "What is my role in changing the system? A new model of responsibility for structural injustice". *Ethical Theory and Moral Practice* 21 (2018): 869–85.

6

Disobedience and seeing like an activist

Erin R. Pineda in conversation with Robin Celikates

There are few movements more firmly associated with civil disobedience than the civil rights movement. In the mainstream imagination, civil rights activists eschewed coercion, appealed to the majority's principles, and submitted willingly to legal punishment in order to demand necessary legislative reforms and facilitate the realization of core constitutional and democratic principles. However, as political theorist Erin R. Pineda argues below, this familiar account of civil rights disobedience not only misremembers history; it also distorts our political judgements about how civil disobedience might fit into democratic politics. This conversation coincided with the publication of Pineda's book, *Seeing Like an Activist: Civil Disobedience and the Civil Rights Movement*. It looks at civil disobedience from the perspective of an activist rather than the dominant liberal political theorists, raising numerous important questions about how civil disobedience ought to unfold in the present.

ERIN R. PINEDA is Assistant Professor of Government at Smith College, Massachusetts. Her research interests include the politics of protest and social movements, Black political thought, race and politics, radical democracy and twentieth-century American political development.

ROBIN CELIKATES is Professor of Social Philosophy at Freie Universität Berlin and a member of the editorial team of *Critical Times*. He specializes in critical theory, civil disobedience, democracy, collective action, recognition, migration and citizenship, and methodological questions in political and social philosophy.

Robin Celikates (**RC**): I think it is fair to say that civil disobedience is back on the agenda, both on the streets – with Black Lives Matter, the climate justice movement, anti-austerity movements, and so on – and as a topic for philosophical discussion. And it raises a lot of fascinating theoretical questions, from definitional questions that ask what civil disobedience is and how it differs from other forms of protest, to questions of justification and legitimacy, to questions about its role within more or less democratic systems. Your recent work has focused around a critique of mainstream political theory, especially of liberalism. Despite being a very narrow perspective, liberalism has been hegemonic in political theory for quite some time. But it appears to be losing its hegemonic grip. What you refer to as "seeing like a state" or even "seeing like a white state" involves operating from within this hegemonic liberal perspective, and this is what you think political theorists have for the most part been doing. You, however, urge us to see "like an activist". How does that work, and what does that actually mean for you?

Erin R. Pineda (**ERP**): When I began writing about this back in 2012, I was thinking a lot about the Arab Spring, Occupy Wall Street, and the modes of direct action, civil disobedience, and forms of protest that were happening globally in that moment. And while we may typically think that the civil rights movement of the 1950s and 1960s provided a blueprint for civil disobedience, I began to ask whether this might no longer be the case. After all, the world has changed substantially, so the kinds of structures that activists are confronting might require different forms of action; or activists might attribute different meanings to their actions, understanding them in new and distinctive ways. But once I started engaging closely with the literature on the civil rights movement, I became fascinated by the way that mainstream liberal and democratic philosophies of civil disobedience – many of which emerged in the 1960s and 1970s – interacted with and used the example of the civil rights movement. There seemed to be a gap between what I was seeing as the representation of the civil rights movement reflected in mainstream philosophy, and what I knew sociologically and historically about the movement. And I wanted to better understand that gap.

The liberal and democratic philosophers of that time – those who went on to create these influential theories of civil disobedience – were very interested in and invested in the civil rights movement. They were sympathetic to its aims and its tactics. They sought to defend the movement from the conservative critique that civil disobedience creates lawlessness and results in the breakdown of democratic constitutional orders. Being politically motivated in this way, they took up the question of whether citizens have an obligation to obey the law, and they wanted to theorize that obligation in such a way that there would still be room for something like civil disobedience within democratic, liberal societies. But in adopting that framework – by starting with the question, "when are citizens of good, liberal, democratic orders justified in breaking the law in protest?" – they saw the movement through the lens of their own motivations, their own concerns for the obligation to obey, and their own assumptions about the kind of society the Jim Crow United States was.

This way of seeing prioritizes the stability and maintenance of the constitutional order. These theorists tended to take it for granted that the context about which they were writing – the US in the 1960s – was *already* meaningfully democratic. They wanted to theorize civil disobedience as this limited exception to an otherwise legitimate, healthy democratic order. And this caused them to theorize the problem of racial domination in a very narrow and specific way, as a relatively anomalous, purely domestic form of exclusion. Segregation was a serious injustice, of course, but it was not conceptualized as something that would affect or seriously threaten the overall legitimacy and integrity of the constitutional order. This framework strongly shapes the way that they saw civil disobedience unfolding, the kinds of normative meaning that they ascribed to it, the kinds of limitations that they put on its use, and the kinds of actions with which they associated it. Most problematically, they then tended to impute this view to the civil rights activists that they were writing about. It is this tangle of issues that I refer to as "seeing like a white state".

Methodologically, the key question for me was how to think about it otherwise. If I don't find the existing literature to be an adequate characterization of what was going on, what are my alternatives? The methodological commitment that I made was to investigate the frameworks, the vantage points, and the questions that activists themselves were working with rather than trying to simply retheorize civil disobedience from a different theoretical angle. I wanted to think about the activists themselves as engaging in political theorizing, in making public political sense of what they were doing: identifying and problematizing political structures; thinking about how racial domination functions and how it shapes subjects, relations and institutions; and forging a course of action to remediate a problem or to transform oppressive structures. As theorizing, all of this involves abstracting away from the complicated reality of political life, conceptualizing forms of domination, and then making political claims about how action can affect the shape of the world.

RC: To flesh this out a bit, it would be useful to look at a specific feature that is often taken to be central to civil disobedience. There are many definitions of it, but it is pretty standard to think that civil disobedience is non-violent, that it seeks change while also accepting the general legitimacy of the political and legal system. And insofar as civil disobedience always involves breaking the law (which differentiates it from legal protests, demonstrations, and so on), one of the ways in which this acceptance of the legitimacy of the political system is often taken to be expressed is through the readiness to accept the legal consequence of breaking the law. Many liberal theorists think that this readiness to accept the consequences of one's actions is important to signal one's continuing loyalty to the constitutional order. Furthermore, it serves to underline the seriousness of one's intent: you are not just doing this because you are an anarchist or have an irrational desire to smash things; rather, you are a serious political agent, even in some ways an exemplary citizen. We find such claims in the writings of Martin Luther King Jr, as well as in how the civil rights movement operated. What do you think is wrong with this liberal picture, and how does seeing like an activist help us to understand what is wrong with it and provide an alternative perspective on how these issues of loyalty and accepting punishment should be reconsidered?

ERP: The way that you set up the question is exactly the way that I would think about it. What is foundational to the liberal perspective is the presumption that the constitutional order is democratic, is legitimate, and ought to be maintained – and, furthermore, that activists themselves have a primary interest in maintaining it because it is the guarantor of their rights and democratic citizenship. John Rawls noted that it is not an easy thing to be taken as sincere by your fellow citizens;

your actions, however sincerely undertaken, do not automatically read to others as serious acts of conscience or as signs of a deeper commitment to justice and democracy for all. Consequently, he argued, activists have to find ways of communicating not only their sincerity, but also the limited nature of their intervention: they have to somehow broadcast that they intend their lawbreaking to be targeted, confined to the issue at hand, and not an assault on the rule of law as such. Proper Rawlsian activists have to convey that though their actions may be dramatic or disruptive, they are nevertheless intended in the spirit of reform; they are intended to remediate specific injustices that all citizens should have an interest in addressing. The point is not to tear down; it's to reform.

There are a couple of things that I would say about that framework. The first is to simply grant that this account might sometimes be true. I would not want to deny that you could easily find examples in which activists expressed themselves in that way, saw their own actions in that way, and adopted those ends as their own. However, I believe that it is a problematic reading of the civil rights movement in particular, as well as many other movements. It certainly cannot be *the* theory of civil disobedience, and it's a questionable theory of injustice in liberal democratic states. If we take seriously the idea that the states that we call liberal democracies are nevertheless built on various nested forms of domination that make people substantively – and, often, formally – un-free within them, then I think it becomes problematic to say that this is how civil disobedience works within them, or to impute that set of claims to activists contesting their domination. In the end, even as Rawls and his liberal interlocutors criticized conservatives who rejected the "lawlessness" of civil disobedience, their own theories accepted and operated within a quite conservative framework in which dissent in liberal democracies is, by necessity, severely circumscribed in the interest of stability.

The other issue that I see with this framework is that it treats liberal-democratic states as having nothing of consequence in common with contexts we categorize as colonial or authoritarian. In other words, if one problem is that Rawls gets liberal democracies wrong (or gets the United States wrong as a liberal democracy), the other problem is that liberal democracy is theorized in isolation from other political contexts that were actually historically and politically linked. Activists themselves often speak across those contexts, borrowing tactics and cultivating ethical languages amongst each other; they also make arguments about how two contexts that appear distinct are actually related. In my work, I try to show that civil disobedience emerged within a civil rights movement that was deeply in conversation with, and tied to, anti-colonial movements around the world. For this set of global activists, Jim Crow was fundamentally tied to colonial rule through histories of racial capitalism, through the continuities between US racial terror and colonial rule. In this way, the language of radical non-violence and civil disobedience became a shared language and a shared framework. The civil rights activists certainly did not see the world as bifurcated into democratic states and everywhere else.

In the example that you brought up about accepting arrest and punishment, there are alternative ways of understanding what those tactics might mean. I have done research into the student sit-in movements of 1960 and 1961, as well as the Freedom Riders of 1961. In these examples, the activists allowed themselves to be arrested, but then chose to serve out jail sentences rather than accepting bail. From the liberal perspective, we can say that this is just the way that they are showing their sincerity and reformist intentions: they are choosing the harsher of the two punishments in order to demonstrate their investment in both the cause and the legitimacy of the legal system. But looking through the archival documents and trying to trace out the strategic and ethical conversations that activists were having amongst themselves, I found that they defended their strategy of accepting arrest and refusing to pay bail (what they called "jail, no bail") as a way of signalling their deep break with the legal architecture of Jim Crow. In their view, "jail, no bail" *radicalized* their protest rather than tempered or limited it. They argued that they should refuse to contribute funds to the legal system by accepting bail, because doing so would be equivalent to paying their jailors, paying their captors, paying to prop up a system of Jim Crow injustice that did not stop at the courthouse door but was society-wide. They were thus attempting a much more radical critique of the political and legal system than the liberal account gives them credit for.

When they talked about why it was important to go to jail and what could happen by going to jail, they used this evocative language of self-emancipation and self-liberation. They argued that there is something materially and symbolically important about showing courage and fearlessness, about refusing to comply within the Southern jail – a site that represented the epicentre of Jim Crow racial violence. These jails were not just sites of a legal order at work, but were also sites of intense extra-legal violence and terror. They were extremely vulnerable in that setting. For them, then, choosing to go to jail and choosing to stay was an act of defiance and self-liberation; they were not going to be submissive to this system or captured by its techniques of racial terror. Through this dramatic refusal, activists could build solidarity with each other, they could spur on solidarity protests, and they could build the movement from the Southern jail cell outward. This provides a wholly different normative or theoretical constellation than the liberal model, but it's a constellation that is very difficult to see if we are so committed to the liberal model that what we are trained to look out for is reformist intent or signals of investment in the constitutional order as it exists.

RC: In your work, you also discuss how the civil rights activists learned about how non-violence works, and how effective it can be, from anti-colonial movements elsewhere, especially from Gandhi and the Indian independence movement. In the context of what you just said, with activists rejecting the claim to the legitimacy of the constitutional state and disputing that it has the democratic credentials it presented itself as having, this seems to open the way to more militant, maybe even openly violent, forms of resistance that would seem legitimate in a context where the state does not have a claim to your obedience because it systematically violates your freedom and subjects you to racial domination. In the colonial situation, there was not only the non-violent form of anti-colonial struggle, but also, in many cases, openly violent and militant movements whose legitimacy today seems out of the question due to the specificity of that particular context. Was the question of violence within the civil rights movement settled in advance or were there discussions about its legitimacy under these circumstances? If the state is not really a democratic one, then why restrain yourself in these ways? Was that a tactical choice or a principled one?

ERP: The question that the activists posed was less about the threshold at which something more than non-violence becomes legitimate, and more about what non-violence *does*: What does mass non-violence do, what does it enact? What effects does it have, both inwardly in relation to the self, and outwardly in relation to others and to institutions? The flip-side of this question is what violence might do instead of, or differently than, non-violence. Once again, the problem with the question of whether (or when) violence is legitimate is what it presumes about the contexts in which activists chose non-violence: is it really the case that their choice indicates a judgement that Jim Crow, or colonialism in India or Ghana or wherever, was not unjust enough to justify doing something more extreme or radical? Are we suggesting that non-violence is reformist and violence is revolutionary? Historically and theoretically, that presumption is dubious.

With all that said, activists did argue about what different forms of action would do, what effects they would have on the world, and how those actions corresponded to the structures and conditions as they saw them. Within that framework, questions about violence or non-violence came up repeatedly for civil rights activists. And the choice of non-violence was disputed the entire way through.

The activists that I focus on in my work thought about mass non-violence as having this twin face. On the one hand, it cultivates this practice of fearlessness and performs libera-tion in the ways I was talking about earlier. But it also works outwardly on the world by using techniques of disruption and direct action to intervene in ongoing practices of domination and to interrupt the functioning of existing institutions. This in turn creates the space for other citizens, particularly white citizens, to reorient themselves toward what is going on and to take up the question of their own investment in the revealed architecture of domination. Do they wish to be associated with it or do they wish to be associated with the movement that is fighting it? For Martin Luther King Jr, as for others, mass non-violence held out this possibility of radically transform-ing colonizers, occupiers and dominators into wholly different kinds of subjects, into citizens *for the first time*. Those like King, those who insisted on non-violence, felt that violent strug-gle cut off that possibility. That was why non-violence was important. It had ethical stakes, but they were tied to political ones.

We could view this as capitulating to the white perspective by trying to appeal to white people in a way that will not leave them feeling so threatened. I think that this idea gives too little credit to the radical nature of this way of seeing non-violence.

The ambition to transform people who are cast into the role of occupiers, colonizers and dominators, and to think about what it would mean for them to become democratic citizens for the first time – to really inhabit relations of mutuality, equality, respect and reciprocity with Black citizens – is an ambition of radical proportion.

RC: You seem to want to liberate current protest movements from the burden that is often imposed on them to somehow conform to the idealized (and highly non-factual) standards associated with the civil rights movement. How are we to break this spell that conservative forces, in particular, try to cast on current social movements by continuously invoking this idealized version of the civil rights movement that is in fact completely whitewashed and watered down?

ERP: I have always been very interested in the ways that the civil rights movement is invoked politically, not just by conservatives but also by liberals, by almost everybody in fact (even in cases where it clearly does not belong). To take one example, something that caught my attention when I was in graduate school was the invocation of Martin Luther King Jr to criticize Edward Snowden for not accepting arrest. In a variety of ways, this seems like an odd example to reach for as the cases are so incommensurate: you have a mass movement for racial justice on the one hand and a lone whistleblower outing government surveillance on the other.

As the Snowden example shows, one use of the civil rights movement is to suggest that contemporary activists are not doing it right: they are not living up to their obligations, they are not behaving in the right ways, they are too disruptive, rude, violent, and so on. It's a kind of disciplining rhetoric. But, at the same time, we also get really opportunistic invocations of the civil rights movement due to the legitimacy that it confers. Over the past year within the US, for example, anti-lockdown protestors and anti-maskers have been arguing that they are modern equivalents of Rosa Parks or that they are resisting in the tradition of Martin Luther King Jr. It is no accident that they turn to these exemplars and try to claim them for themselves: the example, domesticated though it is, carries with it the idea that it is a legitimate form of resistance.

One thing I wanted to understand through my work was how and why the civil rights movement example started to circulate like this, and how this circulation might be tied to the ways the movement is used and evoked in academic philosophy. I want both to suggest that the example of the movement is still exceptionally fertile ground for theorizing and thinking radically about tactics, strategy, ethics and politics, while also suggesting that it is not a model or a blueprint of any kind. It cannot just be slapped down on other movements to suggest that their approach is not the right way to do it.

My way of tying these two aims together is to think about what the civil rights activists who undertook these kinds of activities thought they were good for, and why. What were the questions for which it provided an answer? We are then in a better position to understand the extent to which those questions are still (or are no longer) our questions. To what extent are these still the questions that activists themselves face? In what ways might the analyses of contemporary activists overlap with – or diverge from – the analyses of white supremacy and colonialism that civil rights activists devised? In what ways do activists have room to differ and come up with their own social and political theories of what they are up against? Rather than being left with a model that is good for all times and for all places, I try to think closely about what it might mean to see like a contemporary activist, and to accept that this might mean seeing quite differently than a civil rights activist.

RC: Just to clarify: why would anti-lockdown protests that claim to pick up the mantle of the civil rights movement *not* count as engaging in civil disobedience in that kind of tradition?

ERP: There is of course a real risk in just taking up the movements and the claims and the causes that we ourselves endorse as legitimate forms of protest! My point was not that anti-lockdown protests would definitely not qualify as forms of civil disobedience. Rather, I think that part of the problem with the invocation of the civil rights movement as so tied to what legitimate civil disobedience looks like is that it rules out all kinds of things. It works as a kind of litmus test: the question of whether a form of protest looks like the civil rights movement tends to answer the question of whether it is legitimate, and even whether it counts as civil disobedience at all. But the civil rights movement cannot possibly carry that kind of interpretive, political weight; it cannot relieve us of the burden of judging in each particular case what is happening, why it is happening, and what effect it has on the world. The anti-lockdown protests may well be a case of civil disobedience, and, depending on how you articulate what is at stake in them, they may well be legitimate. So, the way that I would look at this question is by thinking quite seriously about what the anti-lockdown protestors want and what effect they think their actions should have on the world. However, we cannot just invoke the civil rights movement to circumvent the work of judging the anti-lockdown protests politically, on their own terms, by figuring out what kinds of freedom they want, and articulating its stakes and consequences.

RC: As a final question, what do you think would have to change in public and higher education for the example of the civil rights movement, in all its complexity, to be integrated into our current situation?

ERP: I grew up in the US and when I look back on my own education and the ways that I first encountered this example, it is clear that it was already packaged within a narrative that seemed to predetermine the outcome. The civil rights movement tended to be paired with the abolitionist movement as an example that proves the gradual perfection of American democracy, the unceasing progress towards greater and greater inclusion, towards the formation of a more and more perfect union. It was always framed within this very patriotic and ideological narrative. This framework might tell you that the civil rights movement is important and inspiring, and it might familiarize you with some of these figures, but it already pre-empts the question of what the civil rights activists themselves were up to: why they thought it was meaningful to connect with anti-colonial activists, how they thought about Jim Crow, and so on. This rules out in advance any interpretation of their actions other than this standard liberal one. The short answer to your question is that I think the entire way that racial history in the US is packaged and taught would have to change in order to make sense of the US as a longstanding racial state. We can characterize it as a constitutional democracy in some ways, but it is also a racial order durable over several centuries. Understanding this is crucial to understanding what citizenship means here; it is crucial to understanding what activism means here. And it is so central that it cannot just be repackaged into a story about how this is a democracy from 1776 slowly perfecting itself over time.

FURTHER RESOURCES

Robin Celikates, "Learning from the streets: civil disobedience in theory and practice". In Peter Weibel (ed.), *Global Activism: Art and Conflict in the 21st Century*. Cambridge, MA: MIT Press, 2015.

Erin R. Pineda, *Seeing Like an Activist: Civil Disobedience and the Civil Rights Movement*. Oxford: Oxford University Press, 2021.

Erin R. Pineda, "Disobedience". *The Philosopher* 110:1 (2022).

Eraldo Souza dos Santos, "Violence". *The Philosopher* 110:2 (2022).

"William Scheuerman and climate activism". The Philosopher and the News podcast, 28 October 2021. https://newsphilosopher. buzzsprout.com/1577503/9446219-william-scheuerman-climate-activism.

PART II

LIVING TOGETHER

As actress Gal Gadot found out to her cost in assuming that "we're all in this together" during her preamble to the widely ridiculed celebrity rendition of John Lennon's "Imagine" in the early days of the global pandemic, there is a certain recklessness in harbouring any great ambitions for the first-person plural.

In asking, "What Is We?" in her 2020 essay for *The Philosopher*, Ragini Tharoor Srinivasan captures the tension that lies at the heart of any assumption of shared subjectivity, perspective, or experience. More conventional forms of that question, such as "who are we?" or "what are we?" take it for granted that "we" already are. Srinivasan, however, is not convinced.

It is a commonplace that universalisms exclude. The pseudo-universalisms that shape the modern world blur the interests of the powerful with the interests of all. The ever-expanding call for rights and recognition from the excluded is at the same time a call to keep the universalist promise. But what if modernity is in fact *constituted* by its exclusions? Where are we to go from here?

The felt absence of a common world in our time of radical upheaval has led to interpersonal and political deadlock. The twin crises of Covid-19 and anthropogenic climate change have not served to collectivize us; rather, they have served to amplify the staggering differentials of power and advantage that could more easily be papered over in normal times.

Amidst all this, can we cultivate an art of living together, however provisional and unstable? There is no art of polarization, to be sure (just look at Twitter). Rather, the art of living together involves reaching out across ever-expanding categories of difference – human, non-human, vegetal, robotic, earthly. And despite emerging narratives of relationality and interdependence from feminism to physics, nothing feels harder. The cocoon-like embrace of our echo chamber feels terribly attractive when faced with "them" in all their strange, inscrutable otherness.

Polarization is easy, but, to quote Spinoza, "all things excellent are as difficult as they are rare".[1]

----

1. This is the famous final line of Spinoza's *Ethics* (1677).

7

What is "We"?

Dan Zahavi in conversation with Luna Dolezal

Towards the end of 2020, *The Philosopher* published an issue asking, "What is We?" As part of a series of events to celebrate the launch of this issue, Luna Dolezal interviewed Dan Zahavi about the main themes in Zahavi's essay for that issue, "We and I". They explore the ways in which "I", "You" and "We" interact; the nature of selfhood; the politics of group identity; and the work of thinkers like Jean-Paul Sartre and Martin Buber. For Zahavi, if we wish to understand what it means to share a belief, an intention, an emotional experience or, more generally, a perspective with others, we also need to look at how we come to understand and relate to others in the first place.

DAN ZAHAVI is Professor of Philosophy and Director of the Center for Subjectivity Research at the University of Copenhagen. He is an authority on the work of Edmund Husserl and has written on numerous topics, including selfhood, subjectivity and empathy.

LUNA DOLEZAL is Lecturer in Medical Humanities and Philosophy at the University of Exeter. Her research is primarily in the areas of applied phenomenology, philosophy of embodiment, philosophy of medicine and medical humanities.

Luna Dolezal (**LD**): One of the most fundamental philosophical concepts related to the idea of "we" is collective intentionality. Could you tell us what philosophers generally mean when they use this term?

Dan Zahavi (**DZ**): A simple way of thinking about intentionality is that it amounts to *object-directedness*. Examples of individual intentionality include: I perceive a tree; I remember a summer vacation; I love somebody; I feel ashamed about something. This individual intentionality can also extend to actions: I move a chair; I bake a cake. And, crucially, it can also come in a collective form: we make food together; we move furniture together; parents love their children or feel ashamed about how they have treated them. In everyday life, there are many instances of shared emotions, shared experiences and shared actions. This is what is typically meant by collective intentionality.

LD: One way of interpreting this is that through having a collective, intentional experience, we are thereby constituted as a "we", as a group subject. I was wondering whether you think of the "we" of collective intentionality as having primacy over the "I" of individual intentionality?

DZ: If we consider the idea that collective intentionality or the "we" takes precedence, the claim could be that individual action is actually the exception rather than the rule – it is something we have to learn, something that departs from the collective actions that we have undertaken with others. An extension of this line of thinking would be that it is our *separateness* rather than our togetherness that is in need of an explanation. One area where this kind of thought is commonly found is in the psychoanalytic literature where we sometimes find the claim that the infant is *literally* incapable of distinguishing itself from the caregiver. On such an account one might say that the infant is initially part of an undifferentiated "we" that is not yet decomposable into "I" and "you".

Another slightly looser way of considering this would be the claim that the "I" or the self is communally grounded. We might, for instance, say that we initially experience ourselves as part of a family, or tribe, or group. We partake in its way of life, and this precedes the development of our own individuality, of our own distinct perspective on the world. This is probably a much more commonsensical way of talking about the primacy of the we.

LD: If we want to understand the notion of the "we" better, it seems to be of paramount importance to get a clearer idea of what exactly we mean by "I", by self, by individuality. How do you think of the "I" in terms of its relation to the "we"?

DZ: The plausibility of the claim that the "we" or the community has some kind of primacy might make sense if we operate with a certain conception of self. Consider certain questions related to our individual identities: What defines us as person? What do we care about? Which norms and values and preferences do we have? It makes a lot of sense to think about our identity in terms of these kinds of notions. And if *that* is what we mean by "I" or self, then it clearly makes sense to claim that the "I" is formed, shaped and enabled by our community membership. To assume that we somehow have a very fixed grasp of what matters to us or what preferences we have independently of any kind of social interaction or cultural history does not strike me as very plausible.

But there is another way of talking about the "I" that I have written about extensively. According to this "minimal self" position, it is quite appropriate to already talk of a self when considering the very structure of experience, when considering the fact that experiences are not just anonymous, un-owned events, but rather always *somebody's* experiences. If this fundamental subjective component of experience is what we have in mind when we talk about selfhood, I think it is much harder to make sense of the claim that such an "I" should be socially constituted or that we would only come to possess subjective experiences as a result of communal membership. I frankly don't really understand how that argument is supposed to run. So, in order to make headway with this kind of discussion, it is important to disentangle different notions of self and to be very clear about which one we have in mind.

LD: What about the fact that interactions with caregivers who ensure survival are the conditions for the possibility of experience? There is no infant who is going to survive to the point of self-conscious experience without at least one caregiver who will bring them to that point.

DZ: From the first moment of experience, the infant is together with others and it could not survive if it was not supported by others. I don't really think anybody would dispute that. But if the claim is that phenomenal consciousness, or experience itself, is somehow constitutively dependent upon others, this is certainly a more theoretically interesting claim, but I find it quite implausible and have never seen a convincing argument in its defence. So again, it is true that the infant would die if it was not supported by others, but is it also the socially supporting environment that imbues the child with experience? I doubt it.

LD: Another common argument for the primacy of "we" seems to be motivated by a critique of individualism. What do you make of this kind of critique?

DZ: If individualism is taken to mean the idea that one should valorize individual preferences or exclusively focus on maximizing the quality of one's own life, I don't think that has anything to do with the view I am defending. I think it is useful to distinguish between egoism and, for want of a better word, an "egological" view of consciousness. When I defend the view that consciousness is necessarily subject-centred, this has nothing to do with defending the view that concern for one's well-being overrules other concerns. One is a metaphysical discussion about the nature of consciousness, while the other is an ethical discussion about the values we should pursue and about what is important in life. I think those two things don't overlap.

LD: One thing this discussion brings to mind is Jean-Paul Sartre's discussion of "the Look" in *Being and Nothingness*, and how reflective self-awareness is awakened through interactions with others. For Sartre, this is an ontological relation – the self is awakened by the other. So, when you talk about the fundamental subjective component of experience, does this include reflective self-conscious experience?

DZ: It is a very specific kind of externalized self-consciousness that Sartre thinks comes about as a result of being looked at by others. Sartre is well-known for having defended the idea that pre-reflective self-consciousness is part and parcel of consciousness per se. He certainly does not argue that pre-reflective self-consciousness is brought about as a result of experiencing yourself being viewed by others. So, it is important to distinguish different levels and different types of self-consciousness. I have absolutely no problem with the view that there are lots of very important forms of self-consciousness and levels of selfhood that are socially mediated and enabled. My concern is about whether it goes *all the way down*.

Another issue is that if we really assumed that the "I" is socially constructed all the way down, if all of us are co-constituted, intertwined and co-dependent from the very start, this wouldn't only put pressure on the role of the subject, it would also put pressure on the role of the *other*. But in my view, we need robust conceptions of both if we want to arrive at a proper conception of the "we"; one that is very different from, say, any fantasy of an undifferentiated, fusional oneness or some kind of totalitarian uniform "we".

LD: We have discussed dependency on others in childhood, but there are numerous examples of the severe mental disturbances experienced as part of, say, forced isolation in prisons. Is this not an example of how phenomenal consciousness remains constitutively dependent on others into adulthood?

DZ: I think it is very important to distinguish externally enforced social isolation from voluntarily chosen social isolation. I remember reading about a Buddhist nun who spent several years alone in a cave in the Himalayas as part of her spiritual practice, and who subsequently reported that this was one of the richest experiences she had ever had. So, social isolation can actually mean a lot of different things. So, we should distinguish between the idea that sociality can *influence* the content of our experience and help us become psychologically robust individuals, from the more radical (and, in my view, wrong) claim that when deprived of social interaction we would not have experiences and would transform into some kind of non-conscious zombies. There are theorists who defend such a view, but I don't know of any evidence – empirical or otherwise – that supports it. I am not saying that social interaction and caring relations are not extremely important, but I think the wrong way to argue for their significance is by considering them a necessary condition for experience per se.

LD: We have talked about the first- and third-person perspectives so far, but I am interested in your thoughts on the second-person perspective. This has been famously discussed by thinkers like Martin Buber and Emmanuel Levinas in relation to the "I-Thou" or "I-You" relationship. What is the significance of the second-person perspective in your conception of how we form a "we"?

DZ: If we want to understand the "we", it is not enough just to try and think about the relationship between the "I" and the "we" because a "we" always involves more members than myself, and whether I qualify as a member of that "we" is not just up to me. I think it is in the nature of a "we" that it involves some kind of recognition or acknowledgement by the other members as well. One way to develop that thought is to say that if we wish to understand what a "we" is, we also need to look at the relationship between the prospective members; we need to understand how we come to understand others in the first place. How do we acquire social cognition? How do we acquire interpersonal understanding?

A further and related question is: are all forms of interpersonal understanding equally significant? If members of a group are engaging with each other from a third-person perspective, would this be sufficient to constitute a "we"? Or does relating to and addressing the other as a "you" play a special role in the formation of a "we"? My basic idea would be that constituting a "we" with another person involves relating to that person as a co-subject, rather than merely as, say, a mental object or an entity with a mind. A "we" is a first-person plural – it is about sharing a perspective with others. And relating to another as a "you" is a way of highlighting or emphasizing precisely the status of the other as a co-subject. When I relate to the other as "you", I relate to the other as somebody who has a perspective on myself as well, and I think this is crucial in order to establish a "we".

LD: Given that the concept of the "we" is applicable in so many different realms, from intimate family relationships to nation states, how does your account work with the differentiation of "we-formations" across durations and sizes?

DZ: One problem with some of the most influential discussions of collective intentionality is that the main focus has often been on very simple archetypes: how do we decide to go for a walk together? How do we make food together? How do we paint a house together? It's not that these kinds of joint actions are unimportant, but rather that they do not touch upon the types of "we" that are most important politically. We certainly do need a proper account of larger group-formations, of the communities of which we are part, and it will not do to simply focus on dyadic face-to-face relations. Having said that, I doubt we could ever understand such larger we-formations, let alone become members of them, were it not for our more intimate face-to-face encounters. Thus, I would still maintain that the dyadic "we" is a precondition for larger and more anonymous we-formations, and it is in accounting for the former that I want to appeal in particular to the second-person "you" relation.

LD: Thinkers like René Giraud argue that a "we" can only be constituted by processes of exclusion, for example sacrificing scapegoats to maintain social cohesion and confirm community conventions and mores. Can a "we" only be a "we" if it demarcates itself from those who are not part of it?

DZ: The answer to this question would depend on which "we" is being considered. Take the example of two people alone in a house dancing together – this clearly does not presuppose a simultaneous exclusion of others. But when we consider more enduring and consolidated "we-formations", they often involve very interesting structural features, relations of power, and so on. In these cases, the contrast to competing groups might help consolidate the "we" identity, and, indeed, it may be the case that such a "we" is primarily defined and held together by animosity vis-à-vis outsiders. This of course raises the interesting question of whether there might be (more open and tolerant) ways of securing the endurance of the "we" that avoided such exclusion and demarcation.

LD: Being excluded from a "we" raises the question of how membership of a "we" is constituted. For example, an individual may think of themselves as part of a "we", but they may then come to be excluded and realize all along that they were mistaken in assuming this membership.

DZ: To touch on something I was saying earlier, it is very important not to view the "we" as a kind of fused unity; rather, a "we" is always something that preserves plurality and difference. And one outcome of this is that a "we" is also potentially fragile; it is something that has to be negotiated over and over again. So, if the very nature of the "we" requires the acknowledgement and recognition of the others, membership of the "we" is not something that I can decide for myself. That someone has a "we experience" is not sufficient for we-membership, since they could be mistaken; this is regrettably a fact of life. We can sometimes think that we are part of a group, and then realize that the others never actually recognized us as proper members. A "we" is a fragile formation, but this is precisely what also makes it so valuable.

LD: Another scenario is that you are recognized as belonging to a particular group but you don't feel that you are part of that group at all. In effect, you are ascribed to that group from the outside.

DZ: This example shows that it is very important to distinguish the "we", which I take to be a very particular social formation, from other types of groups. As you just pointed out, there are certain groups that we are members of, regardless of whether we care about it. We might even be members of these groups unbeknownst to us. For example, we might be a member of a certain blood type group, and our membership of this group might be determined exclusively by certain objective criteria. But I do not consider such groups appropriate candidates for "we" groups, since a "we" group is one that involves and requires identification, appropriation and participation. This, in turn, serves to enrich and affect the member's self-experience, their engagement with the world, and their understanding of others.

LD: How has the pandemic and related social distancing conditions impacted on the sense of "we"? For example, ubiquitous forms of communication mediated by platforms like Zoom?

DZ: You could of course say that platforms like Zoom offer an excellent example of a face-to-face relationship, but what many people typically mean when they talk about a face-to-face relationship is not these floating faces decoupled from the rest of the body. I think that the notion of *inter-corporeality* captures what is important in our encounters with others far better than the notion of a face-to-face encounter, and this is something that our many Zoom meetings have made us realize. There are two things that we are missing out on in Zoom encounters, both of which I consider very important for the constitution of a "we": one is that even though we have some kind of eye-to-eye contact, we lack the kind of shared environment that normally characterizes proper inter-corporeal encounters. We are not free-floating subjects, but are constantly engaging and interacting in a shared environment that contributes significantly to the process of understanding one another. The other thing that we find in encounters via platforms like Zoom is typically a structured agenda. What we do not find, and what I think is also very important for promoting a sense of community, is the kind of unstructured "just being together" with one another that characterizes normal social interactions. As a result, I do not consider these digital platforms to be optimal when it comes to developing a real community or "we".

FURTHER RESOURCES

Martin Buber, *I and Thou* [1923]. London: Bloomsbury, 2013.
Luna Dolezal, "Intercorporeality and social distancing". *The Philosopher* 108:3 (2020).
Jean-Paul Sartre, *Being and Nothingness* [1943]. Abingdon: Routledge, 2018.
Dan Zahavi, "We and I". *The Philosopher* 108:4 (2020).

8

Polarization and talking across difference

*Elizabeth Anderson in conversation
with Alexis Papazoglou*

This conversation with Elizabeth Anderson asks what it means to be a democratic citizen in a time when we find ourselves divided not only over values, but over facts. As lies, propaganda and fake news have hijacked political discourse on polarizing issues and distracted the electorate from constructive engagement of the problems we face, Anderson looks to thinkers like John Dewey and Susan Neiman in order to reframe democracy as a kind of culture that must be kept alive through civil society.

ELIZABETH ANDERSON is Arthur F. Thurnau Professor and John Dewey Distinguished University Professor of Philosophy and Women's Studies at the University of Michigan, Ann Arbor. She specializes in moral and political philosophy, social and feminist epistemology, and the philosophy of the social sciences.

ALEXIS PAPAZOGLOU is an Editor at the Institute of Art and Ideas, London and host of "The Philosopher & The News" podcast. He writes on the intersection between philosophy, politics and current affairs.

Alexis Papazoglou (**AP**): In his inauguration speech, President Biden said, "Let's begin to listen to one another, hear one another, see one another, show respect for one another". Your 2019 Uehiro Lectures at the University of Oxford are about the ethics of communication, and you try to articulate the conditions that would make possible a constructive discourse across political and identity divides in order to enhance our democracy. One of the things you focus on is what has gone wrong with our discourse around facts, with talk of "alternative facts", "fake news", and even a "post-truth era" in which a shared reality of facts is no longer available as a starting point for political discourse. How did we arrive here?

Elizabeth Anderson (**EA**): This kind of polarization of facts has been going on for several decades now. Much of it was initially driven by right-wing media, but the more recent driving force has been social media and their use of algorithms to amplify polarizing voices and outrage. The algorithms have discovered that polarizing discourse holds people's attention on these sites, and the longer you pay attention to something, the more money social media companies make on their advertisements. So those are the voices that get amplified. How do you generate polarization? By telling lies or presenting facts in a very misleading way that arouses fear and anger. This process has been commodified and commercialized. It's driving us into unreality.

AP: You mention certain emotions that can be problematic in how we conduct speech and communicate with each other, like anger and fear. But when it comes to certain marginalized, even brutalized, communities, might one argue that some of that emotional response is justified? And, if so, how do we try and manage these emotions and bracket them in some way so that we have a more constructive discussion about changing things?

EA: It is of course totally justified for people to, say, be outraged at police violence against people of colour – and indeed against anyone. The issue here is which emotions to express and to foreground when one is communicating to fellow citizens who disagree. To throw back anger at them is ineffective because it's just going to raise their hackles. It also represents a failure to understand where they're coming from because they've got fear too. Just look at "Defund the Police" or discourse about gun control. What we have to understand first is *why* the other side finds it important to support the police and to purchase guns. Fear is driving this, and when people are afraid, their cognition shuts down. They don't want to hear statistics about how people use guns mostly to kill themselves, their family members, or their friends and neighbours. Rather, what they feel is that there is a lot of real crime and real danger, so police and guns are part of the solution to that. In order to have an intelligent conversation across differences, you have to be receptive to and show empathy for the fact that other people are in other situations that they perceive as threatening and dangerous. If you don't hear that, they just think that you don't care about them.

AP: One of the things you diagnose as part of the current discourse is something you call the *populist economy of esteem*, where esteem is represented as a zero-sum game. If you gain esteem and I don't like you, then I thereby lose esteem. Can you tell me a little bit more about this concept and its impact on current discourse?

EA: Let's step back and think a little bit about right-wing populism, which is now a worldwide trend across almost all democracies. Right-wing populism is a mode of activating or mobilizing political support through a rhetorical strategy that explains the meanings of political events in terms of "elites" who are betraying the "real people" by promoting the interests and esteem of historically subordinated groups above them. Now, what's important about populist discourse is that it doesn't really put forward policies that offer material benefit to the people they're appealing to. Instead, it's symbolic, it's representational: it's addressing the feeling of cultural decentring and cultural demotion; it's addressing the resentment that white Christians feel because they believe that elites hold contempt for them because they're so transphobic, homophobic, racist, and so forth. But this resentment also extends to the people "beneath" them – trans people, gay people, immigrants, people of colour, and so forth – because they feel that those people are being promoted above them in the scale of social respect and esteem. Almost all populist discourse is actually taking place in these symbolic and cultural terms, rather than in material terms, related to, say, how much money people actually get.

AP: One of the other things you identify is that when we talk about facts these days, there's always a subtext. We're not *really* talking about facts; rather, we're expressing our identity. You call this *identity-expressive discourse*, and consider it to be prevalent on both spectrums of the political divide. What exactly is identity-expressive discourse? And is it always bad?

EA: Identity-expressive discourse is any kind of expression that serves to uphold a sense of the dignity and worth of the identity group to which one belongs. Of course, there is nothing inherently wrong with such discourse in general. Think, for example, of someone wearing a sweatshirt with the logo of their favourite sports team on it. Rather, identity-expressive discourse goes wrong when you use the medium of (purportedly) factual claims to express pride in your own side. In so doing, you are hijacking empirical discourse that is supposed to be attentive to the facts and using it for some other purpose. One of the key features of populist discourse is that it's *all* identity-expressive. It has trained people to think that whatever somebody says is simply an attempt to raise the esteem of their own side by means of putting the other side down. So, if you are in that mindset, you are always going to interpret whatever the other side says as some kind of insult, and you are never going to hear the facts for what they are.

One clear example of this is the idea that Covid is a hoax. Trump repeatedly said that the only reason that liberals/Democrats/elites are talking about Covid is to make *him* look bad! And, of course, because his followers identify with him, when somebody tries to make him look bad, they feel that it is also an attempt to put *them* down. Through this kind of lens, even the simple act of wearing a mask is perceived as an insult. It is interpreted not as a prudent public health measure based on facts and evidence, but as an insult aimed at a particular group.

AP: Apart from facts, we obviously also disagree about moral values. What are some of the fundamental disagreements around moral values that you see as especially pertinent right now?

EA: I think that disagreement about facts *is* driven by disagreement about values. If you look at, say, climate change denialism, the question of whether human beings are heating the earth to catastrophic consequences is simply a matter of scientific fact. But people still resist this idea because they are looking ahead to the seismic political implications of this. It is obviously outrageous and horrible to let millions of people die from rising sea levels and burning forests, and the only credible way to deal with climate change is via a massive scaling up of state capacity, changing environmental regulations, changing how utilities work, mandating alternative energy, and so forth. But people who oppose the view that society should be organized in terms of state-directed collective action just do not want to go there. They find it threatening to institute a mode of political organization that is more democratic and egalitarian. They feel safer in a hierarchical mode of organization that stresses the individual, rather than the collective. So they resist. This all comes from what the psychologist (and law professor) Dan Kahan refers to as "cultural cognition".

There are many ways to measure social identity. But the way Kahan and colleagues do it is through the intersections of two values. The first one is individualism versus collectivism, i.e., do you think that we should just rely on our own resources to deal with problems, or do you think that we need to get together in larger groups and cooperate in a more collectivist way? The second one is hierarchy or egalitarianism. The strongest disagreements are between the hierarchical individualists and the egalitarian collectivists. The former like free markets, hierarchically-organized corporations, and so on, while the latter like equality, democracy, large state capacity, social insurance, and things like that. In short, we have a values war! We all resist threats to our social identities or our fundamental value commitments. As a result, factual information that threatens these identities is something we resist. This is a universal.

AP: In terms of bridging this divide, you reference a social experiment to facilitate constructive discourses across political divides along the lines of a citizen jury. You get people to discuss "hot button" issues in a context that strips away the kind of partisan language that fosters negative or positive reactions. In such a context, people can share their personal stories of how they have been affected by certain policies. For example, people who live in metropolitan areas probably don't know how the policies that they favour can affect farmers, and so on. What is special about these forums that manage to facilitate discourse?

EA: We have excellent evidence both from deliberative polling and from actual assemblies of citizens that it is possible to moderate discussions of politically significant issues in such a way as to orient people to the facts, rather than trying to jockey for position and asserting their moral superiority at the expense of the other side. If the focus is on people talking about their own personal experience, their own lives, and their own struggles – what they know in person, rather than what they have heard on some media source – what you find is that people share those concerns. *Everyone* is worried about making a living in a pandemic, about the flourishing of their families, about staying safe, about affordable healthcare. These are all common concerns. And once you see that the other side cares about and are coping with the same issues, then you can start a more fact-oriented discussion. The key to opening people's minds to the facts is to reassure them that their identities are not being threatened, and you do that by listening – *seriously* listening – to their personal troubles and concerns.

In Republic of Ireland, for example, they adopted a constitutional reform that opens up opportunities for citizens' assemblies to deliberate on major issues over which, typically, the legislature is gridlocked and cannot move forward. One of the most widely discussed citizens' assemblies was over whether to liberalize abortion law. The most moving and important elements of these citizens' assemblies were when they presented testimony from women who had had or had contemplated an abortion. These women talked in rich detail about what was going on in their lives and what was going through their minds when they made that decision one way or another. Some of the women had had an abortion, while some had decided against it. And people listened very respectfully and then they discussed it.

AP: Throughout your lectures, you present the obstacles to a sensible form of public discourse as a problem that is caused by both sides of the political divide. But surely it matters in the end that one side is more often right about the facts – about whether the elections of 2020 were fraudulent or whether climate change is real? Or that one side happens to support a political framework that is more compassionate and more empathetic to begin with, that is likely to be more conducive to addressing questions of justice and suffering?

EA: The biggest point I am addressing is that both sides are looking at what I call second-order questions – i.e. who is better than who? – rather than first-order questions, i.e. those related to problems we need to solve like the pandemic, unaffordable healthcare in the United States, or long wait times to access healthcare in Britain. *Everybody* has a stake in these problems. We should never ask public policy to adjudicate over who is better than who, especially at the group level. For politicians to do so would be totally contrary to democratic norms. An obvious example of this is Hillary Clinton's infamous speech in her 2016 election campaign in which she referred to the "basket of deplorables" made up of those elements of Trump's supporters who she characterized as racist, sexist, homophobic, xenophobic, Islamaphobic, and so on, before dismissing them as *irredeemable*.

This is absolutely appalling – and not simply because it didn't work (although, of course, it didn't), but because it is so contrary to the democratic ethos to do that. Clinton campaigned on the idea that *we* are better, more empathetic than *them*. But is she *really* more empathetic to the people who are gripped by fear? In his 2016 campaign, Trump had a group of so-called "angel moms" follow him from one campaign event to the next. These were women who had family members who had been murdered by undocumented immigrants. So, Trump is stoking fear, he is repeatedly saying that immigrants coming over the Mexican border are murderers and rapists. And of course this is just propaganda. But that doesn't mean that the fear this generated wasn't genuine. So, to address people on immigration, the first thing you have to do is to take their fear seriously, *even if* it is ungrounded. Because to dismiss it is to make them think, "You don't care about people like us. Don't tell me you're the empathetic one, because you don't care about me".

AP: That is a really important point. Even if you believe the concerns are unjustified or wrong, you still have to take them seriously or you will fail in talking to the other side. I thought we could close our discussion by turning to your favourite philosopher, John Dewey. Dewey is affiliated with the American pragmatist tradition, and you consider the approach you are taking to the problem of citizen communication to be rooted in a Deweyan pragmatist approach. What do you mean by that? In what way is it pragmatist?

EA: In the context of ethics and political philosophy, pragmatism takes a sceptical position on the question of whether we can figure out through pure reasoning what the fundamental moral principles are. Instead, it wants to replace the quest for a purely rational deduction of first principles of morality with a *method* of enquiring about which rules we should live by. Dewey thinks (and I endorse this view) that we can test moral propositions in the same way that we test scientific claims. If you propose a certain moral principle, the idea is that you act in accordance with it and see if you are satisfied with the results. People have been advancing certain ideas on how to live for millennia, but when people try to live in the ways they mandate, they tend to learn that there are all kinds of unanticipated and undesirable consequences. We may be able to tinker and modify the framework, to add exceptions here and there, but sometimes you just come to the conclusion that this is not an acceptable way to live. And when it comes to moral enquiry and questions of what we owe to each other, this testing has to take place collectively because a certain rule might be perfectly satisfactory to some, but not to others. And this latter group has to be able to communicate that – sometimes in strident ways. But if the people who are happy with the status quo are also those in a position of power, then they just don't listen. This is why we need social movements, this is why democracy is on the streets.

AP: For Dewey, democracy isn't just about voting every four years, or about the institutions of democracy like parliaments, legislatures, and so on. Rather, it is a kind of culture that must be kept alive through civil society. Apart from demonstrating in the streets, what are the ways that we can contribute to the culture of democracy in our day-to-day lives, before we exercise our democratic voting rights when the time comes?

EA: The most important thing is to recognize the democratic obligation to engage with people on the other side. But this process is fraught with risk and needs facilitating conditions. Consider the fact that the geographical segregation of the sides has made this extremely difficult because it is expensive and time-consuming to travel to engage with one's political opponents. Furthermore, social media is optimizing for values that are actively hostile to democracy. This is why we are in desperate need of other forums where people get together – and not even necessarily to talk about politics, but just about their lives. In fact, it would be even better if we had *non*-political activities around which we could engage. But, as things stand, we don't even go to the same *churches* (if we go to church at all). Everything has been sorted and segregated so that people of different political parties have no opportunities to engage one another.

AP: One of the things that struck me in one of your lectures was your idea that philosophy is a terrible model for public discourse! Philosophy is combative, it looks to decisively refute the other side. Philosophy doesn't care about where people are coming from, it doesn't care much about lived experience. So, if this type of debate is terrible for our politics, is it also terrible for our philosophy?

EA: I do think that there is way too much philosophical argumentation that's just oriented toward refutation and one-upmanship. But I'm not going to condemn philosophy. I am a philosopher, after all! And there are many ways to do philosophy. Somebody who offers a really beautiful example of doing engaged political philosophy is Susan Neiman in her 2019 book, *Learning from the Germans: Race and the Memory of Evil*. She is writing as a white Jewish woman who grew up in the American South, and who has been living in Germany now for a number of years. She was struck by how the Germans had come to terms with the evil of the Holocaust, morally speaking, and encoded it in their historical memory in a way that white Americans (and America generally at the political level) have never managed in relation to slavery and its contemporary legacies of systematic racism. There has been no moral accountability, no apologies, no reparations. Much of the toxicity of politics today is a product of the refusal to come to terms with this.

Neiman does not just offer abstract arguments. She is out there talking to people – to Germans and to people in the American South – who are trying to move to a better way of being. As a philosopher, Neiman is making arguments in the course of her reporting. But these arguments are all embedded in the lived experience of coming to terms with the legacies of gross injustice in one's own society. It is thus rooted in a way that purely abstract argument over principles is not. It is a beautiful piece of philosophy. In standard analytic philosophy, we are used to formulating isolated premises, and then looking at objections and replies to our narrowly constructed premises that we can express in a single sentence. But moral life is too messy to encapsulate in a single moral principle.

FURTHER RESOURCES

Elizabeth Anderson, "Can we talk?" Neubauer Collegium, 11 November 2019. https://www.youtube.com/watch?v=NGVgvFERgqA.

John Dewey, "Creative democracy: the task before us" [1939]. Short essay readily and freely available online.

Susan Neiman, *Learning from the Germans: Race and the Memory of Evil*. New York: Farrar, Straus & Giroux, 2019.

Robert Talisse, "America's real polarization problem". The Philosopher and the News podcast, 4 February 2022. https://newsphilosopher. buzzsprout.com/1577503/10012968-robert-talisse-america-s-real-polarization-problem.

9

Misinformation and the right to know

Lani Watson in conversation with Aidan McGlynn

With the rise of social epistemology over the past decade, epistemologists have for the most part moved beyond the purely analytical task of defining knowledge, with their work today touching on almost every aspect of our lives. This conversation between social epistemologists Lani Watson and Aidan McGlynn coincided with the publication of the "Authority and Knowledge" issue of *The Philosopher*. In that issue, we asked how what counts as knowledge both depends on and supports authority, as well as what forms knowledge has to take (objective, expert, etc.) in order to be authoritative. Lani Watson's idea of "epistemic rights" expands the question of rights to include the right to goods such as information, knowledge and truth. Using the US pharmaceutical company Purdue Pharma as a case study, Watson argues that epistemic rights violations harm individuals, diminish the quality of the debate, and lead to increased polarization.

LANI WATSON is a Research Fellow with the Oxford Character Project at the University of Oxford. Her research is in applied social and virtue epistemology, with a focus on the nature and value of questioning.

AIDAN MCGLYNN is Senior Lecturer in Philosophy at the University of Edinburgh. His research focuses mainly on issues in epistemology, particularly where it intersects with other areas such as the philosophies of language and mind, and social and feminist philosophy.

Aidan McGlynn (**AM**): In your work, you make a case for the importance of the notion of epistemic rights. But this isn't a particularly familiar phrase to us in law or politics or other areas of social significance. How do you understand the notion of epistemic rights and what are some examples of the kind of phenomena you're trying to understand in these terms?

Lani Watson (**LW**): The term "epistemic" has always been a hard sell outside of academia, and I think that is a great shame because it is a very useful term. We can use it much more widely outside of universities and the academy than we in fact do. Epistemic rights are simply rights to epistemic goods like information, knowledge, understanding, truth, maybe even wisdom. They are rights that concern these epistemic goods and, in particular, they are rights that govern and protect the quality, the accessibility, and the distribution of these goods. As an example, take the right to know the results of a medical test. This is what is called a *claim right*, meaning that you have actually got a claim to that information. Claim rights are central to my work because they are necessarily social, they necessarily involve other people. In the case of my medical test, the doctor has a duty to convey the results accurately, not to mislead me, not to misinform me, not to give me false information, not to withhold the information, and so on. If she did any of those for no good reason, that would be a violation of my right to that information. But there are examples of epistemic rights all over the place: rights to data protection, rights to privacy, rights to true information in the mainstream media, rights to information about the food or drinks we are consuming or what is being used in cosmetic products, as well as rights to bigger picture things like education. Then there are interpersonal epistemic rights, such as the right to know if your spouse is having an affair or if the person that you are sleeping with has a sexually transmitted disease. These are the kinds of thing that we can talk about if we are talking about epistemic rights.

AM: You mentioned a couple of examples of epistemic rights related to healthcare, and you have written extensively about the case of Purdue Pharma and their drug OxyContin. What is the significance of this example for you?

LW: Purdue Pharma is a huge pharmaceutical company that produces and markets the opioid-based painkiller OxyContin. And in a very well-known legal case that's been going on for several years, Purdue Pharma and its top executives have been taken to court for the way in which they have marketed

OxyContin. Purdue eventually admitted that OxyContin was marketed "with the intent to defraud or mislead" (that is a quotation from the case). The misinformation campaign at the heart of the marketing of OxyContin is a case study that I draw on extensively to illustrate a huge number of very clear epistemic rights violations across a wide range of situations.

AM: One thing you focus on in your work is how to understand the harms involved in violations of rights where these harms are in part epistemic, but have other aspects to them as well – for example, they might be moral harms. To stick with the Purdue Pharma example, what kind of harms might be involved in the epistemic rights violations that you see present in that case?

LW: Something that I really want to emphasize is that epistemic rights are *both* legal and moral rights. I do not want to carve out a distinct category of rights in addition to legal and moral rights; rather, I am trying to draw attention to a distinct class of legal and moral rights which are epistemic in nature. When we violate epistemic rights, we have the potential to create all sorts of harms. In the Purdue Pharma case, there are so many harms that we can identify: some of the obvious practical harms are addiction and death, as well as financial harm. Then there are those hybrid practical-epistemic harms, such as the harm done to one's capacity as a decision-maker. We make decisions on the basis of what we know, and those decisions can be hugely corrupted if we have false information. And when decisions result from violating someone's epistemic rights through false information, the perpetrator of that violation bears responsibility for any harms caused by decisions based on that violation. In the Purdue Pharma case, they sent out a press release claiming that OxyContin was much safer, much less subject to abuse, than any other opioids on the market, and that this was supported by robust empirical research. This position was reinforced by promotional materials, conferences in Hawaii for medical professionals, financial incentives to prescribe the drug, and numerous other ways of influencing the prescribing habits of doctors.

The doctors (rightly or wrongly) take this information in good faith, which leads to them making certain decisions about which opioids to prescribe to patients. And then the behaviour of patients themselves is influenced by the belief that OxyContin is a safer option, that it is much less subject to abuse than other opioids. For example, one of the key claims made by Purdue Pharma in relation to OxyContin was that it has a special time release formula, meaning that the number of times you have to repeat taking the drug was twelve hours as opposed to the standard eight hours for other opioids on the market at that time. In fact, it turned out that all along they had studies showing that for at least half of the people taking OxyContin, the typical eight-hour interval was still applicable. If you only have a certain number of pills because the doctor also believes in the twelve-hour interval, then you have potentially a four-hour window characterized by excruciating withdrawal symptoms and an intense craving for the drug. This is what led to enormous amounts of addiction in the case of OxyContin. In focusing on the Purdue Pharma case, I wished to draw this really direct line between the spreading of that false information, the decisions that people make on the basis of that false information, and the massive harms resulting from those decisions.

AM: Talk of rights more generally gives us a powerful set of resources for talking about certain issues and, perhaps, intervening in them. But doesn't this also carry some dangers when the language of rights more generally, or epistemic rights in particular, are appealed to in ways that we perhaps don't want to endorse?

LW: As you say, rights talk can be abused, precisely because it is familiar and it is powerful. It has a certain rhetorical force that other types of moral and legal language can lack. Rights talk, or the notion of rights, has a unique power to direct conduct because rights are about telling us what we can and cannot do. If we take them seriously, then we need to do certain things and hold back from doing other things. This is part of what makes rights language particularly open to abuse. At the heart of what I am arguing is that rights talk is incredibly powerful, it has been used successfully to advocate for various crucial rights over the past century (women's rights, black rights, disability rights, LGBTQ rights, and so on), so there is no reason why we should not deploy it in the epistemic domain, especially as information is a huge part of our lives and our cultural landscape. We need some rights advocacy in order to protect ourselves from a whole range of harms and wrongs that take place in the epistemic domain. And precisely because of its capacity for abuse, it is especially important to get really clear about what epistemic rights are, what we can and cannot do with them. If we do not have the vocabulary and the language to articulate that, then we are going to be much more open to the kinds of harms and wrongs that we have discussed already in the case of Purdue Pharma, as well as in numerous other overlapping contexts.

AM: Issues related to epistemic rights are particularly pressing in the "information age", and this raises vital questions about authority and power, and how these interact with epistemology. How do power, authority and knowledge interact within the framework of epistemic rights?

LW: In a sense, this problem is as old as talking and thinking and spreading gossip itself, but it has also started operating at a new scale in the information age. One of the people whose work I have engaged with is Kent Cooper, who was the executive director of the Associated Press in New York during and after the Second World War. At that time, he was responding to what he saw as the malicious control of the spread of information by national medias across the world, including in Germany. Looking back to Cooper's work shows that ideas of controlling information, particularly via mass media, were with us before, during, and after the Second World War. Cooper argued for a restatement of the first amendment in terms of the right to know rather than press freedom. I think that is really interesting because his point is that they are not conceptually tied to each other: you can have press freedom without having protection of the right to know, because it cannot be taken for granted that press freedom is going to deliver us truth and accurate information. This is what I think we see on a massive scale now with mass media and social media controlling the spread of information at such a pace that is proving impossible to keep up with it legislatively.

AM: I thought that we could turn now to the question of who has epistemic rights. We may all accept that small babies have the right not to be treated in certain harmful ways. But you argue that a creature with rights in general also has epistemic rights. According to your account, then, a baby has the right to know. While it seems far from the case that small babies do not know anything, they certainly do not seem capable of knowing the outcome of, say, a diabetes test. So, this seemed like a slightly odd claim to me. Could you say a bit more about these kinds of cases and what motivated this slightly un-intuitive choice about who has rights and when they start?

LW: I am interested in the question of how we limit the allocation of rights in general. Human history is littered with instances where we have limited rights when we should not have. It is a testament to the past one hundred years that the allocation of rights has grown to cover many more people who were previously vulnerable and marginalized in terms of their status as rights holders. Being a rights holder is a marker of moral status, and babies have moral status, so we need to assign them rights, including epistemic rights. I do not want to attach the question of whether someone has a right more generally, or an epistemic right more specifically, to their capacity for knowing, believing, understanding, and so on, precisely because there are cases where we might start to lose that capacity over time, for example cognitive aging, Alzheimer's, or dementia. Generally speaking, it is not the case that we take rights away from people on the basis of their mental health or physical health, and this is something that we should bear in mind when we are assigning epistemic rights. We cannot take epistemic rights away from people based on the deterioration of their cognitive capacities; rather, we need to notice the deterioration of their cognitive capacities and assign them appropriate epistemic proxies, just as in the case of very young children when their parents or carers can act as their proxies. All this is to say that if you pull apart capacity from right-holding status, then you end up with the conclusion that a baby getting a diabetes test *does* have a right to know. I am much more comfortable with that than I am with taking away those rights on the basis of any kind of capacity.

AM: I am interested in epistemic harms that appear to be akin to treating a person as an object – a kind of epistemic objectification, rather than the sexual objectification we're more familiar with. The legal philosopher Joel Feinberg, for example, contrasts right bearers with "mere things", noting that "mere things have no conative life; neither cognitive wishes, desires, or hopes; nor urges and impulses; nor unconscious drives, aims, goals; nor latent tendencies, directions of growth, and natural fulfilments".[1] I wonder if you see any connection between treating somebody in a way that violates their epistemic rights and treating them as, in some sense, "mere things"?

LW: I am interested in the question of who has epistemic rights in general, not just in particular cases. I wanted to find out how big this category is, and ultimately came to the conclusion that it is in principle as big as the category of rights holders. But the category of rights holder excludes mere things: it does not include tables or rocks or rainbows. I think that treating someone as not having rights serves to lower them below this threshold, thus treating them as in some sense closer to an object rather than a rights holder. One of the really interesting emerging cases at the threshold between object and rights holder is artificial intelligence (AI). Advances in AI have brought ethical questions about the use of AI to the fore in recent years. As AI becomes increasingly sophisticated, questions about how we interact with and treat AI machines become increasingly salient. Should we be permitted to verbally abuse AI home assistants or act violently towards near-future AI robots in the street? Is there a point at which AI machines become rights holders? We might be tempted to think that such a point is a conceptual impossibility. However advanced, AI machines will always be machines, and machines can only ever have instrumental as opposed to final value. There might still be good reasons not to verbally or physically abuse them but those reasons are not derived from the final value of the machines themselves. If they cannot have final value, then they cannot have rights. Either way, if we do end up assigning rights to AI machines, these should prominently include epistemic rights.

AM: At what point should we draw a line between rights to know that should be protected by law and those that should not? For example, should a person's right to know if her spouse is having an affair be written into law? And if not, why not?

LW: We can usefully distinguish three different levels of protection for epistemic rights: (1) direct legal protection, (2) indirect legal protection, and (3) moral (but not legal) protection. These

---

1. Joel Feinberg, "The rights of animals and unborn generations" in W. Blackstone (ed.), *Philosophy and Environmental Crisis* (Athens, GA: University of Georgia Press, 1974), 49.

are all important forms of protection for epistemic rights. And in each case, we can ask a particular question regarding whether or not that protection is sufficient. To return to the Purdue Pharma case, many of the harms have been recognized through exposure in investigative journalism and in the media, and through activist organizations. All of this exposure serves to apply a moral pressure and protects our rights in a moral sense. In lots of these cases, there are good reasons to upgrade from merely moral protection to actual legal protections. However, in the spouse case that you mentioned, my personal view is that such an epistemic right should not be written into law. I think we can understand it quite a lot better if we think about the nature of these epistemic rights as *relational* rights. If I am married, for example, that does afford me certain moral rights, including epistemic ones. This is why we can hold people to account for lying about having an affair, and certainly we should be doing that. But I do not think that we should legislate for that. That said, there are certainly many cases in which we should be upgrading epistemic rights to legal rather than merely moral protection.

AM: I thought we could close by looking at epistemic rights in two particular contexts: (1) the media, and (2) education. In the media case, I am interested in the question of who has epistemic authority over the media when an epistemic right is violated. And in the education case, I am interested in the extent to which children can and should be protected from misinformation when they're being taught at school.

LW: In relation to the media, I think that we massively under-regulate and under-legislate the mainstream media, certainly in the UK. The epistemic rights of audiences are not well protected by the regulation and legislation that we currently have. That being said, however, there is also an important role for the consumer to take some responsibility for seeking out certain types of information and not exposing oneself to obviously false information or information that you have got good reason to think is not reliable. There is a tricky balance to be had between responsibility for epistemic rights from the point of view of the people pushing the information out through mass media, and those consuming it through social media, online, or even just print newspapers.

AM: So the consumer has a responsibility to weigh up what they are being told?

LW: Much of my work has to do with intellectual character, with traits like curiosity, open-mindedness, rigour and honesty. It also foregrounds being able to ask good questions. I think of good questioning as a key line of defence against the violation of epistemic rights. If we can ask good questions, curious questions, open-minded questions, honest questions, then we can have some kind of autonomy over the information that we receive and not be passive recipients of the information that people want us to see.

This links to your question about education, because it is a responsibility of educators to educate such that they produce adults who can engage in this kind of reasoning and be intellectually autonomous so that they are less likely to be subject to epistemic rights violations. Looking at education more generally, there are well-known cases in some states in the US where there are clear state-sanctioned laws around teaching creation and/or evolution, and the two are butting heads. So, what we put on our curricula is certainly a massive epistemic rights issue. But I think our focus should be much broader than these really controversial cases. I want us to be thinking about the very focus of our education: should we be focusing on only STEM (science, technology, engineering and mathematics) subjects to the exclusion of the arts and humanities? Should we teach philosophy to five-year-olds? In this latter example, I absolutely think that we should, but we don't. These are all important questions about epistemic rights; it is about what we teach on the curriculum full stop, including in those really controversial cases.

There are many things that we can actively do to defend and protect epistemic rights. Part of this is about having the kind of open-minded, curious, rigorous approach to information I was just talking about: being willing to ask difficult, challenging questions. These are really important ways to take ownership over the kinds of everyday epistemic rights violations that we find in areas like the media and education.

FURTHER RESOURCES

Nima Bassiri, "The force of scientific authority". *The Philosopher* 109:2 (2021).

Patrick Radden Keefe, *Empire of Pain: The Secret History of the Sackler Dynasty*. London: Picador, 2021.

Lani Watson, "Epistemic rights in a polarized world". In Alessandra Tanesini and Michael P. Lynch (eds), *Polarisation, Arrogance, and Dogmatism: Philosophical Perspectives*. Abingdon: Routledge 2021.

Lani Watson, *The Right to Know: Epistemic Rights and Why We Need Them*. Abingdon: Routledge, 2021.

Other people working in the field of social epistemology include Franca D'Agostini, Miranda Fricker, Kay Mathieson and Mervi Pantti.

10

Decolonial ecologies

Malcom Ferdinand in conversation with Romy Opperman

Because of the work of researchers like Malcom Ferdinand, we are increasingly beginning to think of ecological issues as inseparable from anti-racist and anti-patriarchal demands for equality. This conversation coincided with the English language publication of Ferdinand's book *Decolonial Ecology*. Building around the idea of a politics of encounter, the conversation explores what a non-colonial way of being in relation with one another might look like, extending this vision to include non-humans and the earth itself. In the face of the growing storm of climate catastrophe, Ferdinand invites us to build a world-ship where humans and non-humans can live together on a bridge of justice and shape a common world.

MALCOM FERDINAND is a researcher in political ecology and environmental humanities at the Centre national de la recherche scientifique (IRISSO/University Paris Dauphine). He has published on topics such as climate justice and the struggle against the toxic legacies of slavery and colonialism.

ROMY OPPERMAN is a Mellon Postdoctoral Fellow in Philosophy at the New School for Social Research, New York. Her research bridges Africana, continental, decolonial, environmental and feminist philosophy to foreground issues of racism and colonialism for environmental ethics and justice.

Romy Opperman (**RO**): How do you understand "decolonial ecology"? I ask this in the context of your book, but also because the terms "decolonial" and "decolonizing" often get used quite freely within academia.

Malcom Ferdinand (**MF**): I titled my book *Decolonial Ecology*, and, as you point out, there are often confusions between the terms "decolonizing ecology" and "decolonial ecology". To me, decolonial ecology argues that ecological issues are not separate from socio-political ones. So, I argue that the ecological imperative to preserve the ecosystem – for instance, to limit pollution and reduce biodiversity loss – should be fought together with what is often called the "decolonial demand"; that is, the anti-racist demand for equality and to be treated fairly. The goal of decolonial ecology is to think them together. I am not the first one to bring these two ideas together, but the reason why I make this connection – and especially in the context of France where I live and work, and where the book was first published – is because ecological issues have typically been thought of as separate from the anti-racist movement, from Afro-feminist demands, and even, to some extent, from the struggle against gender discrimination.

I would not use the phrase "decolonizing ecology" because of the movement that it implies. Some people today think that we have a set understanding of what ecology is, and the task is then to decolonize it. This tends to involve some makeover, or adding something (usually some colours!) to what we already have. Then we're awakened, we're decolonized, we're good to go! This approach presents the issue as if the existing institutions and organizations are already valid, as if they just need to be reformed or modified a little bit. One very disturbing example of this was when I talked to some French ecological NGOs [non-government organizations] who effectively said, "We haven't worked in impoverished suburbs around Paris, so let's go there now. And then we'll be decolonized". Their attitude could instead have been, "How about we encounter and interact and talk with the people that are already there, the people who know their suburbs more than us, who have an understanding of what it means to live and inhabit the world from these spaces".

What I call for is the recognition of all points and sources of ecological discourse, which should be taught and included in the conversation; a full exchange of what we know. That is why I am more in favour of recognizing the plurality of decolonial ecolog*ies*, rather than simply having this single framework of decolonizing ecology.

RO: You just used the word "encounter" in your example, and it is a really important term in the book. How are you using it?

MF: My book details, or presents, what I have called the "politics of encounter". I start with the divide between the scholars and the body of work that engages with ecological and environmental issues but not with anti-colonial, decolonial, post-colonial, and anti-racist issues, and vice versa. In many ways I'm trying to bridge this divide. I go over the ways of encountering both sides of this divide – the "encounter" between these two currently divided theories and thinkers. That's one way of looking at it.

But, more importantly, the question I ask is: what would a non-colonial way of being in relation with, of encountering, one another – whether that "other" is a human being or a non-human being – look like? In my opinion, the answer to colonization is not that all of us should stay in our respective corners of the earth. Rather, it is to understand what it would mean to encounter the other, to meet the other, and what kinds of conditions are necessary for such encounters to take place in a dignified, humane manner. As you know, France still has the remains of the colonies, including French Guiana, Guadeloupe and Martinique, which are today referred to as "Outre-mer" (overseas territories of France). I'm inspired by Aimé Césaire, the famous poet and philosopher from Martinique, who defended this political path for these overseas territories. Césaire has been harshly criticized for defending this path, but one could look at his position as a way of saying that the relationship that we build with one another is the necessary condition for equality demands. I am trying to imagine a different way of meeting the other than what has been typified by the colonial encounter.

RO: One common tendency that you're arguing against – particularly in the history of abolition, but also in animal ethics – is the move of placing ontology prior to ethics, for example by having to show that Black people count as human in certain terms *before* they're worthy of, say, freedom or recognition, or that animals are sentient in a certain way before they might also be worthy of freedom or recognition. Does that resonate with you?

MF: The abolitionists engaged in a very important study of what a human being is, as captured in the famous medallion by the abolitionist Josiah Wedgwood with its inscription, "Am I not a man and a brother?" (as well as its other version, "Am

I not a woman and a sister?") I think this started from a good intention – a discursive strategy in the struggle to end slavery. Yet, it does present the ethics of the relationship you have with someone as in some way dependent on an answer to the onto-logical question of what that person *is*. And that's problematic.

RO: Given this critique of ontology, what is your relationship, or the book's relationship, with philosophy? And, more specif-ically, what role does, or can, philosophy play in your worldly ecology? Finally, is it important to you that this book be read as philosophy?

MF: I would not presume to tell the readers how they should read the book! They can read it as a work of environmental pol-itics, or as a piece of literature, or as philosophy. I am actually trying to do a bit of all of the above. To write this book in France, I had to let go the idea of this work as a classical philosophical work. When I did my PhD dissertation, I was told that the two subjects – coloniality and ecology – that I was working on were either not considered philosophical at all or were considered questionably philosophical. To this day, post-coloniality and decoloniality are more accepted in literature studies than in philosophy. Although philosophy is becoming more interested in ecology through placing it within environmental ethics, this connection with decoloniality remains very much on the mar-gins. However, it is slowly beginning to gain acceptance thanks to the work of scholars like Norman Ajari, Elsa Dorlin, Matthieu Renault, Hourya Bentouhami and Françoise Vergès.

Philosophy has great importance to me, and the book is in constant dialogue with many philosophers, yet it was not my goal to have it accepted as a philosophical work. My main focus is on the ways that we think about ecology and the world. But I also wished to go beyond ecology to think about how we can produce knowledge about certain topics that have been excluded not just from academic philosophy, but from the entire history of philosophy. I believe that colonialism, and par-ticularly the history of slavery, has yet to be fully understood and recognized in terms of the type of thinking, conceptions and philosophies that the enslaved adopted and practiced.

Another difficulty I would have faced if I had tried to write the book as a philosophical essay is that the traditional Euro-centric approach necessarily references a philosophical literature. However, my goal was to engage in thinking from the Caribbean (the book's subtitle) and I could not find much traditional philosophical work or many philosophical institutions from the Caribbean world. So, I instead made use of different materials, for instance looking at the work of thinkers like Jacques Roumain and Édouard Glissant, looking at the philosophy present in Caribbean literature and novels, as well as carrying out numerous interviews with local NGOs to see what their ideas were.

When you actually wonder about why we can't find philosophical work on Caribbean ecology or why we are led to believe that the Caribbean has not really produced a philosophy, you realize that it is because we have institutionalized the idea that certain knowledge or philosophy *only* comes from European institutions, from European people. That's where Africana philosophy and post-colonial/decolonial theory come in handy. They allow us to change the focus, change the place from where the discourse, the knowledge and the philosophy are produced.

RO: There is a wonderful feminist vein that runs throughout your work. You engage with a number of eco-feminist and you address a number of core feminist questions, such as reproductive injustice, as well as issues of racialized gender and sexuality. You show how racist misogynistic hetero-patriarchy isn't accidental, but is in fact fundamental to what you call our "colonial earth inhabitation". You also use the term "matricide" not only in relation to the violence against those gendered as women – particularly non-white colonized women – but also in relation to violence against Mother Earth. And you then develop this beautiful concept of "matrigenesis". What is the role of feminist voices, as well as these feminist-inflected terms, in your work?

MF: Many anthologies of environmental thought start with two people: Jean Jacques Rousseau and Henry David Thoreau. And at the same time as these two white men were educated, were moving around, were perceived to be present in nature, there were men, women, and children imprisoned in the holds of slave ships. These people also had an idea of what it means to inhabit the earth, to live with one another, or not to live with one another. At the beginning of each of the chapters of the book, I tell the story of a slave ship – true historical slave ships. I use details from the archives but tell the stories with some freedom, in a manner that sheds some light on each chapter. One reason to do this is to try and access the personal histories beyond the numbers, beyond the many millions transported in slave ships, but another reason is because I situate my work in the imaginary. Political understandings of ecological issues are always accompanied by a certain imaginary of the world and earth, where the imaginary is the precondition of the images we use. The imaginary of Eurocentric theories like the Anthropocene and Gaia hypothesis carry the image of the world as a ship, one that resembles a colour-blind Noah's ark. I wanted to provide a different imaginary, an alternative to the Noah's ark framework. We may be on the same boat, but not everybody is treated equally – and some are jettisoned at the first gust of wind. It was through trying to shift my viewpoint to these people, especially women, that I came up with different concepts and different tools to analyse the world today, especially the ecological crisis. This is where the terms "matricide" and "matrigenesis" come from.

In trying to adopt a feminist perspective, I realize that I have to proceed with humility, knowing that my experience is not that of a woman, that I will not have the same understanding of many issues. Through feminism, I learned that in my upbringing I was taught to have a male gaze, including on the history of slavery. For example, I was led to believe that with the second liberation of slavery in France in 1848 the enslaved were now free and equal, with new rights like the right to vote. But that was only true for men. As men, we need to ensure that when we look for freedom and equality, it actually includes women. So, my feminist perspective is a method through which I continually ask: Does my thought apply to women? Will this make sense for women? Just asking this question opens up new answers and possibilities.

My feminist method is also informed by women's description of their experience. Take, for example, Wangari Maathai, the Kenyan environmental activist and Nobel Peace Prize winner, who founded the green belt movement in 1977 to stop deforestation in Africa. I was very moved by her autobiography in which she wrote that in the anti-colonial struggle in Kenya, both the colonial forces and the anti-colonial forces were engaging in aggression and dominating practices against women. I felt, then, that my task was not just to describe domination and these dominating practices throughout history, but to look for conceptual alternatives.

The term "matricide" allows me to talk about how people are made motherland-less and lands are made childless. For the colonizers of America, specifically the Caribbean, these lands were claimed as the motherlands of no-one, and this "matricide" – this denial or death of the motherland – set the scene for the genocide of the indigenous peoples. Furthermore, the people transported from Africa, the enslaved, the dehumanized and demeaned, have also suffered matricide. Because we have been brought here, our first motherland is elsewhere. And many of us have not been able to own land and continue to be prevented, to this day, from making this new land our motherland. So, my work is not just about the socio-political elements of slavery and colonialism, but also about showing that when people are motherland-less, it leaves our land motherless.

Regarding the term "matrigenesis", I wanted to reclaim a relation to Mother Earth. When thinking through this concept, I took inspiration from the Maroons, who not only manifested a powerful opposition to slavery, but also lived in defiance of the way of inhabiting the land that I call "colonial inhabitation" – a mode of inhabitation dominated by extractivism, by plantations, and by unequal conditions for men and women. The Maroons were the enslaved who fled the plantations and tried to live in secluded places, such as hills, mangroves and mountains. They created a different relation with the environment, a relation in which they had to live "with" and within the space, caring for the trees and the land. They offered a way of recreating a motherly relation with the land that I found very inspiring (even though it has its limits, particularly regarding the conditions of women). Not motherly in a sense of essentializing "mother", but a nurturing, caring relation.

I want to offer these different concepts not to just paint a colonial, decolonial, or anti-colonial horizon, but to paint a horizon of the world that is truly beyond coloniality.

FURTHER RESOURCES

Aimé Césaire, *Discourse on Colonialism* [1950]. New York: Monthly Review Press, 2000.
Malcom Ferdinand, *Decolonial Ecology: Thinking from the Caribbean World*. Cambridge: Polity 2021.
Malcom Ferdinand, "Coloniality". *The Philosopher* 110:1 (2022).
Wangari Maathai, *Unbowed: A Memoir*. New York: Knopf, 2006.
Romy Opperman, "Racism". *The Philosopher* 110:1 (2022).

11

Listening to animals

Eva Meijer in conversation with
Darren Chetty and Adam Ferner

The Philosopher ran a series of three events in partnership with Adam Ferner's and Darren Chetty's podcast "Do You Even Vegan?" scheduled to coincide with each of the three daily meals, and the "breakfast guest" was Dutch philosopher, novelist, and artist Eva Meijer, a pioneering thinker on the political rights of animals. In this conversation, Meijer argues that the political turn in animal philosophy allows us to look at animals not just from an ethical perspective but also from a political perspective, which opens up many new and difficult questions about how to form democracies with other animals and how to conceive of them as political groups. For Meijer, a true interspecies democracy will only be possible if humans begin to listen in a different way to animals and to the natural world. Crucially, such a listening is not just for their survival but also for our own.

EVA MEIJER is an artist and postdoctoral researcher at Wageningen University in the Netherlands, and the author of many books, including *Animal Languages* and *When Animals Speak*.

DARREN CHETTY is a teacher, doctoral researcher and writer with research interests in education, philosophy, racism, children's literature and hip hop culture.

ADAM FERNER is a writer and youth worker based in London. His books include *The Philosopher's Library* (with Chris Meyns) and *Notes from the Crawl Room*.

———————

Adam Ferner (**AF**): You argue that humans massively underappreciate the extent to which non-human animals are engaged in intelligent and meaningful communication. For example, you describe Prairie dogs meeting each other with a "French kiss" and the extensive greeting ritual monogamous seabirds perform with their partners when they return to their nest, with the males often bringing gifts for the females such as flowers to decorate their nest or to use as a necklace. These descriptions offer a picture of non-human animals with human characteristics – French kissing, gift giving, and so on. But does this not run the risk of flattening non-human animal interactions by likening – or reducing – them to human interactions?

Eva Meijer (**EM**): The first answer would be that denying certain capacities to non-human animals is an ideological construction that has been very popular in animal research. The Dutch primatologist Frans de Waal called this "anthropo-denial". For a very long time, it was thought that only humans were capable of certain emotions and forms of cognition, language and culture, while the other animals were not. This was taken to be the neutral position from which to study whether they may in fact be capable of such cognitive achievements, and also to model such abilities in relation to human capacities. But, to take one example, the Belgian psychologist Vinciane Despret shows that animal research is subject to ideological preconceptions similar to the kinds that we find in research into different human groups, and that these mutually reinforce one another. For example, bias with regard to gender influences how nonhuman animals are studied. So, the question of anthropomorphism cannot be seen in isolation from our historical and current engagement with other animals.

As a philosopher, however, I am interested in something else. I see concepts as a starting point for understanding what goes on in certain types of relationships. Ludwig Wittgenstein saw language as a kind of tool box for understanding the world, and I find this idea of language very fruitful for understanding engagements with other animals. When using concepts such as love or language in relation to other animals, the idea is to try not to start out by asking how our human interpretation of these concepts fits with the other animals. To take language as an example, we have traditionally denied other animals the capacity for language use. We understood language simply as human language, and when studying other animals we would ask, "How good are they at learning human language?" If they were good at it, they had some kind of language; if they were not good at it, then they are basically mute. But if you turn it

around and see language as something that we use to interact with others and build worlds with others – even others
of different species – and investigate how this works for the
other animals, then language suddenly becomes a question; it
becomes a conceptual framework that allows us to see other
animals differently. They may not be writing novels like us, but
there are many similarities in their language use. For example,
humans always think that naming is a uniquely human phenomenon, but dolphins name their children, and they give
these names throughout their lives; parrots use names for their
children; bats use names. Investigating these phenomena can
give us a better grasp of what goes on in non-human animal
minds, and it also allows for a certain kind of humility because
the other animals can teach us about these things as well. As
humans we are limited: we have a limited sensory apparatus,
we have a limited notion of concepts. But this does not mean
that we cannot engage with those who are other from us.

Darren Chetty (**DC**): Two things come to mind in relation to
what you have just said. Firstly, you made the joke about animals not writing novels, but it does seem that there is an
important difference in how language is being used by humans
and non-human animals, not just in terms of writing but in
terms of storytelling; not just immediate communication, but
what is often called "culture". And the other thing is that what
you have said sounds a bit like the way anthropology began,
with Europeans going out into other cultures and noting that
"some of what they do is quite like us". So, even though on the
one hand what you say has got this sense of being quite emancipatory, the animals are probably not taking the same interest
in humans, so there is less of a cross-cultural, cross-species
engagement. Rather, humans are looking out at the other animals. This risks reinforcing the sense of human superiority,
albeit a more benign one than has traditionally been the case.

EM: I think that animals are looking much more at us than we
are looking at them. For a lot of animals, this is simply because
their life depends on it. If you move around in cities and you
look at the pigeons and the mice and the city birds and the
rats, they are basically looking at humans in order not to be
killed. There are also a lot of non-human animals – compan-
ion animals, farmed animals, and so on – who co-evolved with
humans, so their genetic make-up is formed by humans. But

humans' genetic make-up is similarly formed by them. For example, there is a lot of research about how humans and dogs not only have this sort of co-culture, but that humans have been formed physically by living with dogs for a very long time.

I think that the function of animal languages is to make people more attentive to what is going on around them, and to present them with a picture of a world that is alive and in which different beings are talking about different beings. Adam very briefly mentioned the Prairie dogs who greet each other in a certain way. But they also have a very significant set of alarm calls through which they speak about humans; additionally, elephants have words for humans. This raises the question of who is doing the looking. My feeling is that right now animals are doing the looking at us and we are not paying enough attention. We should pay much more attention and listen to them in a different way. I hope that this offers some kind of answer to the anthropology question. Touching on the novel-writing comment, we know that certain whales sing love songs that go on for 20 hours. These are epic creations, you know! What are they saying? We don't know. We don't have a clue. We don't know a lot about these other beings that we share our planet with.

DC: You seem to be saying that we should become *more* involved with animals than we currently are. But our involvement with animals has typically led to destruction of their habitats, and so on. How are we to negotiate this tension between involvement and over-involvement?

EM: I'd love to be an abolitionist. I think Peter Singer once suggested something to the effect that humans should all go and live in Australia and leave the rest of the planet to all the other animals. But of course that is just not going to happen. I do think that humans should withdraw more and leave more space for the other animals, but as it is – and as it is going to be for a long time – we are also going to have to negotiate all of the encounters we have with the other animals. We have to be really careful in figuring out how to learn about animals in non-violent ways, and how learning together goes hand-in-hand with living together in new ways. We have ignored an animal agency for a very, very long time, and we are now trying to figure out how to deal with it in a way that is respectful. My argument is that it is not up to us humans to define what the perfect political society would look like. For that we definitely need to engage with other animals, but this does not mean imposing new political experiments on them as we have always done. Rather, it means taking seriously the encounters that are already there and seeing them in a new light, engaging with them in different ways. A lot of people are currently grappling with the question of what we do with animal subjectivity, with language and culture. I'm not presenting an answer, but rather trying to reformulate the question.

AF: I wonder if there's a tension here. On the one hand, I get the impression that you think we can get on the same wavelength as some animals, that we can communicate with them and have really meaningful relationships with them. You have already given the example of dogs as animals with whom we have co-evolved and with whom we share some kind of culture. On the other hand, you have suggested that there is something fundamentally inscrutable about certain types of animals. You gave the example of whale song which is beautiful in a very abstract way – but it is very difficult to even begin to understand how we may make sense of it. I find myself persuaded by the thought (which is central to much feminist theory) that the way that we think about the world is intimately connected to our physicality: we are embodied beings rather than Cartesian minds floating in space. And if we accept this view of ourselves, then it is hard to resist the idea that communication across species boundaries is going to be very difficult, and may not be possible at all. It would be helpful if you could clarify exactly how you think that we can get on the same wavelength as some other animals and why they are not obscure alien intelligences.

EM: There are both many kinds of differences and many things that we share with the other animals. I think that a lot of people have an immediate "folk knowledge" or understanding of other animals that can be driven by empathy or by cognition. When you see someone of a different species suffer, then you feel it. I think that humans have been obsessed with species in a similar way to how they have been obsessed with, say, gender differences. This is not to deny that there are significant differences between different groups of beings, but rather to highlight that these differences are not simply biological, but are also cultural and historical. Maurice Merleau-Ponty wrote that difference is actually a *prerequisite* for understanding someone because if you are completely the same you do not need to understand each other. And this difference generates a space in between that you can choose to cross or not. For example, we all know the feeling with an intimate human partner that sometimes they feel very close and familiar to you, and at another point you can feel like they are a complete stranger. I think that the same is true with dogs, for example. With dogs too there can be this intuitive understanding that is not bound to species in any sense.

The danger in the kind of binary thinking that posits a radical separation between humans and the other animals is that we make them so different that we don't end up engaging with them at all. Jacques Derrida, for example, warns against using the word "animal" for all other animals. He argues that this word separates all humans from all other animals, and that this serves not only to flatten out the differences within the different species of animal, but also to flatten out the similarities between humans and the other animals. For Derrida, there is not one gap between all humans and all animals; rather, there are many kinds of gaps. We need to be very specific about the types of non-human animals we are discussing and about the sorts of differences that exist between them and humans. Furthermore, the words that we have to describe these relations can sometimes reinforce the problem. I think that the idea of embodied thinking, as developed in feminism as well as by thinkers like Merleau-Ponty, can give us a different perspective on the situation. In some instances that might help, but for other things we need different conceptual tools.

AF: I was hoping you could say a bit more about the extent to which cross-species communication compares to intercultural communication. For example, Jason Hribal positions animals as members of the working class and there are highly controversial comparisons between the treatment of non-human animals by humans and the treatments of prisoners in Nazi death camps.

EM: When we compare different groups, we have to be very specific about what it is that we are comparing. When I write about animals as a social or a political group, I am not looking for any essentialist comparisons with other social or political groups. If, for example, I was to compare the political position of non-human animals to that of women a hundred years ago,

I would not do this to argue that animals are *like* women, but rather to bring to light certain aspects of the animal condition. Take the Holocaust comparison that you mentioned. I understand why some vegans or animal rights theorists will invoke this comparison: they think of the worst thing they can think of and then say, "It's like this for the animals". It seems to me that this comes from a position of powerlessness on the part of the person using it. They are saying, "Please see how bad this is!" But when you use that comparison you also completely alienate other people because they consider the two situations to be radically different and find the comparison extremely troubling. In human language we have to be as precise as possible. A metaphor is meant to illuminate something about a topic by comparing it to something else, which clarifies the topic at stake both with regard to its similarity to and difference from the metaphor. That sensitivity towards language and images is sometimes lacking in political and activist contexts. Furthermore, searching for non-violent relations in language and politics with other animals includes humans, and learning to listen and be sensitive to others is part of that.

On the other hand, it is, for example, perfectly legitimate to discuss non-human animals as workers. There is a new and emerging field in academia that focuses on animal labour in very careful and important ways. The beautiful thing about the political turn in animal philosophy is that it suddenly allows us to look at animals not just from an ethical perspective but also from a political perspective, and this opens up many new and difficult questions about how to form democracies with other animals and how to conceive of them as political groups without falling into the anthropological-colonial traps that we discussed earlier.

This all relates back to the question of imposing certain concepts onto other animals. We have human interpretations of a concept and we have lots of new understandings and discoveries about other animals, but how do these interact? Should we try and mould human concepts to fit with the other animals or is this something that would not be of any interest to them? I think that a good starting point for addressing this kind of question is to recognize that the animals have been speaking all along. Recognizing this encourages us to see our own blind spots and change our own attitude as humans. The experimental composer Pauline Oliveros wrote about "deep listening" as an attitude we can take towards the world. As humans, we often think that we have to understand the world with words, by speaking about it. But Oliveros is suggesting that we need to listen much more – not simply as you would listen to a conversation, but through adopting a very different kind of attitude. We are now at a point in our existence as humans in which we have discovered that we need to begin to listen in a different way to animals and to the natural world – not just for their survival but also for our own survival as humans. We are not this wonderful exception that we think we are. We are poor, embodied, vulnerable creatures but also sometimes wonderful and loving beings, and we can do better and we should do better. But this doing better cannot be based on our own perspective alone, because we are not alone. We are with all the others.

FURTHER RESOURCES

Nicolas Delon, "The meaning of animal labour". In C. Blattner, K. Coulter and W. Kymlicka (eds), *Animal Labour: A New Frontier of Interspecies Justice?* Oxford: Oxford University Press, 2020.

Jacques Derrida, *The Animal That Therefore I Am*. New York: Fordham University Press, 2008.

Eva Meijer, *When Animals Speak: Toward an Interspecies Democracy*. New York: NYUP, 2019.

Eva Meijer, *Animal Languages: The Secret Conversations of the Living World*. London: John Murray, 2019.

Pauline Oliveros, *Sonic Meditations*. Sharon, VT: Smith Publications, 1974.

12

Relationality and political commitment

Lewis R. Gordon in conversation with Olúfẹ́mi O. Táíwò

Our Euromodern philosophical inheritance via thinkers like Hobbes, Locke and Mill is of an atomistic and non-relational being who thinks, acts and moves along a course in which continued movement depends on not colliding with others. In this conversation, Lewis R. Gordon proposes a relational model of humanity inherited from southern Africa, Asia, South America, and even parts of continental Europe. For Gordon, this relational understanding of ourselves allows for the opening up and transformation of the possibilities of being human, all the way through to rethinking our institutional and political relations. While the Euromodern model views political commitment through the self-interested prism of success and failure, the relational model represents a profound critique of how most of us have come to fix action at an individual level. Seen in this light, Gordon argues that we must rethink the philosophical anthropology at the heart of a specific line of Euromodern thought on what it means to be human.

LEWIS R. GORDON is Professor and Head of the Department of Philosophy at the University of Connecticut. His work spans Africana philosophy, existentialism, phenomenology, social and political theory, postcolonial thought, theories of race and racism, philosophies of liberation, aesthetics, philosophy of education and philosophy of religion.

OLÚFẹ́MI O. TÁÍWÒ is an assistant professor of philosophy at Georgetown University. His theoretical work draws from the Black radical tradition, anti-colonial thought, philosophy of language, contemporary social science, and histories of activism and activist thinkers.

Olúfẹ́mi O. Táíwò (**OOT**): In your work, political responsibility is something that goes beyond moral responsibility, and certainly beyond moral*ism*. You use the example of Harriet Bailey to exemplify one model of political responsibility. Harriet Bailey was the mother of abolitionist and political thinker Frederick Douglass, and the two of them were separated at birth, which was a common aspect of chattel slavery at the time. When Douglass was around seven years old, Bailey found out that she was enslaved on a plantation 12 miles away from where he was growing up, and she walked the distance in the evenings to spend time with him into dawn, when she returned to the fields. Shortly after this, she died. Why do you see Harriet Bailey as an exemplar of your idea of political responsibility?

Lewis R. Gordon (**LRG**): In my work, I tend not to think in terms of liberation but in terms of liberation*s*. I love the plurality in liberations because to me liberation is a very relational idea. You never arrive *at* liberation; rather, it is an ongoing praxis. But today there are so many people who want the outcome before the performance; they want guarantees; they want their actions rendered entirely risk-free via some kind of epistemic algorithm. But this evacuates action of praxis. Praxis is the world of the contingent; it is dialectical; it doesn't have its synthetic conclusion before its performance. In the case of Harriet Bailey, this remarkable woman had no reason at all to expect this child to love her as he had been kept away from her for the first seven years of his life. Furthermore, she acted in a world that said her point of view, even her very life, did not matter except as a commodified instrument in the production of wealth for her masters. At sunrise, she is put out into the field and at sunset she comes in. She barely has any nutrition, and yet she carries the little food she has to her child and, as you pointed out, she died shortly after she was reunited with him. My argument is that from the point of view of instrumental rationality, of the reductive logics through which we understand notions of "human nature" (a notion that I strongly reject), Bailey was a conundrum; her actions made no sense. And so, the question I asked was, "Why did she act?"

Bailey offers a clue to political action because when I act politically it's not about what is in it for me. When I act politically, it is because of the collective responsibility of "us". And this "us" transcends the present – it includes our ancestors and our descendants, as well as conceptions of life in the future that may be radically different from ours. Through the example of

Harriet Bailey, I try to bring political responsibility out of the realm of the pessimistic, out of the narrowly rationalistic, egotistic, narcissistic models of society and action, in order to foreground the idea that political responsibility produces actions that reach beyond the self to an anonymous "we". Being accountable to the political means being so to what is to come, even though one may not be able to demonstrate a direct causal and epistemological understanding of what will emerge. This is an understanding of political responsibility that is premised on a political form of love, as embodied by Harriet Bailey, whose actions reverberated in directions she could not have possibly predicted. In her extraordinary efforts to spend time with her child, Harriet showed she loved him. In doing so, she was also saying, "Frederick, you're valuable". Douglass' love of freedom was also an expression of his love for his mother.

OOT: In line with someone like Iris Marion Young, you argue that political responsibility is always about the future; it is not about us individually but instead is about what depends on us while transcending us. As you put it, "The future is never *ours*. It is a love always committed to the life and freedom of others". I was wondering if you could say a little bit more about the act of choice and the mentality of choice that comes from this commitment to political responsibility.

LRG: One of the distinctions I like to make is between substance metaphysics and relational metaphysics. A lot of narcissistic philosophical anthropologies are premised upon substance metaphysics because it deals in an identity relation to the self as well as the ongoing reproduction of the self. This atomistic and individualistic substance-based view, as articulated by Thomas Hobbes, John Locke, John Stuart Mill, and many others, is of a non-relational being that thinks, acts and moves along a course in which continued movement depends on not colliding with others. Under that model, the human being is a thing that enters into a system that facilitates or obstructs its movement. This is the philosophical anthropology at the heart of a specific line of Euromodern thought on what it means to be human. Relational metaphysics, by contrast, is a position shared by many groups across southern Africa, Asia, South America, and even parts of continental Europe, and offers a model of the human being as part of a larger, open-ended system of meaning. And part of liberatory practice is to increase the options available through which people can act and live meaningful lives.

My idea of "disciplinary decadence" deals with the reductionism, the idolizing, the closure, the ontological and epistemic locking-in that we find with substance-based metaphysics. This can happen at disciplinary and epistemic levels, but also at social levels when we treat a society or identity like a god. This quest for purity in these various contexts always involves a turning away from reality in a quest for controlled outcomes. Reality becomes problematic, in other words, because it is "impure" and resistant to complete control. Political life, to take one obvious example, is not a formula or a closed system. Instead, it is open, which means that when we are willing to go beyond the arbitrary constraints of a substance-based metaphysics, when we are willing to expand the normative reach of human reality through our actions, we thereby make ourselves into conditions of possibility for what is to come. And this pulls us full circle back to Harriet Bailey and many people like her. As we face what may look like the futility of our times, as we behold a world in which it seems like our actions don't matter, we have to understand that we don't have advance knowledge of the implications of our actions. Political action thus becomes an existential challenge or, in the language of Kierkegaard, a leap of faith. This is why I place such emphasis on the concept of political commitment without foreknowledge of outcome. Because the commitment is expressed in the action that becomes a condition of possibility through which others can look back, and, like Frederick Douglass, be able to say, "Thank God my mother acted".

OOT: Presumably this kind of orientation towards the future, towards possibilities that exceed us and exceed what we can predict, is equally open to optimistic as pessimistic readings?

LRG: Optimism and pessimism are two sides of the same coin, because they both require us to say and predict and do things that we are absolutely unable to access. As a result, they elide the human ability to act on the basis of commitment – in other words to act because I *must*. The presumption that what is at stake is what can be *known* in order to determine what can be done *is* the problem. If such knowledge were possible, the debate would be about who is reading the evidence correctly. Such a judgement would be *a priori* – that is, prior to events actually occurring. The future, however, is *ex post facto*; it is yet to come. Facing the future, the question is not what will be or how we may know what will be, but instead the realization that whatever is done will be that on which the future will depend. We don't want to be stuck in an endless debate between optimism and pessimism that results in impeding our capacity to act. Political commitment is the supervening alternative that rejects this oscillation between optimism and pessimism. As I see it, this ability we have to be committed and to say, "I'm doing this not for me but due to an understanding that it needs to be done, whether I succeed or not" is the *sine qua non* of liberatory political action. And this also doesn't mean that we act *irrationally* because while reason has to be able to evaluate actions, reason is never complete.

OOT: The idea of humanity as itself incomplete is a central part of your existential philosophy. Could you say something about this line of your thinking?

LRG: Etymologically, the word "existence" is rooted in the idea of *standing out*. Existence is to stand out from being, and the moment you stand out from being you can raise the question of being in a way that is always making you other than being. Human nature arguments are always premised upon trying to squeeze human reality back into being. I agree with people like Keiji Nishitani that the problem with ontology is that it strives to encompass reality. But reality is greater than being, it transcends being. If human nature were to be a real thing, it would require a causal mechanism behind our actions in such a way that eliminates the freedom in our actions. The thing about human reality, however, is that you could put human beings (I am using the term "human being" here for convenience, despite the fact that a human being is not properly a being) into situations without having any idea in advance of what they will do, because we live in the sphere of meaning, culture, and so on, which brings a fundamental ambiguity to whatever actions may ensue.

If you throw a tied-up animal in front of a starving human being, you cannot predict the outcome. Some human beings may instantly kill the animal and eat it, while others may stick to being vegetarian, and others still may be vegetarian but will still eat the animal, and so on. In other words, once you get into the realm of human reality, you're dealing with a mediating condition of meaning that raises the question of responsibility for the action. If a crocodile doesn't eat the animal, your response is going to be something like, "That's a sick crocodile. What's wrong with the crocodile?" You're not going to look for the question of whether the crocodile decided to become a Zen Buddhist! But the human being who doesn't eat the animal is not necessarily a sick human being. This is one of the reasons why within the sphere of human reality you cannot use the notion of your nature as an excuse for your action of committing harm on another. Responsibility is part of the human condition precisely because freedom is part of the human condition. I don't reject the notion of human conditions; I don't reject the notion that human beings are terrestrial creatures with biophysical features, and so on. But those are just our conditions, and human reality is always more than that.

By way of an analogy, consider the abstraction of "the market". Elided in such an abstraction is the understanding of markets as human relations constructed through the human capacity to produce social worlds or systems, communicate them, and transform them. Treating the market as a deity makes it stand outside of human agency and, thus, offers the illusion of its ontological completeness and the futility in attempting its transformation. Missing here is that as a human system, the market requires human agency for its creation and maintenance. What human beings bring into being we can also take out of being. And what is true of markets is just as true of ourselves. So, any notion of human nature that elides this capacity for freedom and ambiguity is simply an abstraction that limits our imagination and political capacity.

This relational understanding of ourselves allows for the opening up and transformation of the possibilities of being human. And we are already seeing this happening. Right now there are different kinds of people who are challenging the old norms, unlocking the possibilities by which human beings could live otherwise, all the way through to rethinking our institutional and political relations. If we think of ourselves dialectically *as* relationships, then we begin to understand that our actions are always affecting things and are part of something other than ourselves. We are a paradoxical being whose natural condition is unnatural, whose being constitutes *the unnatural* or, as I prefer, *queer*. In our efforts to keep in check this queer aspect of human reality, we have given rise to numerous varieties of avowed stabilizing efforts such as class, gender and race (among many others). At the heart of the various strategies we seek to undo these dehumanizing structures is the unlocking of possibilities by which human beings could live otherwise.

OOT: To close our conversation, please can you say something about Black consciousness and how it is reshaping our idea of what it is to be human?

LRG: Unsurprisingly, I look at consciousness relationally! So, I reject models of consciousness that are locked in a failure to see the inter-communicative sociality of consciousness – in other words, how we're affected by each other. When I talk about Black consciousness, I distinguish between black consciousness and Black consciousness. The former is mostly affected and sometimes immobile, while the latter is effective and always active. The former suffers, while the latter liberates. I think of Black consciousness as a consciousness that is fundamentally linked to political reality, that addresses the choking contradictions of anti-black societies. If we pick racism as an example, racism ultimately depends on blocking us from setting the conditions for the irrelevance of racists. This is why there is such a fear of Black consciousness in anti-black racist societies, and why all racist societies devote a lot of energy to disenfranchisement, to illiteracy, to creating all the mechanisms to erode the capacity for black people to act and transform. All racisms, all oppressions, all forms of degradation of human beings rely on disempowerment; they all have in place mechanisms to block the options through which people can act.

Black consciousness is about understanding the mechanisms of power for *em*powerment, because it makes no sense to say you're fighting against racism if you're going to avoid getting rid of the conditions of disempowerment. It is about cultivating a humanity that is reaching out for the dignity and freedom of all, but is rooted in political commitment because you don't know what the consequences of your actions will be at the moment you act. This is the existential paradox of commitment to action without guarantees. The slave revolts, micro and macro acts of resistance, escapes and returns to help others do the same, the cultivated instability of plantations and other forms of enslavement, and countless other actions, were waged against a gauntlet of forces designed to eliminate any hope of success. The claim of colonialists and enslavers was that the future belonged to them, not to the enslaved and the indigenous. Such people were, in colonial eyes, incapable of ontological resistance.

What is important for political commitment is that it is not about success or failure; rather, it is about the ongoing commitment to the actions to be done. From the egotistic self-interested model, failure is very self-referential. According to this model, Harriet Bailey would have to have died saying, "I failed"; Martin Luther King Jr would have to have died saying, "I failed"; Malik el-Shabazz (aka Malcolm X) would have to have died saying, "I failed", and so on. But none of these people failed because Black consciousness understands political reality as the connection of actions over time, so these actions are the conditions of possibility for other actions. This is not an optimistic point; instead, it is a critique of how most of us have come to understand action, because we tend to lock action at an individual level. Consider Frantz Fanon's notion of *constructive failure*, where what does not initially work transforms conditions for something new to emerge. To understand this argument, one must rethink the philosophical anthropology at the heart of a specific line of Euromodern thought on what it means to be human.

If we are going to change the game, we have to change what we think human beings are. If we look at human beings as individual, isolated things, the game continues. But if we look at human beings as not beings, but as living realities and relationships facing conditions, we then know that we have to change the game as we have to change the conditions. And if we change the conditions, we also change ourselves. The moment when it is just mundane and ordinary for you and me (and many other people towards whom society's phobias remain directed) to be in the room means that a lot has changed and that new relationships are developing. The reason that you and I are having this conversation in this forum is precisely because of those people's actions that set the conditions of possibility for us to be here.

FURTHER RESOURCES

Frantz Fanon, *The Wretched of the Earth* [1961]. London: Penguin, 2001.
Lewis R. Gordon, *Fear of Black Consciousness*. London: Allen Lane, 2022.
Lewis R. Gordon, *Freedom, Justice, and Decolonization*. Abingdon: Routledge, 2021.
Lewis R. Gordon, "Racialization and human reality". *The Philosopher* 109:3 (2021).
Iris Marion Young, "Political responsibility and structural injustice". 2003 Lindley Lecture. https://philpapers.org/rec/YOUPRA.

PART III

***

LIVING WITH TECHNOLOGY

Finding ourselves somewhere between the ideological extremes of techno-optimism and techno-pessimism, we are somewhat ambivalent and just a little confused.[1] Everyone is still on social media, but it seems that there is an emerging art of living with social media that involves something like: *delete all your accounts right now!* While social media giants stick by their stated ambition to unify the world, they are in fact, as Brad Evans and Chantal Meza point out, "creating islands of isolation, the likes of which we have never seen before".[2] Perhaps the art of resistance in the face of ever-more refined and numbing tech seductions is simply (to channel both Bartleby and Žižek) *preferring not to*?[3]

Tech visionaries have a venerable history of cheque-in-the-mail promises: in the 1960s, Marvin Minsky promised us Hal-style robots "in a generation"; in 2005, Ray Kurzweil declared that "the singularity is near" (Kurzweil sets the date as 2045, which conveniently means he will probably have died shortly before he is proven wrong); prophecies of a forthcoming AI apocalypse get tongues wagging. The reality, however, is

***

1. In the spirit of Part II, I acknowledge the contested nature of this "we" I have just assumed . . .
2. From their 2022 essay, "Have we finally become ghosts in the machine?", published in the summer issue of *The Philosopher*.
3. The Bartleby reference is to Herman Melville's 1853 short story, *Bartleby, the Scrivener: A Story of Wall Street* from which Žižek has gleaned much inspiration.

far more mundane. Even the LaMDA system that made global headlines last year when a Google engineer claimed it was sentient is, once the stardust settles, just an impressive text production programme. It seems that the art of living with technology is also the art of cultivating a good nose for bullshit.

Iris Murdoch noted that we are creatures who make pictures of ourselves, and then come to resemble that picture.[4] Seemingly oblivious to the long history of using the latest technological innovations (from catapults to telephone switchboards) as a model for understanding the mind, the hypothesis driving most modern cognitive science these days is that our minds are literally computers or algorithms. The plausibility of the transhumanist dream of liberation from corporeality and finitude depends on this. But what do we give up and how do we distort our natures when we acquiesce to the powerful, gendered fantasies of a rather bloodless tribal creed?

Despite these misgivings, we all know that *it* is coming, no matter what...

---

4. See Murdoch's *Existentialists and Mystics: Writings on Philosophy and Literature* (London: Chatto & Windus, 1997).

13

Misunderstanding the Internet

Justin E. H. Smith in conversation with Alexis Papazoglou

We tend to think of the internet as an unprecedented and overwhelmingly positive achievement of modern human technology. But is it? This wide-ranging conversation coincided with the publication of Justin E. H. Smith's book *The Internet Is Not What You Think It Is*. It looks to Leibniz, transhumanism, and mycorrhizal fungus to help us better understand the part of the internet that is continuous with what we have always done and conducive to our thriving, and to fight back against the part that is a distortion of who we are and non-conducive to that aim.

JUSTIN E. H. SMITH is Professor of History and Philosophy of Science at Paris Cité University. His research interests include Leibniz, early modern philosophy, history and philosophy of biology, classical Indian philosophy, the history and philosophy of anthropology.

ALEXIS PAPAZOGLOU is an editor at the Institute of Art and Ideas. He hosts "The Philosopher & the News" podcast and writes on the intersection between philosophy, politics and current affairs.

Alexis Papazoglou (**AP**): What is the internet is and how have we got it wrong in the ways we think about it?

Justin E. H. Smith (**JEHS**): The internet is not nearly as new-fangled as most people think. It does not represent a radical rupture with everything that came before, either in human history or in the vastly longer history of nature that precedes the first appearance of our species. As a result, we tend to overlook the natural analogy that thinks of the internet as being in continuity with the instantaneous transmission of signals across living nature. In other words, it is more productive to think about the internet as an outgrowth of a species-specific activity. Animal and plant signalling – for example, lima bean plants giving off methyl jasmonate that floats through the air across significant distances to their conspecifics; mycorrhizal fungus networks that attach to the roots of trees, enabling them to communicate with one another; sperm whales clicking; elephants stomping; – are true forms of telecommunication. Throughout the living world, telecommunication is more likely the norm than the exception. The main difference between these and our forms of telecommunication is that we haven't always been doing it. The ecology of the internet is only one more recent layer of the ecology of the planet as a whole, which overlays networks upon networks.

AP: This sounds appealing to me, but how would we be able to distinguish between what is natural and what is technological, or between what is part of human nature and what is transforming it in some way? There is a lot of talk about how the internet is literally changing the way our brains are wired, how much attention we can give to things, how we absorb and process information. And then there is also the transhumanist position, which is built around the speculative hypothesis that at some point we will be able to implant the necessary microchips, and then the internet will be directly accessible through thought. So how do we know whether something is just an expression of our nature, and when it is something that is changing or distorting it?

JEHS: While it is obvious that sperm whales have always clicked, we have not always "clicked", so to speak. And so there is a significant disanalogy there. It's not clear to me if you read, say, paper correspondences in the seventeenth century Republic of Letters, that they are experiencing the kind of time lag between sending and receiving any differently than we do with emails. What counts as simultaneity is itself conditioned by the state of technology. As long as there have been exchange networks, there has been long-distance signalling. Whether you actually have to walk across that distance in order to send the signal, or whether there are other technological means, what you still have, in a species-specific way, is an experience of a broader community of simultaneously dispersed similarity, i.e., a network. They may get faster and better in some respects, but in other respects we're still doing something very species-specific.

Now, of course, we're also messing up our brains and our faculties of attention, and this is leading to severe cognitive disruption. The best evidence suggests that this is temporary and reversible: you can retrain your brain pretty fast to start memorizing epic poetry. So it is hopefully not leaving an evolutionary mark in the manner of, say, industrial agriculture. After all, eating is also something we do naturally, and so you could ask, "Isn't McDonald's a distortion of that?" Well, in some respects it is, but in other respects it's still eating. Maybe that's a good way of thinking about how far this can be pushed.

AP: So you don't think transhumanism is a possibility for us? Are we incapable of transcending our nature?

JEHS: Well, let's take an extreme case. I don't believe that what David Chalmers charmingly calls "DigiDave" is a real possibility. You cannot transfer your personal identity to a silicon substrate because your personal identity fundamentally depends on your embodied experience. You might programme a computer to talk like you, but it's not going to *be* you. That just won't happen, and I am confident in saying that. Obviously, if we have implants and augmentations of various sorts, there is always going to be the question of whether this is in fact the transhumanism dream realized or just more of the same. But transhumanism implies scenarios in which the human exits the picture altogether, because you no longer have a lived, embodied experience. In the absence of that, however, you no longer have yourself, you no longer have a subject to talk about who is human. In that respect, I think transhumanism is based on science fiction enthusiasms that don't really stand up to conceptual scrutiny.

AP: You referenced the impact of the internet on our attention – what has been termed "the crisis of attention". Have philosophers thought about the nature of attention before, or is it something that we're only becoming alerted to now because we can observe its effects? It's definitely harder for me to read long books than it was five or six years ago!

JEHS: The philosophy of attention really started with William James. It then developed over the course of the twentieth century in various schools of thought, including experimental psychology and phenomenology. But it's safe to say that at the present moment we do indeed have a crisis of attention, which is rooted in the fact that those things that place demands on our attention are at the same time reading us. This feedback loop serves to maximize harmful exposure to the inane advertisements and quasi-advertisements that dominate the online landscape. Furthermore, the great engine that is fed upon countless little nibbles of individual human attention, and that must constantly solicit such attention if it is to get fed, runs much more effectively when it appeals to human passion than to human reason, when it entices our first-order desire for dopamine-fuelled gratification, than when it invites us to cultivate moral character or pursue long-term goals of betterment of self or world.

Theorists like Yves Citton – who wrote a book called *The Ecology of Attention* – argue that the way the internet is now set up is as an attention extraction economy. Our attention is being extracted in the same way that one would extract oil or precious metals, because that's where the money is. If true, then it's a particularly significant economic revolution, because while people have always been exploited, they were not typically exploited as the source of the natural resource.

AP: You host a podcast in association with *The Point* magazine called "What Is X?" So, I was thinking of asking you: what is the internet? But what I have read of your work on this topic suggests that you would not consider the internet to be amenable to a necessary and sufficient conditions kind of answer; rather you would want to introduce a more historical perspective to help answer the question. But why do you think we need to understand the history of the internet in order to understand something that we use and interact with every day of our lives, and how far back do we have to rewind in order to give an account of what the internet is?

JEHS: As we have seen, the history of the telecommunication side of it goes back hundreds of millions of years. But telecommunication is not the full definition of the internet – the other part is machine information processing. For that, you have to go back to 1678, with Gottfried Wilhelm Leibniz's idea of a reckoning engine and the possibility of translating information into sequences that could be mechanically processed.

Although this is not actually developed until the 1830s with Charles Babbage and Ada Lovelace, there has been a concept of machine reasoning since at least 1678, and this started to connect with dreams of telecommunication in the mid-nineteenth century.

This might sound like an idealist history of technology, and one might oppose it for that reason. But that's how you start to understand why people were trying to make this happen in the first place. What you detect in someone like Leibniz is that they think it fits – or would fit – with the nature of reality itself – that the world *is* an interconnected network, and that if we were to develop a technology that depended on that, it would tap into what the cosmos already is like, rather than an artifice where one *constrains* nature to do something that it wouldn't ordinarily do. In that respect, if we take Leibniz as our ancestor figure for the history of the internet, then the internet really is doing something quite natural.

AP: That brings me to the opening quote of your book, in which Leibniz talks about how each thing that exists is in some way connected to everything else, and that therefore everything is an expression of everything else: a "perpetual living mirror of the universe", as he calls it. And I take it that you think this is a good metaphor for the internet. But then you also talk about the internet as a *distorting* lens. To what extent, then, can we think about the internet as a mirror of reality, as representing the way things are, and to what extent is it a distorting mirror or lens through which reality is filtered rather than mirrored.

JEHS: My history of the internet would go something like this: chapter 1 extends from 1678 to about 2011, and chapter 2 extends from around 2011 to today. Around 2011, the original Facebook model (which basically involved having a list of friends whose posts you would see in the order they posted them) was abandoned. Following this, things started looking like a distorted image of the information that the people in my network were actually trying to communicate. It got worse to the extent that by the middle of the last decade, the general perception was that social media were not a neutral medium of communication, but rather a "distorting mirror" (to use Jia Tolentino's phrase) – something that was essentially misrepresenting the reality around us. We still tend to underestimate the extent to which the internet is currently perverted and dominated by economic interests, and, in particular, the fact that we are constrained to communicate and debate through media that are explicitly profit-driven. Indeed, it was in the interest of extracting more profit that the former social media model was abandoned.

We are now in the terrible situation where this is de facto the only choice you have if you want to be heard or noticed. Of course, you could still publish pamphlets or stick posters on trees, but this is even less effective than if you fire off tweets that fail to go viral. What we have, then, is closer to a deliberation-themed video game where the real function is to rack up points in the game. But we don't refer to the points *as* points; rather, we call them likes, or follows, or retweets. And we're supposed to pretend that it's *not* a video game, but the actual public space in which rational deliberation can be pursued. We think we're exchanging ideas, but we're not. We're playing a game.

AP: This is not really what Leibniz planned, then?

JEHS: Leibniz sincerely believed in a rationally governed society freed of passionate human conflicts through the outsourcing of decision-making procedures to machines. We humans could then, he believed, use our reason for relaxation, recreation, and enjoyable things like geometry. With the appropriate machines at our disposal, we could, for example, outsource hard problems like diplomatic deadlocks. So, with two empires about to go to war, they would just enter in respective arguments, and the reckoning engine churns out some kind of ticker tape and tells you which empire is right. And both sovereigns say, "Alright. No more war. We know who's right". This is, of course, absurd! War simply doesn't work that way.

And even as recently as the 1990s I can remember people talking about the idea of being a "netizen", as if deliberative democracy and everything underlying civil society could be transferred to the internet – and therefore improved. The initial hope after the Arab Spring, which was said to be proof of concept that social media was a force for democratic political change, disintegrated quickly into violence, and then by 2016 you have Brexit, Trump, and the painful evidence that these tools were not doing what some optimistic people until very recently believed that they were going to do. The 1990s and early 2000s were really the swan song of Leibnizian optimism. The world is vastly different now.

AP: How does understanding the internet and its history help us protect ourselves from it?

JEHS: Frankly, I don't know what should be done. I think social media are going to have to be reconceived as a public utility with democratic oversight, in particular over how the algorithms favour certain declarations over others. Until that happens, we are in a bad situation. On the other hand, I wouldn't like to see governments seize social media corporations overnight and proclaim them officially a public utility. It's a serious question of political economy beyond my understanding. I see my role, however limited, as helping to diagnose the problem and urging other people to come up with a positive programme for what comes next. What we are doing is in one sense species-specific and continuous with what we've always done, and in another sense that it is a massive distortion of who we are. I hope that we can better understand the part that is species-specific and conducive to human thriving, and fight back against the part that is distorting and non-conducive to that aim.

FURTHER RESOURCES

Johann Hari, *Stolen Focus: Why You Can't Pay Attention – and How to Think Deeply Again*. New York: Crown, 2022.

Justin E. H. Smith, "It's all over". *The Point*, 3 January 2019. https://thepointmag.com/examined-life/its-all-over/.

Justin E. H. Smith, *The Internet Is Not What You Think It Is: A History, a Philosophy, a Warning*. Princeton, NJ: Princeton University Press, 2022.

Jia Tolentino, "The I in the Internet". CCCBLAB, 19 February 2020. https://lab.cccb.org/en/the-i-in-the-internet/.

14

Will artificial intelligence transform ethics?

Shannon Vallor in conversation with John Zerilli

Artificial intelligence (AI) has generated a staggering amount of hype in the past several years. But is it the game-changer it has been cracked up to be? And, if so, how is it changing the game? John Zerilli's 2021 book, *A Citizen's Guide to Artificial Intelligence*, explores the implications of AI for our lives as citizens across a number of different domains, including political, legal and economic ones. In this conversation with Zerilli, Shannon Vallor, one of the world's leading AI ethicists, explores the interplay between the ethical and the political, the scope of AI ethics, the dangers posed by our increased reliance on AI systems, and much more.

SHANNON VALLOR is the Baillie Gifford Professor in the Ethics of Data and Artificial Intelligence at the University of Edinburgh. Her research explores how emerging technologies reshape human moral and intellectual character, and maps the ethical challenges and opportunities posed by new uses of data and artificial intelligence.

JOHN ZERILLI is the Chancellor's Fellow in AI, Data and the Rule of Law at Edinburgh Law School. His research interests include the interplay between cognitive science, artificial intelligence and the law.

John Zerilli (**JZ**): I am interested in addressing more than just what we would consider to be questions of an ethical nature pertaining to the individual and how they confront moral dilemmas in their own lives. So, my first question is about AI ethics as a discipline, and how it connects to politics. There is this meme that suggests that AI ethics really isn't a very interesting specialization at all, because the questions that pop up are just questions whose answers are uncontroversial. The meme states that, "The ethics of AI is no different from the ethics of a pencil". The idea is that you shouldn't go around stabbing people with pencils, you shouldn't use pencils to write racist or sexist things, you shouldn't throw pencils at people, and so on. Similarly: don't be racist with AI technologies, don't be sexist, don't write and perpetuate discriminatory stereotypes using AI. Is there anything more to AI ethics than just this sort of bland vision?

Shannon Vallor (**SV**): There are two things I want to pick out from your opening comment and question. So, the first is about the ethical and the political. The way you described ethics I think is an accurate description of what we've done to ethics, particularly in the last few hundred years in the western philosophical tradition. But I actually don't think it's a good description of what ethics *is*. I'm a virtue ethicist in part because Aristotle understood that the ethical is political, and there is no sense in the minds of most Greek philosophers that ethics made sense as an individual practice separated from the political realm. Now, in part, that was because they associated the individual outside of the political realm with the domestic, which they devalued as a sphere of gendered responsibility and care and intimate family life. And so, when Plato and Aristotle are talking about ethics and the political realm, it's partly because they think that is where manly men use their intelligence, doing manly political things. But they weren't wrong that the ethical is political. What they overlooked is that it is political at home as well – and of course, that women are perfectly capable of practical wisdom in the politics of the state!

The point is that I have never been able to understand ethics as separable from the political, and I think that to the extent that AI ethics has been in some contexts depoliticized or politically denatured, this has been a tremendous loss to what AI ethics is about. Fortunately, there are many voices pushing back against that denaturing and depoliticization of AI ethics. The fact is that when we talk about justice, we cannot avoid talking about power and its legitimate uses, we cannot avoid talking about equality, we cannot avoid talking about violence and harm and oppression. Similarly, we cannot talk about justice without also talking about what is right, what is good, what is moral.

With respect to the question of whether AI ethics is doing anything unique or special, I think it is. AI is not like a pencil in the following sense: I've never had to ask the question, "Why did the pencil do that?" Nor do I think I'm ever going to have to ask such a question! Pencils do things that are not mysterious and not in any sense autonomous. They have a relatively well-defined scope of purposes: I can write with a pencil, I can draw with a pencil, I can also stab with a pencil. But AI can be used in virtually every domain of human activity, and we increasingly see its expansion into the realm of the creative arts, into finance, into health, into education. AI systems are still always extensions of human power and choice and decision-making, but the agency between us and them has been stretched out to such a degree that we often lose a clear sense of *how* our will is being enacted by this system or machine or algorithm. It *is* still enacting our will, but in a way that is opaque and often not subject to our immediate moment-to-moment control. With AI systems, there are increasingly so many human agencies involved in their operations that it can be very difficult to assign responsibility to one particular agent. So, we've started talking about the "responsibility gap" in AI that happens when it is difficult to take a particular AI action and find the human being, or even a definite set of humans, who is responsible.

JZ: What about if we replace the pencil with a more complicated artefact, for example a desktop computer. Of such an artefact one could ask, "Why did the computer do that rather than this? Why won't my software programme accept this instruction?" You pointed out that AI has attained a sufficient complexity that we can no longer just treat it as a passive implement, but it doesn't yet quite set AI apart necessarily as a self-standing discipline. There's obviously such a thing as computer ethics, but it doesn't really mean the same thing as *AI* ethics. We are more or less near consensus that certain things, such as murder, rape, theft, and so on are just wrong to do. Is there anything that AI ethics poses as a question that cannot be answered simply by resorting to the uses the technology is being put to?

SV: You are right that in ethics we have a fairly strong consensus about the kinds of things we shouldn't do (murder, torture, and so forth), but in the realm of AI ethics we are still debating fundamental questions for which there is currently no consensus over what is appropriate. To take one example, affect-recognition tools that aim to detect and classify emotions through monitoring facial expressions are increasingly prevalent in social spaces. But there is no consensus over whether it is scientifically legitimate rather than just three phrenologists in a digital trench coat, or, if it *is* scientifically legitimate (even in a minimal or provisional way), whether it is ethically legitimate to deploy these technologies in certain contexts. So, one way to talk about what's distinctive or necessary about AI ethics is that certain technologies are presenting us with ethical situations that we really haven't had to wrestle with before. This does not mean that there won't be parallels with already existing ethical situations, but it does mean that the work in this field is qualitatively distinct from other fields of ethical inquiry.

There are also some really interesting metaethical questions that are implicated by AI. For example, the rise of increasingly sophisticated AI technologies puts increasing pressure on us to talk about what is distinctive about human reasoning and what is missing in machine reasoning. In philosophy of mind, we have long addressed questions relating to whether the mind can be understood analogously with a computer; there has been a lot of debate about the validity of that comparison, and rightly so. But in metaethics, we are increasingly being challenged to re-examine what we mean when we talk about the ability to respond to reasons as a property of moral agents. One of the reasons that my dog is not considered a moral agent is that my dog cannot respond to reasons in the same way as I can. But what if we are talking about an artificial agent? We are not at this point yet, and I don't think that we will be any time soon, but let's assume that we have an artificial agent with advanced machine learning skills that has developed a dialogical capacity to be responsive to reasons within certain bounded areas. Is it a moral agent in that domain? And how do we answer that? The kinds of questions that this scenario raises suggest that there is some underspecification in our notion of what it is to be responsive to reasons.

JZ: To continue the discussion of moral agency, in what ways do you think that trust between humans is different from trust between AI and humans?

SV: I don't think there can be trust between AI and humans in the real sense. We may use the word "trust" but I think what we mean is that we *rely* on AI systems. The reason why this distinction matters is because trust involves putting something that you value – whether it is your body, your thoughts, your money – in someone else's care. The problem is that a machine *cannot care*. None of the machines we have today can care, and they cannot care for the things that you put in their power. Therefore they cannot be objects of legitimate trust. If there is a person using the machine to care for something, then we can talk about trust, where the trust is really passing through the machine to the agent that is responsible for it. Trust always comes with the possibility of being disappointed or betrayed. When I am betrayed, I feel anger because my trust has not been treated with the value that it warrants in human relations. But that kind of response makes no sense when we are talking about a machine. However, because machines increasingly *represent* agents, it is going to get harder and harder to keep this clear. And I do worry about that.

JZ: How about in the case of robots? The extant social psychology literature on how humans interact with robots is interesting and markedly different from how humans interact with what we could call embedded AI like Alexa, Siri, and so forth. With robots, we tend to anthropomorphize a whole lot more, and the trust, including the affective component of trust, seems to be more prominent in our interactions with them. This raises the worry that as robots themselves become better dissimulators or emulators of human conduct, we might start thinking that it *cares* for us because it is saying all the right things when in fact it is just a machine, a zombie, the lights aren't on.

SV: If you look at some of the studies on social robotics, people were initially worried about the possibility of deceiving children, deceiving the elderly, and so forth. But then there were all these anecdotal reports of *engineers themselves* reporting that they found themselves talking to their robot or leaving the lights on around it so that it didn't have to sit in the dark! These were the people who *built* the thing, who *knew* it was dead inside. So, when we talk about deception in this context, it is not deception in the traditional sense; rather, it is just the activation of a certain kind of affective desire that we project onto all kinds of objects. It's not intrinsically wrong, but I think that the problem is the potential for it to be exploited. These robots are increasingly being deployed without the kind of regulatory protections that can protect us from having those emotional responses exploited.

JZ: All of what you have discussed suggests that AI can change us and change our own moral capacities. How do you see AI changing us beyond our moral capacities?

SV: Our technologies have always changed us, and our technologies have always resulted in shifts not just in our moral reasoning, but our political thinking and our scientific understanding of the world. We have co-evolved with the world we have built with our technologies. We build ourselves, our values, our expectations, our framings of reality into the built environment, and then they are reflected back into us, sometimes in surprising ways that cause further changes, and so forth. In a sense, AI is just continuing this pattern. But I do think that the growing agency of AI, the growing power of it to do things and change things at previously unimaginable scales and speeds and levels of complexity, makes it hard for us to map our individual choices onto a discrete set of effects in the world that we can track, as well as to know what the effects of this kind of technology are on us. To take an example, think about the ways that AI is been used in the workplace to monitor, to predict, to manipulate, to judge, to rank, to nudge, and so on. We don't just have a single AI system changing us, we may have ten different AI systems changing us – from the chatbots that we're interacting with, to the predictive analytics that are being used to feed us our statistics in real time, to the facial recognition software that we might be scanned with in order to get into our office. And we have no real way to understand the collective impact of this on our psyche, on our moral capabilities and skills, unless we start thinking about this impact and studying it far more rigorously.

FURTHER RESOURCES

Shannon Vallor (ed.), *Oxford Handbook of Philosophy of Technology*. Oxford: Oxford University Press, 2022.

John Zerilli *et al.*, *A Citizen's Guide to Artificial Intelligence*. Cambridge, MA: MIT Press, 2021.

Mark Coeckelbergh, *AI Ethics*. Cambridge, MA: MIT Press, 2020.

Mark Ryan, "In AI we trust: ethics, artificial intelligence, and reliability". *Science and Engineering Ethics* 26 (2020), 2749–67.

15

The algorithmic is political

Annette Zimmermann in conversation with Matt Lord

There is a widespread assumption that the continued deployment and incremental optimization of AI tools will ultimately benefit everyone in society. But perhaps it is time to critically interrogate the value and purpose of using AI in a given domain in the first place? In 2021, political philosopher Annette Zimmermann published an essay for *Boston Review* called "Stop Building Bad AI". In this conversation with *Boston Review* editor Matt Lord, Zimmermann expands on many themes from this essay, offering a clear overview of the key social and political questions that philosophers are addressing in the face of AI-related problems, such as algorithmic injustice, lack of democratic accountability for powerful corporate agents, and the kind of learned helplessness that results from coming to see AI development as inevitable.

ANNETTE ZIMMERMANN is Assistant Professor of Philosophy at the University of Wisconsin-Madison and a Technology and Human Rights Fellow at Harvard University. Their research focuses on the ethics and politics of artificial intelligence, machine learning and big data.

MATT LORD is senior editor at *Boston Review*. He studied literature, mathematics, and philosophy at MIT and Harvard and is editor, most recently, of *Thinking in a Pandemic: The Crisis of Science and Policy in the Age of COVID-19* (2020).

Matt Lord (**ML**): One way of telling the story of philosophy's long engagement with artificial intelligence is to see a transformation from an earlier focus on logical, epistemic and metaphysical questions – "What *is* AI? Is it even possible?" – to a growing discussion of ethical, political and social questions. To put it crudely, there was a time when the field was once little more than footnotes to John Searle's Chinese room argument. Now, following significant advances in machine learning and computing power over the last decade, we have this well-defined new subfield of philosophy, the "ethics of AI", to which a lot of scholars, including you, are contributing. What explains the change? And what does it mean to think about AI from within the perspective of ethics and political philosophy, in particular?

Annette Zimmermann (**AZ**): One of the reasons for this is that there is a growing body of work, which is identifying problems of clear normative – not just technical – significance, coming from computer science and applied statistics, as well as applied mathematics. This research community has been looking into the technological sources of phenomena like algorithmic injustice, i.e. errors that generate unjust outcomes, such as privileging one group over another within a particular domain. So, given that we now have more information about these kinds of technological problems, the ethical and political questions associated with them are becoming much more salient and urgent. Moral and political philosophers of AI are asking questions like: What is this phenomenon of algorithmic injustice? Who is wronged by disparate output distributions, and what should we do about that? Who should play a role in making decisions about where AI should be deployed?

I am especially interested in questions related to algorithmic injustice, and think that it is really important to have an accurate and sufficiently encompassing notion in mind of what algorithmic injustice *is* in the first place. For example, we might think of it as a fundamentally new phenomenon that requires entirely new philosophical concepts. But when we look at existing cases, what we actually see is that the kinds of long-standing, deeply entrenched social, political and economic injustices with which moral and political philosophers are familiar are resurfacing in often surprising and conceptually interesting ways. In other words, structures of social injustice are being replicated – but also amplified in a philosophically interesting and ethically objectionable way – by AI. This is an important opportunity for us to investigate how we can actually draw on longer-standing work in moral and political philosophy that has to do with different notions of justice, and see how it applies in this very urgent domain.

There are two other especially urgent questions for political philosophers to address in this area. The first one has to do with control over AI, i.e., who should be able to make judgement calls about where and if AI and machine learning tools ought to be deployed? The problem that we are wrestling with at the moment is that there is currently a complete devolution of control to the tech industry because of a lack of government expertise on the policy side. The tech industry moves much faster – and often more efficiently – than any government agency and the wider citizenry can, but that fact alone does not resolve the normative question of who *ought* to be able to make decisions about the really consequential judgement calls that we need to make here. In this context, exercising much more democratic control in relation to the goals that we as a society are trying to pursue with AI in the first place is crucial.

However, rather than every citizen needing to become a computer scientist and understand the detailed inner workings of every single machine learning tool, what we need is democratic citizens deliberating about what we are trying to achieve when we automate. That is a *value-based* question that ought to be at the forefront of people's minds – and increasingly is. The second question is how and why we ought to *improve* technology. Optimization is a big buzzword in the tech industry. And optimization sounds really great – there is nothing obviously worrying about making things better! But, as it turns out, making things better can often move us further away from our bigger political, moral and social goals. Approximating one type of ideal – such as making complex decisions fast and at scale – might actually make us compromise on another set of ideals – such as fair decision outcomes across all socio-demographic groups. Therefore, we must have a clear view in mind of what we are actually aspiring to when we talk about "optimization".

ML: What are some of the ways AI technologies can be morally or politically objectionable? What exactly does injustice mean in this domain?

AZ: There is a real temptation, particularly in the more technical communities working on this topic, to think of these normative problems as purely technical ones that ought to be addressed first and foremost via technical interventions, for example by imposing particular quantifiable constraints on our AI systems. However, there are serious limitations to what we might call this "quality control" approach to algorithmic bias.

For example, a lot of influential computer science research has been pointing out that it is actually mathematically impossible to reconcile multiple intuitively plausible fairness measures with each other in the same system. This is where moral and political philosophers of AI can come in to advance arguments about what kind of conception of justice we ought to be working towards.

Because forms of social injustice exist along many different axes, we cannot just look at one type of algorithmic decision scenario in isolation and resolve the problem by picking the right mathematically-defined conception of fairness. So, as AI becomes more and more enmeshed in all kinds of different decision scenarios, there will still be this interplay between social injustice broadly construed and things like algorithmic bias. In this sense, we cannot fix algorithmic bias by just fixing the algorithms; rather, larger-scale social, political and legal interventions are required here in order to transform the kinds of institutions and decision-makers that choose to deploy AI. If we were simply to accelerate what we are already doing and try to make sure that this process runs smoothly, this would fall short of a plausible conception of social justice.

ML: Facial recognition technology is a case in point: in response to work on racial and gender bias by Joy Buolamwini, Timnit Gebru, and many others, there has been this claim that the solution is purely technical: just train the algorithms on better data or tweak some code.

AZ: That's exactly right! And when the focus is simply on improving the data, we completely overlook important questions such as whether we should be trying to accelerate existing policing practices with the help of facial recognition tools in the first place. Given the severity of structural injustice that plagues the criminal justice system, is the most just decision we can make really to support and accelerate the *existing* set of law enforcement practices? We urgently need to rethink the institutions and practices of criminal justice at a more fundamental level, and remain open to the idea that *not* deploying facial recognition tools at all in this domain is the more just option.

There are also important political questions that arise when thinking about how we get this data in the first place. To take an infamous example, back in 2019 the *Guardian* reported that Google had hired subcontractors who sought out Black, unhoused and economically vulnerable people in multiple US cities to collect data for their new facial recognition tool in exchange for a tiny financial incentive – without disclosing that the image data would be recorded and used to train the kinds of tools that then get used in law and immigration enforcement. Not only is there deception involved in this particular case, but it raises the question of how the data would be collected if there was *not* this kind of deception involved. The particularly disturbing feature of this kind of scenario is that exactly the kinds of social groups that are already at the receiving end of various injustices, particularly in law enforcement, would then have to either volunteer or be forced to provide their image data in order to make these tools run more smoothly. There is an independent wrong at stake here that is politically urgent and that cannot easily be subsumed into discussions about data accuracy. If we can only get better datasets by exploiting those who are already oppressed by existing structures of injustice, narrowly construed optimization of this kind does not sound like a feasible and desirable moral and political ideal.

ML: You have identified some issues that are genuinely distinctive, but others seem like generic concerns that have always been raised about emerging technologies. What, if anything, makes AI special? Or, to turn the question around, what can we learn by refusing to think about AI solely conceptually and ahistorically – by considering it, that is, in relation to other technological revolutions? There is now widespread consensus that "move fast and break things" isn't good policy when it comes to nuclear technology or biotechnology, say; most people think those domains ought to be carefully regulated. Should we be optimistic that some similar consensus will emerge around AI?

AZ: One obviously unique feature of AI is the conceit that AI development is too important or distinctive to be stifled and thus should be exempt from the caution and regulation we apply to other technological innovations. Only very rarely before have we seen so much reluctance and timidity – both from regulators but also from citizens – to intervene critically in discussions about the purpose of automating various domains of social life. There are many economic and sociological reasons for this state of affairs. For example, tech industry companies are able to attract an immense amount of talent as there are really strong economic incentives for talented young researchers to move into that industry. And the kinds of corporate papers that these researchers publish to address questions related to the moral and political implications of AI are obviously rather different to what they would publish if they were employed in a government agency, in an activist role, or within academia.

One of the scenarios we currently face in this domain is a form of what psychologists have called "learned helplessness". This often surfaces in relation to the idea that we just know too little about AI and there is too much uncertainty around it, so it would be wrong and unreasonable to make any strong value-based judgement calls about it, particularly from the perspective of industry-based developer teams. There seems to be a common view in the tech industry that essentially says, "Let's just deploy, and then wait and see if any ethical problems arise". However, if AI technology really is so shot through with uncertainty and unpredictability, this gives us all the *more* reason to exercise caution and moderation in deploying these technologies, rather than defaulting to rapid deployment in all domains.

Another strand of this learned helplessness stance relates to the *inevitability* of the rise of AI within our societies, coupled with the fear that AI will eventually grow out of our control. Despite the fact that AI is very much the result of human decision-making, and thus necessarily a product of choices that are currently within our control, this stance risks creating a self-fulfilling prophecy: thinking that we *cannot* steer technology in the right direction, and simply *opting out of trying* to steer it in the right direction even though doing so would be feasible, ultimately amounts to the same thing.

A third part of this picture is concern over a lack of ethical expertise. This form of learned helplessness is very common amongst computer scientists and tech industry practitioners: understandably, many AI experts without ethical (or more broadly, philosophical) training feel that they are simply not equipped to tackle normative problems – and conclude that normative problems, such as properly understanding the nature and scope of algorithmic injustice, are outside of the scope of their own responsibilities. In a way, it is good to see recognition of the fact that developing ethical reasoning skills might take training, rather than being a mere matter of exchanging spontaneous opinions and intuitions. But overall I am sceptical of the more general idea that we need ethical *experts* in order to reason well about ethical AI, and that those experts must necessarily and exclusively be moral and political philosophers of AI. Rather, I think that tech practitioners and computer scientists should dare to ask themselves these complicated and often not quantifiable ethical and political questions, because they are often the ones best placed to intervene in these questions.

But of course, there is a major risk inherent in allowing tech practitioners and the private sector more broadly to navigate the ethics of AI by themselves, as they could dangerously *over*estimate their ability to make representative and democratically accountable decisions. Furthermore, it is unclear whether corporations will actually empower their ethical AI teams to intervene in the development and design of new technology. AI ethics efforts can often be limited and outweighed by competing corporate goals.

ML: We have said a lot about the risks and harms associated with AI, but of course many people also talk about the good that it can do. (Here again there is nothing special about AI; every technology has its utopians.) Take one common argument for *more* AI: that it can correct bias in human judgement and the limitations of human processing power. Proponents of this view emphasize that human reasoning suffers from unconscious bias, overt prejudice, limited information, and all kinds of cognitive fallacies, whereas algorithms are "objective" or "neutral". A machine won't deny you a loan simply because it does not like you, nor will it overlook some crucial piece of information in your medical chart because it is tired or distracted. Sophisticated AI, so the argument goes, promises to liberate us from all this mess. What do you make of this view? Does AI have a role to play in helping to *advance* justice? What might such constructive uses look like?

AZ: I agree strongly with the concern about fallible and biased human decision-making. It is not as if a human-controlled alternative to algorithmic decision-making and machine learning is necessarily going to be morally and politically superior. However, the kind of logic that dominates these discussions about using AI for good often does not take into account the importance of defining the problem carefully enough, with political and moral values in mind. What often happens when we engage in this comparative logic of looking at fallible human decision-makers and potentially optimizable AI systems is that we ignore this deeper question of setting ourselves a just agenda. There is a range of different political, legal and social interventions that are available to us that we might de-prioritize, or even forget about, if we are simply engaging in this comparative exercise. Neutral solutions might well secure just outcomes in a just society, but only serve to preserve the status quo in an unjust one.

That being said, I do think that there might be some important roles for AI deployment when it comes to *diagnosing* various biases that may occur. Right now, a number of scholars are investigating how we can deliberately deploy AI in a decision scenario that we *know* to be prone to bias, and use AI to locate and precisely diagnose the ways in which that bias plays out. In this scenario, however, it is important to remember that a lot of the classic cases of decision-making scenarios in which we typically see bias are not as complex as supporters of this approach might assume. It is often just not plausible that we need really sophisticated AI to establish support for the claim that bias is prevalent in a given domain.

In the domain of criminal justice, for example, we know that racial bias, gender bias, class bias, and so on, play a really important role: we have quantitative and qualitative social science research on this question; we have direct lived experiences of citizens interacting with the criminal justice system that makes it clear that biases shape criminal justice outcomes in unequal ways. Do we really need sophisticated AI to establish support for *that* claim? Not necessarily. But, of course, it is possible that there may be some domains of social and political life in which we have less clarity about the location and scope of such biases. In those cases, it might be a very good idea to use AI as a heuristic device.

ML: How should we think about various levels of responsibility in this context, from the individual up to the structural? What can be done to start building a more just future for AI?

AZ: Generally speaking, we are not primarily going to worry about holding an individual developer accountable for taking part in the development and design of a tool that ends up causing harm. There are many reasons for that. One of them is just a pure feasibility constraint: given that large teams work on complex tools over long periods of time, it would be really difficult to attribute particular outcome responsibilities to individual agents. This is a familiar problem in philosophy: should we blame members of groups who act together and collectively bring about harmful outcomes?

But there is another reason why we might want to resist the focus on individual accountability, and that is the structural power and influence that big corporations wield in this domain. That's a much more urgent problem to address in comparison to adopting an approach that allows us to sue engineer X or team Y. I view a focus on auditing and holding accountable corporations, as well as limiting their democratic agenda-setting power, as really crucial. And that extends not only to situations in which the deployment of some AI tool causes some disparate output that is really harmful for some groups – it also extends to the ability of corporations to stifle public debate on some issues and steer debate towards other issues. This is a similar scenario to long-standing financial and political controversies (such as debates around campaign financing), in the context of which powerful corporate agents that are not democratically authorized or democratically accountable have the capacity to shape public discourse around certain questions in a way that not only obfuscates their own role in causing harm, but also immunizes them against future accountability and auditing efforts. There is no such thing as "AI for Good" if the group of those who participate in defining "the good" remains confined to a very limited, privileged and unrepresentative group of people.

FURTHER RESOURCES

Daron Acemoglu *et al., Redesigning AI: Work, Democracy and Justice in the Age of Automation*. Big Sandy, TX: Boston Review, 2021. Features essays by Annette Zimmermann, Kate Crawford, Daron Acemoglu, and many others.

Safiya Umoja Noble, *Algorithms of Oppression: How Search Engines Reinforce Racism*. New York: NYU Press, 2018.

Other thinkers working in this field include: Ruha Benjamin, Abeba Birhane, Timnit Gebru and Margaret Mitchell.

16

Artificial bodies and the promise of abstraction

Peter Wolfendale in conversation with Anthony Morgan

What would need to be involved if we want our future robots to be anything more than quiz show champions, phenomenal chess players, and highly efficient killers? An influential answer from many corners of contemporary cognitive science is a body very much like ours, with our needs, desires, pleasures, pains, our kinds of habits, expertise, significance, care, and meaning, our cultural knowledge, practical know-how, and so on. In other words, nothing short of "real meat" embodiment will do. With his characteristic flair and mastery of a great diversity of philosophical traditions, in this conversation Peter Wolfendale clarifies the "real meat" hypothesis and defends the feasibility of isolated human brains animating androids from a distance and distributed artificial intellects inhabiting human bodies from the cloud – without sacrificing any of the cognitive capacities enabled by embodiment.

PETER WOLFENDALE is an independent philosopher living in the North East of England and the author of *Object-Oriented Philosophy: The Noumenon's New Clothes* (2019). His influential blog/website is: https://deontologistics.co.

ANTHONY MORGAN is, among other things, the editor of this book.

Anthony Morgan (**AM**): Please can you start by saying a few things about the rise of embodiment within contemporary philosophy? It seems to me to be mainly used as a corrective against: (1) the Cartesian notion of an immaterial mind, and (2) the materialist tendency to place the mind in the brain. But what are the main positive claims that defenders of embodiment are making?

Peter Wolfendale (**PW**): I think that the meaning of the term "embodiment" in philosophical circles is deceptively diverse, and that those who champion the concept are motivated by concerns that overlap less than is often appreciated. If they are unified by one thing, it is a rogues' gallery of common enemies. Although Descartes is the most reviled of these, his errors are often traced back to some original sin perpetrated by Plato. However, in order to make sense of these conceptual crimes, it is worth first distinguishing the *explanatory* concerns of cognitive science and artificial intelligence from the *normative* concerns of political and social theory, while acknowledging that both of these are downstream from more general *metaphysical* concerns regarding the difference and/or relation between matter and mind. So, although there are many purely metaphysical objections to the Platonic dualism of intelligible and sensible worlds, and the Cartesian dualism of mental and physical substances, what really unites the embodiment paradigm is their objection to the outsized role that Plato, Descartes, and their inheritors give to "the life of the mind" in explaining how we make our way in the world, and establishing which aspects of it we should value. For want of a better word, we might call this "intellectualism".

This "life of the mind" is distinguished by the capacity for *abstract thought*. This is to say that it abstracts away from concrete features of the context in which thinking occurs: it is *theoretical*, or unconstrained by the practical problems posed by our bodily environment; and it is *contemplative*, or independent of the sensorimotor capacities through which we interact with this environment. Both Plato and Descartes take mathematics to exemplify this sort of thinking, and, on that basis, thought *as such*. Mathematical theorems are not strictly *about* anything in our physical environment, and they can be verified even if they're not applicable to it, in ways that needn't involve interacting with it. This being said, what really distinguishes Descartes from Plato is his conviction that the physical world can be accurately *represented* by mathematical models, and thus that our experiences can be treated as internal representations akin to such models. There are other problematic aspects of the Cartesian picture, but this will do for now.

AM: So, what are the main explanatory objections to intellectualism?

PW: There are two. On the one hand, its opponents claim that intellectualism ignores the vast majority of human cognition: most of our lives are spent carrying out tasks and navigating obstacles whose contours are determined by the way our body fits into its environment, rather than reasoning our way from premises to conclusions. Making a cup of tea in an unfamiliar kitchen is a more representative instance of our problem-solving capacity than demonstrating the infinity of primes. On the other hand, they claim that intellectualism has its priorities backwards: rather than treating this sort of "skilled coping" as a deficient form of abstract cognition, we can only understand the latter by showing how it emerges from the former. Even our ability to imagine complex geometric constructions has at some point been bootstrapped from a basic bodily grasp of orientation and gesture.

The most important targets of these complaints are the classical computational theory of mind in cognitive science and what gets called "good old-fashioned AI" (GOFAI). These see cognition as principally a matter of rule-governed symbol manipulation not unlike mathematical reasoning. They are opposed by a range of "4E perspectives", so called because they emphasize some combination of the *embodied*, *embedded*, *enactive* and *extended* dimensions of cognition. The extent to which these diverge from traditional views varies, but, in rough order, the points of contention are: (1) the extent to which cognition is dependent on features of the body outside of the brain (e.g., the structure of sensory organs), and features of the environment outside of the body (e.g., the availability of cognitive resources); (2) whether the concepts of computation and representation are irredeemably intellectualist (e.g., if they can account for pre-linguistic "meaning"); and (3) whether dependence implies constitution (e.g., if my notebook is part of my mind).

AM: What about the normative objections?

PW: Again, there are two. On the one hand, opponents claim that intellectualism reflects and reinforces implicit social hierarchies: those who have historically enjoyed the luxury of theoretical contemplation have done so because the practical problems and bodily processes it abstracts away from have been taken care of for them, often by groups who have been systematically *identified* with their bodies and bodily capacities, such as women, slaves and colonized peoples. The disembodied Cartesian ego is an illusion engendered by ignorance and privilege. On the other hand, they claim that intellectualism devalues significant sources of human knowledge: there are forms of "lived experience" and "situated knowledge" that are valuable even if they aren't (and possibly can't be) articulated in a manner that divorces them from the embodied contexts in which they occur (e.g., their emotional valence). This Cartesian false-consciousness doesn't simply impact the way we treat others, but also the way we treat ourselves, potentially disconnecting us from our embodied existence.

The idea that privileging the mind over the body is associated with other sorts of illicit privilege (e.g., economic, racial, sexual, etc.) is now fairly widespread in contemporary feminist and critical theory. However, there are a variety of philosophical frameworks drawn from the Continental tradition that get used to articulate, elaborate and offer solutions to this problem. Roughly speaking, the main strands are Spinozist (Deleuze, affect theory, etc.), Nietzschean (Foucault, Butler, etc.), and phenomenological (Heidegger, Merleau-Ponty, etc.), although there is much cross-pollination. The first is characterized by the metaphysical tenor of its critique, proposing some form of materialist monism as an alternative to the dualisms of Plato and Descartes. The second is characterized by its focus upon social dynamics, providing an analysis of the way bodies are "ensouled" by the internalization of patterns of thought and action. But the last provides the greatest point of overlap with the explanatory concerns discussed above, as it provides a detailed introspective analysis of the body's involvement in the constitution of experience. Phenomenology has had a marked influence on 4E approaches to cognition, and is responsible for the concept that straddles and sometimes connects all these varying concerns, namely, "the lived body".

AM: The idea of the lived body suggests that the body is not just a causal bridge between ourselves and the world, but rather that the body *is* our engagement with the world in a way that serves as a condition for the emergence of our subjectivity. This suggests that only a "proper" body will be fit for this purpose – no ersatz or artificial alternative will do. Embodiment is in fact "real meat" embodiment. Is this a fair picture, both in phenomenology and in the other frameworks you discuss above?

PW: Although not every proponent of embodiment will go so far as to insist on an essential link between mind and meat, I think it's fair to say that this is where the rhetoric of embodiment leads. To some extent, this is because it aligns with other philosophical and political goals, such as undermining pernicious distinctions between human and animal or diagnosing dangerous fantasies implicit in the very suggestion that minds could be uploaded into computer simulations. However, there are some arguments for the claim, and I'll try to tease out the general pattern of these as I see it. But first, it's worth saying something more about the idea of the lived body.

The cornerstone of the phenomenological tradition is the idea that the *content* of explicitly articulated representations, such as declarative sentences or mathematical models, depends upon a more primitive form of *meaning* implicit in ordinary conscious experience. This gets formulated in slightly different ways by Husserl, Heidegger and Merleau-Ponty, but they essentially agree that our many and varied representations are able to pick out the same *object* (e.g., galaxies, spleens, recessions) across changes in time, shifts in perspective, differences of opinion, and diverging interests, only because the referential frameworks they deploy (e.g., star charts, anatomy, econometrics), are so many layers arranged on top of those simple *unities* that tie together our everyday activities (e.g., places, obstacles, tools). My coffee cup is unified as something I can reach out and grasp, but this grasping is not a carefully planned sequence of muscle movements guided by a mechanical understanding of shapes and forces; rather, it is a single fluid movement in which my fingers fit themselves to the cup's contours without so much as a second thought. What distinguishes the "lived body" from the "biological body" is not simply that it is not yet an object of scientific representation, but rather that it is what ties everything together in the last instance. It is the *origin* of all intentional directedness, and it is experienced as such: an *immediate* awareness of agency. The question remains: if the lived body is *not* the biological body, why is "real meat" so important?

The notion that there is some split between an original and a dependent (or derived) form of intentionality is not unique to phenomenology. Wittgenstein is famous for arguing that the usage rules that give words their meaning ultimately only make sense in the context of some shared "form of life", while John Searle is (in)famous for arguing (in his Chinese room thought experiment) that a mind cannot be built from rule-governed symbol manipulation, precisely because these symbols must already be interpreted as meaningful. Wittgenstein and his followers tend to emphasize the role that social constraint plays in making intentionality possible, while Searle and his followers tend to emphasize the sheer uniqueness of the human body's capacity for intentionality, whatever it consists in. However, they are entirely compatible with embodied phenomenology and other strands of the paradigm, and are often blended together. So a second question emerges: how should we understand the "dependence" between the original (embodied/concrete) and the derived (disembodied/abstract)?

AM: So, the importance of "real meat" has something to do with the way in which "dependence" is understood. How does this work?

PW: I think it is useful to draw two distinctions. On the one hand, we should distinguish *empirical* claims about the workings of the human mind from *transcendental* claims about the workings of any possible mind. On the other hand, we should distinguish *conditions* that enable our cognitive capacities from *constraints* that limit the form they take. When these lines are blurred, it becomes all too easy to mistake significant features of our mental make-up for essential features of any possible cognitive architecture: *de facto* dependence becomes *de jure* constraint.

For instance, there is much experimental research indicating that basic information processing tasks (e.g., determining the direction of a noise) are carried out by *heuristics* closely tailored to environmental and/or bodily parameters (e.g., the distance between our ears). Does this mean that all cognition is heuristic, or just good enough for the environmental conditions it is adapted for? Similarly, there is much phenomenological research arguing that most mental content (e.g., heeding the warning "beware of the dog") is constituted by *sensorimotor expectations* tied to specific sensory modalities (i.e., an imaginary bundle of potential sights, smells, sounds and motions). Does this mean that all thought is parochial, or restricted by the range of our sensory imagination?

AM: I imagine you would want to dispute such conclusions, but why? Has the critique of intellectualism missed something important?

PW: To give Plato and Descartes their due, pure and applied mathematics provide us with a wealth of counter-examples, and not simply because they involve *brute calculation* as opposed to *creative inspiration*. Mathematicians certainly deploy heuristic techniques in searching for solutions to complex problems (cf. George Pólya's *How to Solve It*), and physicists clearly exercise their imaginations in exploring theoretical possibilities (cf. Einstein's "thought experiments"); yet what makes it the case that any two practitioners are thinking about *the same things* (e.g., a twisted manifold or an alpha decay event) has come unmoored from the trappings of bodily immediacy, be it the fingers they count on or the eyes they see with. One way to approach this is to explore modal differences in the analogies physicists find helpful (e.g., visual/auditory takes on particles), but my preferred example is Smale's theorem, which, loosely, proves that there must be a way to turn a sphere inside out without creating creases (eversion). Not only is this physically (and so bodily) impossible, but at the time no one could *envision* a way to do it. It ultimately took several mathematicians working together – one of whom (Bernard Morin) was *blind* – to find one.

I think there's no good reason to assume that there couldn't be similar collaborations between mathematicians with more radical divergences in embodiment (e.g., humans, aliens and AIs). This is the promise of abstraction: that we can repurpose diverse cognitive talents to common representational ends. I think that the error of much work on embodiment is to see this as a false promise: that whatever enables our *immediate* purchase upon the world inevitably constrains any more *mediated* comprehension of its contents; that there is no true escape from the concrete, only misguided escapism. As a consequence, the idea of abstractions anchored to the world in any manner other than our own becomes inherently suspect. Not only is immediate ("lived") experience seen as more authentic than that which is mediated, but the form taken by our immediate ("embodied") purchase on the world – *meat and all* – becomes the only authentic form. I contend that it is this association between immediacy and authenticity that supposedly renders artificial minds and bodies "unreal".

AM: I'm not sure this is enough to dismiss the importance of meat. It seems to me that it's still a salient issue when considering the possibility of minds housed in artificial bodies. Just look at social distancing and the impact that changes to our intercorporeal habits will have on our cognition, on our sense of trust, openness to others, etc. Isn't our flesh incredibly significant here?

PW: I don't think that people are invested in the importance of "real meat" because they have identified some positive feature that makes meat the one true medium of cognition. Rather, it serves as an *index* of authenticity: a stand-in for *whatever it is* that supposedly enables actual human cognition at the expense of those merely possible minds such people would rather rule out. This gets dressed up in various ways, such as insisting that only socialization "in the flesh" can provide the sort of social constraint Wittgensteinians think makes intentionality possible, but there's little reason offered for this beyond its centrality to the current form of life we share. I have no qualms with anyone who wants to analyse this importance. I've no doubt there is much of philosophical interest to be said about the spiritual impoverishment produced by the substitution of virtual for physical contact in life during lockdown. I simply think that elevating it to the status of a transcendental condition is a hyperbolic version of familiar complaints about "kids these days and their smart phones". Meat merely functions as the common denominator of those factors such people deem intrinsic to a "real life", encapsulating everything from our peculiar emotional palette and the centrality of touch, to our inevitable mortality and the significance of suffering.

To put my own cards on the table, I'm entirely convinced that artificial bodies and minds are possible, with or without meat, but I think we can loosen the link between the "lived" and the "biological" by beginning with less controversial examples. If nothing else, there is much of the biological body that simply is not lived. There is no lived experience of my spleen, my lymph nodes, or my mitochondria as distinct unities that bear upon action. Their (dys)functioning is frustratingly opaque. Similarly, though reaching for my coffee cup is a single fluid movement, I can, through reflection, decompose it to some extent: I can separate the movements of shoulder, elbow and wrist in my awareness; consider the motions of individual fingers, and then their joints; but there are limits to this process.

When it comes to bodily awareness, immediacy does not imply transparency. The edges of volition blur as we descend deeper into our own somatic depths. The embodiment paradigm sometimes advertises this as a further departure from Descartes, for whom the inner workings of experience must be fully laid open to introspection. The lived body is no Cartesian theatre.

AM: What about the converse? Can the lived body extend beyond the bounds of the biology?

PW: Yes! Merleau-Ponty was particularly interested in the phenomenon of phantom limbs, or cases in which amputees can still feel the presence of appendages that are no longer there. This is a key piece of evidence for the existence of a "body schema", or an internal model of the body that tracks and organizes our experience. There are disagreements over the nature of this schema (e.g., whether it is a "representation"), but there are other psychological phenomena that let us trace its parameters. Consider the rubber hand illusion, in which someone's hand is hidden from view, but positioned and stroked in the same manner as a rubber hand they can see. This induces the feeling that the rubber hand is part of the subject's body. This shows both that the schema is multimodal, or that it integrates information from distinct senses (i.e., vision, as well as touch and proprioception), and that it can identify non-biological things as belonging to our body. There are a number of other so-called "body transfer illusions", but it's important to see that these are only deemed *illusions* on the assumption that their objects are *not really part* of the body, even if they are felt as such.

This assumption comes into question at the point where phantoms and illusions overlap, namely, in prosthetics. In designing a prosthetic hand, the goal is to exploit the sensory basis of the rubber hand illusion to map the phantom to the mechanism – to put the ghost in the machine, as it were. Thankfully, the human brain is very flexible, and can remap sensorimotor signals so that pressure on a stump can be felt *in* a hand, or flexing of an unrelated muscle be felt *as* a grip. If a prosthetic is to play the role of the relevant body part as well as possible, it must be integrated into the body schema. The deep question is whether this is enough to make it a genuine part of my body. The rubber hand is *felt*, but it is not *lived*. But the prosthetic hand *is* lived, even if it is not strictly living. As far as I can see, there's nothing about the lived body that prevents us from building it to our preferred specifications, as long as it supports an immediate awareness of our agency.

AM: What about the more controversial examples you hinted at?

PW: There's reason to think that the body schema is even more malleable than it seems, and that the sorts of skilled coping mentioned above involve tools literally being appropriated as temporary extensions of our bodies. A seasoned pool player doesn't feel the pool cue hitting the white ball *in* their hands, but feels it *at* the tip of the cue itself. An experienced driver knows the dimensions of their car in the same way they know the dimensions of their body, not in feet and inches, but in the range of movements that feel comfortable. This protean potential of the lived body can be exploited to create prosthetics that diverge from their natural counterparts in form and function, allowing us to embed ourselves in our environments in new and unexpected ways (e.g., thought-controlled computer cursors used by paralysis victims). This should be perfectly acceptable to those 4E proponents that believe in the extended mind (cf. Andy Clark's *Natural Born Cyborgs*), and to those critical/feminist/Continental theorists that endorse certain forms of posthumanism (cf. Donna Haraway's "Cyborg Manifesto").

More contentiously, these mechanisms can be exploited not just to *extend* the physical body, but to *embed* our bodily awareness into new environments, be they spatially remote (telepresence) or purely simulated (virtual reality). This has opened a whole new frontier of technological experimentation; from surgeons operating on patients on different continents, to gamers cooperatively exploring shared fantasy worlds; what it means to "be there" is gradually becoming as flexible as what it means for a hand to "be mine". Of course, there are still those who will insist that we are *not really there* unless we are there "in the flesh", but again, I think this begs the question. What's at stake here is whether we can separate out the different cognitive roles played by the human body, which, in homage to 4E, we might call the 3Is: *incarnation, interaction* and *immersion*. In order, these require: (1) that cognition be physically realized (e.g., in the brain and central nervous system); (2) that cognition be causally entangled with an environment (e.g., in sensorimotor feedback loops); and (3) that cognition be grounded in some immediate practical purchase upon that environment (e.g., skilled coping configured by a body schema).

Although incarnation and immersion may seem essentially united for us, there's no good reason to assume that they cannot be teased apart. It's entirely feasible that isolated human brains could animate androids from a distance, or that distributed artificial intellects could inhabit human bodies from the cloud, without sacrificing any of the cognitive capacities enabled by embodiment. There is nothing in principle preventing a virtual avatar from being a lived body, or its computational underpinnings from being as frustratingly opaque as our own somatic depths. In sum, though the embodiment paradigm has done a great deal to help us understand the functions of the bodies with which nature has equipped us, this very understanding permits us to engineer systems that realize these functions in new and perhaps quite different ways.

FURTHER RESOURCES

Andy Clark and David J. Chalmers, "The extended mind". Analysis 58 (1998): 10–23. https://consc.net/papers/extended.html.

Tim Crane, "Computers don't give a damn". *Times Literary Supplement*, 15 May 2020.

Donna J. Haraway, "A cyborg manifesto". *Socialist Review* 80 (1985), 65–108.

Komarine Romdenh-Romluc, *Routledge Philosophy GuideBook to Merleau-Ponty and Phenomenology of Perception*. Abingdon: Routledge, 2010.

John Searle, "Minds, brains, and programs". *Behavioral and Brain Sciences* 3(3) (1980). In which he introduces the famous Chinese room thought experiment.

Peter Wolfendale, *The Revenge of Reason*. Cambridge, MA: MIT Press, 2023.

17

Intelligence and the future of AI

Stephen Cave in conversation with
Sage Cammers-Goodwin

As Sage Cammers-Goodwin highlights in the conversation below, isn't it curious that those who are seen to fulfil the manufactured tech ideal of intelligence are "so denuded of emotion or caring"? We seem to take it for granted that the most socially and politically prized forms of intelligence lack "those characteristics, such as attentiveness and concern for others, that we routinely connect with being a good human being". What, then, if the much-hyped AI technologies that are promised to be inveigling themselves into ever more intimate corners of our lives are simply an inorganic extension of this highly limited and gendered fantasy of intellectual life as pure information processing? This conversation considers these questions and many more besides, with the aim of clarifying the ethical and societal impact of AI.

STEPHEN CAVE is Director of the Leverhulme Centre for the Future of Intelligence at the University of Cambridge. His research is mostly in the philosophy of technology, with a focus on the ethics of AI/robotics and the philosophy of (im) mortality.

SAGE CAMMERS-GOODWIN is a PhD candidate at the University of Twente. Her research bridges philosophy and computer science, focusing on smart cities, and stakeholder interests and interactions in implementing "smart" enhancements to cities.

Sage Cammers-Goodwin (**SC-G**): What do you consider to be the main problem with intelligence, or the history of intelligence, that introduces it as a matter of philosophical concern?

Stephen Cave (**SC**): Intelligence is such a part of our everyday discourse. This is reflected in assumptions that some people are more intelligent than others, that this matters for what they can or should do, and that this is measurable. But these ideas are quite new. The term "intelligence" wasn't widely used in English until the end of the nineteenth century, and it really rose to prominence with intelligence testing from the start of the twentieth century. It quickly became hugely important because it was useful to a wide range of other political and economic projects. When the term "AI" was coined back in 1955, it was very much trying to ride that particular wave.

So the first thing to emphasize is the need to contextualize and problematize the concept of intelligence. Instead of asking, "What does this concept mean?" I prefer to ask, "What does this concept *do*?" There are lots of papers out there trying to define intelligence, but I prefer to investigate what work the term intelligence is doing in society. That's a different kind of inquiry. It's similar to the method of deconstruction, which assesses the value-ladenness of the concepts we use, and it's a big movement in science and technology studies at the moment. Fundamentally, it challenges things that we might take to be objective, or straightforward, or in the world ready to be measured, and to highlight the ideological baggage they carry.

SC–G: There have been many different ways of categorizing people throughout history – in terms of genetics, for instance. And now we've developed a society where, in order to justify who has power and influence, intelligence has come more and more into play. Can you expand on the nature of this conceptual shift and how it occurred?

SC: The biggest shift involved the adoption of the idea that intelligence is innate, and that people are intelligent to different degrees. For most of western philosophy, concepts like mind or reason were dominant, and were attributes or capacities that everyone broadly had to the same degree – everyone had a mind, for example. And well into the nineteenth century, there was an assumption that our mental abilities were more or less equal. Charles Darwin, for example, thought humans didn't differ much in terms of their intellectual capacities. When his cousin Francis Galton – the inventor of intelligence testing – tried to convince Darwin of his views, Darwin was highly sceptical.

So it's extraordinary that we now take it for granted that people differ in intelligence. And not just that they differ, but that it *matters*. The results of IQ tests matter for people's lives, for their perceived ability to occupy coveted positions, or for their worthiness to receive prestigious educational opportunities. Yet IQ tests were primarily developed and deployed in the United States by academics who were eugenicists, some of whom were motivated to keep the more prestigious universities of the United States white, and to keep immigrants out. The tests that they developed, all the while thinking that what they were doing was objective science, favoured those who had the kind of education that was particular to a privileged social class. They were claiming objectivity for something that was deeply value-laden, both consciously and unconsciously.

These ideas – that intelligence matters, that it's identifiable, that it's a measure according to which people can be shown to vary, and that on its basis people should be allocated a certain place in society – are ones we now accept as normal, but were in fact really radical in the not-too-distant past.

SC-G: I agree that intelligence as a term might be new, but isn't the notion of being clever a longstanding one?

SC: Different cultures have different notions of cleverness, what it means, and what it implies. In *The Odyssey*, Odysseus is clearly portrayed as the clever one, but this is more associated with craftiness or cunning. It isn't implied that he's superior in some way: there's no implication that he'd be a better ruler than Agamemnon, who has immense experience and charisma. Obviously Agamemnon makes a catastrophic mistake in attacking Troy, but he's portrayed as a great leader for possessing other qualities. Then there's Achilles, who is great for completely different reasons, such as embodying the virtues of the warrior. So, different cultures certainly have ways of recognizing differences in mental ability, but not in the unilinear fashion that the modern idea of intelligence assumes. Such differences are not necessarily measurable in a straightforward way, nor is there any universal assumption that they should determine someone's standing in the world. The rise of a concept of intelligence in the nineteenth and twentieth centuries introduced a specific set of criteria about what it means to be intelligent that didn't exist previously.

SC-G: I wonder what role colonialism plays in this. Historically, the assumption was that "the people" really meant those who already ruled or to whom rights had been afforded. The US constitution, with its proclamation of "All men under God", deliberately includes only a privileged class and sex in society. How has intelligence been used as a way to justify segregation, sexism, and the existence of social systems that benefit the "ruling class" over others?

SC: Since its resurgence in the early twentieth century, intelligence has constituted part of what sociologist Patricia Hill Collins calls a "hegemonic ideology": a way of thinking that cements existing power relations and makes them appear natural. Intelligence became a quasi-scientific concept that promised a way of measuring people and allotting them the privilege their intelligence supposedly merited. But it turns out that this actually maintains the social order as it is, ensuring that privileged white men with money and education come out on top, while those who are already disenfranchised and marginalized remain at the bottom.

This has very ancient roots, even though the explosion in interest in intelligence is quite recent. The idea that mental ability can be used to support the status quo is one that emerged in ancient Greek philosophy. Plato's "philosopher king" envisioned the ideal ruler to be someone who was, in effect, the cleverest. He didn't talk of *intelligence*, but he talked about a person who was quick to learn, a lover of truth, and with a good memory. His pupil Aristotle then used similar ideas of mental ability to justify the status quo in his *Politics*, where he says that some people are born to rule, while others are born to be ruled over. Reason is the ability that sets apart those who are born to rule, and is found – surprise, surprise – in educated, wealthy men. And it is on this basis that they have a right to rule over working-class men, over women, and over non-human animals. Just one generation after Plato introduced the idea, we see Aristotle using it as a hegemonic ideology, as a way to justify the privilege of a male class of landowners in Athens.

Interest in this use of mental ability to establish hierarchies takes off again with colonialism. It's impossible to overstate how much the European colonization of other countries has shaped our world. What started as a largely economic enterprise quickly required a political and moral justification to underpin the exploitation and genocide it involved. And

Aristotle's argument that certain people were born to rule was perfectly suited to this ideological aim. Thus in colonialism there exists a mixing together of the ideas of civilization, intelligence and technological prowess as justifications for the domination and enslavement of other peoples. And it's out of these beliefs that the concept of intelligence testing emerged in the late nineteenth century.

SC-G: It's interesting, too, how it becomes a self-fulfilling prophecy. Because those who create what intelligence *means* can then test it and continue to define who is intelligent. College entrance exams, for example, continually ensure only one class or subset of society is admitted. I've also found a similar thing in my research on smart cities where, in order to fix a problem, it has to be justified – and it's always justified from the viewpoint of a certain group. If you are from a disabled community, or a lower-income community, what you know is right for your community is not always seen as true, valid, or smart, because smartness is defined by the city or the corporations. This brings us to the connection between intelligence and AI. How did AI become AI? And what are some of the problems associated with deriving its value using the term "intelligence?"

SC: The term AI was coined in 1955 by the computer scientist John McCarthy in order to get funding for an academic workshop in which he planned to solve the problem of how to get machines to think – to replicate human cognitive functions. And he needed a name for this. There were lots of possibilities deriving from the latest theoretical traditions: computing, automata studies, cybernetic theory, neural engineering, information theory, and so on. But McCarthy was frustrated that none of these existing traditions were really capturing peoples' imaginations. So when he coined the term artificial intelligence, he was consciously breaking with the established traditions of his time. He was saying, "This is not just a continuation of cybernetics, or information theory, or neural engineering. This is something new". And it wasn't a technological invention he was naming; it was the *aspiration* to create machines that can equal or surpass us in cognitive ability.

AI has struggled with its own name ever since. There have been rising and falling waves of hype around AI for a long time. But the reason for the hype is that the term AI never referred to an actual technology; it always referred to an aspiration rather than to a precise term for a concrete technology. And it still suffers from this problem. This is perhaps the first time in history where we have a technology that some people say is absolutely everywhere, and is changing everything, while other people say it doesn't even exist. This is extraordinary. What I am especially interested in is how the importation of this ideologically-laden concept of intelligence might be shaping what we worry about, or hope for, when we think about AI.

SC-G: In my work, I've queried what we are actually using AI for, because it's often heralded as a means of improving society. For example, we'll often say that we want a smart city to improve sustainability or transportation, but it's rarely utilized to increase gender equality, or to improve life for people with disabilities, or to increase education levels. So this technology that can supposedly be used to solve social ills is being applied in ways that often carry over the same biases that the notion of intelligence implanted in the first place. One of the most interesting ideas I came across in reading your work was about those who feel like they have no access to artificial intelligence. Could you talk a bit more about that?

SC: As we've discussed, the concept of intelligence was invented in its modern form by a privileged male elite, largely to defend their privilege (not always consciously, of course). What does this mean for how we think about AI now? Well, it means that AI is emerging from a space that has serious problems with gender and racial bias. Computer science and philosophy are disciplines that prize an ideal of brilliance, of high-intellect. And what's particularly insidious about this in computer science is the myth that the code doesn't lie; that if you're a brilliant coder, the computer doesn't care whether you are privileged or not. There is a myth of egalitarianism around computer science afforded through the supposed neutrality of code. But it just so happens that the majority of computer scientists are white males, and studies have revealed biases that affect every aspect of the discipline. My colleagues and I recently completed a survey of the most influential films portraying AI over the last hundred years, and they portray AI scientists and engineers as overwhelmingly male. This affects the extent to which women might want to go into the field. And beyond that, it affects the hiring panel, who are sitting there thinking, "Well, you don't look like a brilliant computer

scientist to me. You're not a young white man in a hoodie!"
Finally, it affects the workplace culture as there are all sorts of
ways in which women are systematically undermined.

Now, once you introduce into that the rebranding of
everything as artificial intelligence, and the fetishization of
intelligence associated with it, then we have a huge problem.
Because even though the worst days of colonization and eugen-
ics are hopefully in the past, there are many studies showing
that people today have clear prejudices about who is or isn't
intelligent. These associations transfer to artificial intelligence,
and impact and limit who gets to shape the field of AI.

SC-G: When you think of who's seen as fulfilling the manufactured ideal of intelligence, it's curious how denuded of
emotion or caring that ideal actually is. If you watch the Steve
Jobs biopic or *The Social Network* (about Facebook and Mark
Zuckerberg), there's an unspoken agreement that intelligence
involves a lack of those characteristics, such as attentiveness
and concern for others, that we routinely connect with being
a good human being. And, moreover, that this lack should even
be *expected* in the intelligent because they are loftily absorbed
in matters of "higher" concern. Basically it seems we're still not
associating intelligence with abilities other than those that
were originally linked to it over the past two centuries by a narrow group of men.

SC: It is extraordinary how dominant a particular idea of
intelligence became. The claims about the importance of AI
rest on assumptions about the importance of a specific kind
of intelligence. AI is seen as the ultimate technology because
intelligence itself is the ultimate virtue – everything we've
accomplished, we've accomplished because of intelligence. But
this is a claim that throughout most of human history would
have seemed utterly absurd, and still does. If you'd asked someone 500 years ago, or 1,000 years ago, wherever you were in the
world, what they thought the most important virtues were,
they'd mention all sorts of things: teamwork, piety, determin-
ation, will, wisdom, experience, creativity, and so on – only
some of which are tangentially related to the idea of intelligence that we now fetishize. This is not to say that intelligence
isn't important, but that focusing on it to the exclusion of all
else is positively harmful.

SC-G: There is a sense that intelligence modelled on computers is rooted in a gendered ideal of intellectual life as pure information processing. But is any other kind of computer intelligence even possible? Doesn't the technology limit the kinds of intelligence that are possible in this domain?

SC: It might be that AI can only do certain things that we would associate with particular kinds of reasoning. But there are people pursuing forms of computing that depart from classical logical reasoning. For example, some people are very interested in what is sometimes called "affective computing"; that is, the way that computers can read and model emotions. And there's a tradition in robotics that is opposed to the disembodied idea of reason that for some people is an ideal (and itself associated with the IQ test). Instead, they are convinced that embodiment is crucial to realizing AI. So there are different paradigms at play. But if we discover that we can only use computers to do something very specific, and we say, "Well, let's stop calling it artificial intelligence, and just call them calculators", and see them in these narrower terms, we might both better describe what they do, and better manage our hopes and fears and expectations around them.

SC-G: I personally don't think that machine learning is intelligent. We've moved away from symbolic systems, but there are systems now where you type in a caption and a picture is generated. Nothing about that is necessarily logical in the classical sense. If an artist did that, people wouldn't say it necessarily makes them *intelligent*. So I think that the fact that machine learning is being applied to more systems that we don't necessarily categorize as intelligent might lead to new developments. But for now we are still stuck with the term AI.

SC: Machine creativity is a really interesting case, where because we're ascribing intelligence to the machine, which we see as a very general, powerful faculty, we end up *worrying* about machine creativity. For example, we may worry about artists being put out of work. Whereas we could instead be asking questions about how it might enhance human creativity. Looking back, photography caused a great deal of anxiety among visual artists, but the invention of photography didn't end the visual arts. Rather, it spawned abstractionism, expressionism, impressionism, and all sorts of exciting artistic movements, and became an art form in itself. If we were to see a lot of what machine learning does now as a tool that's going to help us in all kinds of domains of human endeavour, we're going to be less anxious and more positive about it.

FURTHER RESOURCES

Sage Cammers-Goodwin, "Revisiting smartness in the smart city". In Shannon Vallor (ed.), *The Oxford Handbook of Philosophy of Technology*. Oxford: Oxford University Press, 2022.

Stephen Cave, "The problem with intelligence: its value-laden history and the future of AI". Proceedings of the AAAI/ACM Conference on AI, Ethics and Society, February 2020.

Stephen Cave, Kanta Dihal and Sarah Dillon (eds), *AI Narratives: A History of Imaginative Thinking about Intelligent Machines*. Oxford: Oxford University Press, 2020.

Malcom Gladwell, "None of the above: what I.Q. doesn't tell you about race". *New Yorker*, 10 December 2007.

18

We and the robots

John Danaher in conversation with Anthony Morgan

We are living through an era of increased robotization, with robots becoming integrated into settings such as factories, hospitals, transportation systems, military, workplaces, households and healthcare. But what are the social and moral implications arising from our interpersonal connections with robots? Can robots have significant moral status? Can we be friends with a robot? When your robot lover tells you that it loves you, should you believe it? In this conversation, philosopher of technology John Danaher considers whether we are robots ourselves; whether we should understand our relationships with robots by analogy with non-human animals; whether robot friendships can complement and possibly enhance human friendships; whether robots have an inner life; whether robots are capable of deceiving us; and much more.

JOHN DANAHER is a Senior Lecturer in Law at the National University of Ireland (NUI) Galway. He researches on a wide range of topics at the interface of philosophy, law and technology, and he is host of the popular "Philosophical Disquisitions" podcast.

ANTHONY MORGAN is editor of *The Philosopher* and commissioning editor for philosophy at Agenda Publishing.

Anthony Morgan (**AM**): In an interview, the philosopher Kevin O'Regan said that he believes he is a robot, and, furthermore, that people get upset when he tells them that they are robots because they feel that they're persons and not robots. He goes on to say that the fact that he is a robot doesn't mean that he doesn't suffer pain or fall in love or appreciate art. It just means that there are no "magical mechanisms" explaining these phenomena, such as free will. What insights do you think we can glean from thinking about whether we are robots ourselves?

John Danaher (**JD**): I consider our world to be a collection of mechanistic structures knitted together in very complicated ways, and so we are in principle very sophisticated mechanisms. Hence if we can create mechanisms that are as sophisticated as us – they may not be exactly functionally equivalent but they may behave and act in much the same way – then they can have all the qualities and attributes that we have, and possibly others too. Thus there's no reason for me to think that we can't create general artificial intelligence or robots that are effectively the same as humans. For people who don't share these mechanistic starting points, this is automatically implausible because they think there is an unbridgeable chasm between the human and the artificial, which I tend to disbelieve. One thing I frequently encounter in debates about the nature of AI and robots is the insistence that humans aren't machines. I always find this a frustrating claim. We're different *kinds* of machines, but there's nothing qualitatively different about us compared to the machines that we create.

AM: You have written on robot friendship, robot love and robot sex, and I hope we will be able to touch on each of them. But to set the scene, one of the people whose work I came across was that of the social robotist Kate Darling. She argues that the best way to model our relationship with AI is according to the ways in which we engage with animals, with one clear point of this comparison being our history of underestimating the mental capacities of beings who are different from us. What do you think are the advantages and disadvantages of thinking about our relationship with robots according to this model?

JD: A key question is whether animals feels pain, and whether your doubts about whether it feels pain mean that you should treat it as if it does. Taking this question seriously recommends a morally precautionary approach to the question of animal pain. One thing that frustrates people about the question of whether robots can think and feel is that we seem more willing to discuss and debate whether machines have moral standing than to cease to exploit animals in harmful ways. I tend to be sympathetic to that because to me it seems obvious that at least some animals are deserving of moral standing.

Part of the reason for the mismatch is that consuming animals is a convenience people are unwilling to forego. Yet when I talk to people about the ethics of eating meat and factory farming, they are uncomfortable about it. They don't want to think about it because it's too convenient or integral to their lives. And certainly, there are all sorts of cultural associations attached to the consumption of meat. By contrast, there is less cultural and personal baggage associated with talking about AI or robots, because there's no grappling with uncomfortable feelings of guilt or responsibility. Robots aren't wandering the streets demanding we consider their welfare – or not yet – and nor are we tucking into them for dinner.

AM: I just read a book called *The Friend* by Sigrid Nunez, which addresses the question of whether humans and animals can have real friendships. The narrator defends an idea of friendship between humans and animals by reference to Rainer Maria Rilke's definition of love in his *Letters to a Young Poet*: "What are we, Apollo [the narrator's dog] and I if not two solitudes that protect and border and greet each other". This vision of love is presented as being built on many of the qualities that we associate with friendships, such as mutual care. What do you make of the possibility of a friendship with robots built upon the standard virtues of friendships, such as mutuality, equality, authenticity, and so on?

JD: This is a complicated debate, but animal lovers or people who have pets will be very sympathetic to the idea. It is a lived reality for them that they have deep bonds with their pets. And there is a reciprocity to those relationships that we also associate with friendship. Part of the issue here is that the concept of friendship or love is loaded with different ideals. Aristotle, for instance, offers a classical framework in which he distinguishes between three levels of friendship. First, there are friendships which are a matter of pleasure. You get enjoyment out of them, but there's nothing more to it. Perhaps you have someone you play a weekly game of tennis with, but you don't share a reciprocal interest in each other's life outside of that context. Aristotle also talks about utility friendships, which are similar except you might have a broader sense of what you're getting out of the friendship. You might, for example, have strategic reasons for being friends with someone because they give you access to exciting opportunities. The last type of friendship

that Aristotle mentions, and which constitutes his highest
ideal, is a virtue friendship in which you are interested in and
care about one another's lives. There's a sense that you're sharing in a journey in which you acquire virtue and meaning.
And it is this type of friendship, according to Aristotle and
his followers, to which we should all aspire. The Aristotelian
framework might be simplistic, but it indicates that there are
different levels of friendship that you can have and desire. And
we can observe this quite easily in everyday speech. We express
the differences in how we connect with others through talking
about acquaintances, casual acquaintances, people that you're
friendly with but who you're not yet friends with, your best
friends as opposed to other friends that you have, and so on.

Bearing this in mind, I think that of course you can have
friendships with animals. And of course you can have friendships with robots. They might just be pleasure friendships or
utility friendships. Whether you can have a virtue friendship
with a robot is a more challenging claim to defend, because
people typically think that this would require that the machine
has capacities that a lot of people think it can *never* have. The
claim here would be that there's always an asymmetry between
you and the machine: you're not on an equal footing and you
can never share a life. Furthermore, the machine simply doesn't
care about you; it has no conception of what your interests
might be and so cannot have your best interests at heart. For
example, it may be created and controlled by a corporation
with a commercial agenda. These are some of the reasons why
people think you cannot have this Aristotelian ideal of friendship with a robot or an AI. I disagree with this. Since we are
all simply sophisticated mechanisms, I see no reason why we
cannot create robots that meet us on equal terms.

AM: There is an intuitive sense in which I can be friends with a
dog, but not with, say, a goldfish, because the goldfish cannot
be friends with me. Can I be friends with a machine if it can't be
friends with me?

JD: I think there is a continuum of different types of relatedness
we have towards objects and beings in the world, and there isn't
necessarily a clear line between them all. When we talk about
having an attachment to something, this doesn't necessarily
mean that the other thing has a reciprocal relationship with
you. An obvious case would be a relationship with an inanimate

object, like the wedding ring of a deceased partner or a beloved childhood toy. Such attachments to objects can still be deep and profound – they can involve a meaningful relatedness – but they involve no reciprocity. The intuition about the goldfish versus the dog is largely to do with the actual or perceived reciprocity in the relationship, where the dog, as opposed to the goldfish, responds to your voice and understands commands. It greets you when you come home, plays games with you, misses you when you leave. It cares about you and takes an interest in your life. This reciprocal behaviour convinces you that this is a real friendship. When it comes to artificial beings, roughly the same standards apply. Take my laptop: despite its importance to me there's no meaningfully reciprocal relationship going on between us. It's very much one way. But there is more reciprocity with a robot which is physical and embodied and can actually talk to me, move around, and play games with me. So, again, you proceed along this relational continuum evaluating the depth and strength of the relatedness that you have with this other being, and step gradually into the world of friend-like relationships.

AM: To pursue this line of thought a bit further, there is a good reason to believe that there is something going on in the dog's head. It's not just its behaviour, but an inference to a mind like ours on the basis of behaviour plus biology. But surely this inference isn't warranted where a machine is concerned?

JD: I've written a few papers defending a position I call "ethical behaviourism" in which I explore this biologically mysterious exceptionalism that a lot of people adhere to. I think it is deeply misguided, because biological similarity is not a robust basis on which to draw a distinction between things, at least not on a normative or ethical basis. To take a thought experiment, imagine you wake up one day and your spouse tells you, "I'm actually not from planet Earth. I'm not a carbon-based life form, but a silicon-based life form, and I evolved in a completely different context to you in another galaxy. Yes, we shared a life over the past twenty years and we had interactions in which I behaved in certain ways towards you. But I'm not made of the same stuff as you are. I don't have the same cellular structure at all". Would this startling scenario suddenly reverse your judgement about whether you had a meaningful relationship with them, or whether they have any kind of moral standing?

I think the answer is obvious: it would *not* reverse or undermine those judgements. My intuition is that learning that they are biologically or mechanistically distinct from me would be surprising but not sufficient to override my presumption either that the relationship I had with them was a meaningful one, or that they have moral standing in relation to me.

AM: When it comes to the prospect of moving beyond friendship to romantic love between robots and humans, people think it sounds quite sad and lonely. I am interested in the question of deception in this context, which I take to be one of the reasons people might pity someone who sought love from a robot. The assumption is that there's only ever a façade of love at work there. So, when your robot lover tells you that it loves you, should you believe it?

JD: This gets to the heart of everything we've been talking about. I think that a lot of people conflate two distinct types of deception here. There's one which we might call "deceptive anthropomorphism", which is based on the notion that it is silly to think that a robot can feel anything for you because machines just don't have private mental states like we do. If you say that you're finding this conversation to be fun, I have reason to believe that's true because you're like me, and I presume that your inner mental life is similar to my inner mental life. But the machine isn't afforded the same presumption: there appears no reason for me to believe that it has an inner life in the same sense. Yet the only way that we have acquired the interpersonal understanding that mitigates worries about deception in the first place is through its verification through external behaviour and representations.

My view is that people don't have good grounds for rejecting the notion that machines or AI can feel things. I don't think they consider the epistemic problem in enough detail. Their argument is that there has to be something on the inside corresponding to the outward behaviour, but we never have any epistemic access to that thing on the inside in our interactions with other people. We only ever have the external behaviour. So, we're landed in the same epistemic position in our relationships with robots. Why would we not apply the same standards in both cases?

I also think the claim that robots are being deceptive when they claim to have emotions is problematic because there's no good philosophical basis to it as an objection. There can be a *practical* objection to it in that, again, the reason why I think your emotional claims are sincere or authentic is partly because I've verified such claims through multiple interactions with other human beings. So, to the extent that I know how human beings behave, I have reason to believe that your claims are sincere. By contrast, no such repository of information or experience is available with robots. But once we do have such a repository of information, we will be in a better position to make more meaningful inferences about deceptiveness and honesty.

The other kind of deception involved in our interactions with robots that I think *is* problematic is what I will refer to in this context as "betrayal". This is not about the robot being deceptively anthropomorphic but is instead about corporations using machines for ulterior motives. They deceive you into thinking that the purpose of the machine is to do one thing when in fact it's designed to do something else. So, it might say it loves you to encourage you to relate to it in a particular way, while at the same time it's building up a behavioural profile that it'll sell to advertisers, and that will later be used to sell you products. I think that is deceptive, a form of betrayal, and something that we should really care about. But it is distinct from the "deceptive anthropomorphism" idea, which is that robots are all surface manifestation and that there's nothing meaningful underneath.

FURTHER RESOURCES

Susan Blackmore (ed.), *Conversations on Consciousness: What the Best Minds Think About the Brain, Free Will, and What It Means to Be Human.* Oxford: Oxford University Press, 2005.

Aifric Campbell, *The Love Makers: A Novel and Contributor Essays on the Social Impact of Artificial Intelligence and Robotics.* London: Goldsmiths, University of London, 2021.

John Danaher, *Automation and Utopia: Human Flourishing in a World without Work.* Cambridge, MA: Harvard University Press, 2019.

John Danaher, "Welcoming robots into the moral circle: a defence of ethical behaviourism". *Science and Engineering Ethics* 26 (2020): 2023–49.

John Danaher, "Philosophical Disquisitions" podcast. https://philosophicaldisquisitions.blogspot.com/p/podcast.html.

Other scholars working in this field include: K. McDowell Adams, Kanta Dihal, Sven Nyholm, Kathleen Richardson and Shelly Turkle.

PART IV

LIVING THROUGH CRISIS

Travis Holloway notes how people "talk casually about the end of the world".[1] We can distinguish an apocalyptic version of the end of the world from the more modest idea of the end of the world *as we know it* (or, more modestly still, *as we want it*). The West certainly finds itself at the end of Fukuyama's end of history, rudely awakened from a complacent belief in the inevitability of a global liberal democratic order. We are in a time of crisis, but still struggle to come up with fruitful ways to think and live our way through it.

"The Anthropocene" has emerged as the most potent western crisis narrative. As Dipesh Chakrabarty (as well as thinkers from many non-western traditions) has noted, we no longer live in a human world shaped by human agency; rather, we have always been geological, we have always been planetary. How long before this idea takes root in the western mind?[2]

Living through crisis promises new forms of collectivity and solidarity: *we are all in this together*. Holloway considers the Anthropocene narrative to offer "a poetics that collectivizes and politicizes us". A less optimistic interpretation is that our common Anthropocene inheritance will be

---

1. See Holloway's book, *How to Live at the End of the World: Theory, Art, and Politics for the Anthropocene* (Stanford, CA: Stanford University Press, 2022).
2. See Chakrabarty's book, *The Climate of History in a Planetary Age* (Chicago, IL: University of Chicago Press, 2021).

little more than increasingly egalitarian exposure to forms of toxicity.[3]

We must be careful when we talk of crises. As Kyle Whyte points out, perceived crises have historically precipitated knee-jerk responses that betray ethics and justice. Furthermore, the presumption that the Anthropocene crisis is *unprecedented* blinds us to the lessons that Indigenous peoples have learned in responding to massive anthropogenic environmental change perpetrated by colonial regimes.[4]

Modernity has been a permanent crisis for various populations, including Indigenous people, Black people in the United States, and non-human creatures. Part of what it means to live through crisis is to realize that some things will never change.

3. See, for example, Simone M. Müller, "Toxicity". *The Philosopher* 110:1 (2022).
4. See Whyte's essay, "Against crisis epistemology" in B. Hokowhitu *et al.* (eds), *Routledge Handbook of Critical Indigenous Studies* (Abingdon: Routledge, 2022).

19

A world beyond capitalism

Martin Hägglund in conversation with Lea Ypi

We all know that it is easier to imagine an end to the world than an end to capitalism. One of the most compelling and ambitious philosophical attempts to snap us out of the solidifying inertia of "capitalist realism" is Martin Hägglund's 2019 book *This Life: Why Mortality Makes Us Free*. In this conversation between Hägglund and Lea Ypi (the only in-person event transcript in this volume), Hägglund builds his argument from an analysis of our most basics needs as humans, and contends that Marx is in fact the strongest defender of key liberal/Enlightenment values such as liberty and equality, and that commitment to such values must inevitably lead us to a world beyond capitalism.

MARTIN HÄGGLUND is Birgit Baldwin Professor of Comparative Literature and Humanities at Yale University. A member of the Society of Fellows at Harvard University, he is the author of four highly acclaimed books, and his work has been translated into eight languages.

LEA YPI is Professor in Political Theory in the Government Department at the London School of Economics. Her research interests include normative political theory, Enlightenment political thought and critical theory.

Lea Ypi (**LY**): I thought I would start by situating Marx, and Martin's reading of Marx, within a particular tradition and within the traditional way in which we think about that tradition. The tradition I have in mind is the Enlightenment and the Enlightenment conception of reason and free agency as something that unfolds in history, through which we reappropriate the world we inhabit, through which we are able to criticize foreign, alien instances like religion or natural circumstances. These are all familiar thoughts in the Enlightenment, carried forward in the Hegelian appropriation of the Enlightenment thinkers. The caricature understanding of Marx is that he was someone who had read the Enlightenment thinkers, who had read Hegel, who was very inspired by the German idealist tradition to which Hegel belonged, but that he was also a rebel, someone who was exposed to different traditions of thought, such as the thinkers of the Scottish Enlightenment and the British empiricists, and became more concerned with day-to-day questions like what we eat, how we reproduce ourselves, how we live in communities – the kinds of day-to-day questions that the German poet Bertolt Brecht captured nicely in his phrase, *"Erst kommt das Fressen, dann kommt die Moral"* ("First comes eating food, and then morality follows after"). Marx is often thought of as a representative of this materialist tradition, which stands in opposition to the idealist tradition I've just described, as someone who concludes that while it is all well and good for the German idealists to think about Reason with a capital R (as he puts it when he writes about Hegel), we ultimately have to think about where these ideas come from historically, what enables them, and what are the material circumstances that enable people to relate to each other.

One of the most productive things that Martin does in his book is to navigate this dualism that is often seen as a contradiction. On the one hand, we have the Enlightenment which is often also associated with the triumph of liberalism, reason and free will – the fact that we are powerful and we can control our circumstances; and then on the other hand, we have this alternative materialist tradition that emphasizes the fact that we are limited, that we live in communities, that we worry about our day-to-day needs and the satisfaction of those needs, that we then establish the institutions required to meet the satisfaction of those needs, and so on. On this reading of Marx, what he's really emphasizing is the bestiality of humans, our proximity to the animal world, the fact that, like animals, we are all vulnerable and dependent on nature, and that we cannot really control nature in the ways that we would like. Martin's book shows us that *both* of these stories can be true, that both can coexist in the socialist tradition, and that what is in fact really interesting about the socialist tradition is that it both appropriates the liberal Enlightenment way of thinking about reason and agency, while also placing it in a particular historical context. Martin offers us a distinctive way of engaging with this relationship between reason and nature, with the way that humans are both natural beings but also beings that engage with nature in a unique way. So I think that the best way of starting the conversation is to ask Martin to unpack this thought a bit, this idea that we're both dependent on nature but also that we can control nature and we can plan and become subjects of history rather than simply being dependent on history.

Martin Hägglund (**MH**): Thank you so much, Lea – that's a very helpful way of framing the issues. One central way in which my book tries to rethink the relation between Hegel and Marx is to show that "spiritual" questions of freedom are inseparable from questions of material conditions. Economic questions are fundamentally spiritual questions, and vice versa, because they are questions about what we value, what we prioritize; economic questions are the very *form* of our material and social life. The precise Hegelian meaning of spirit (*geist*) is here important, since it has nothing to do with something supernatural or immortal. Spiritual life in Hegel's sense does not refer to anything otherworldly. Our spiritual life is rather our social and historical life, which does not leave animal nature behind but constitutes a distinct form of animal life, which can take responsibility for its own practices.

   I bring this question into focus by starting from why Marx was so interested both in what we have in common with and how we differ from other animals. Like all animals, we create a surplus of time ("free time") by virtue of our own activity of living self-maintenance. But unlike non-rational animals, we can take up the question of our free time *as* a normative question – asking what is worth doing with our lifetime, how we ought to cultivate our lifetime, how we should lead our lives. These are traditionally seen as idealist questions, but I provide an account of their conditions of possibility in terms of our distinct form of animality (rational animality) and our social-historical forms of reproducing our lives. It is in and through our material modes of production that we are responsive – for better or for worse – to the normative questions of what is worth doing, what we should do with our lives, and how we should relate to one another.

   So my response to Brecht's claim would be to emphasize that questions of feeding and questions of morality are inseparable in the lives of rational animals. How we relate morally to ourselves and one another is inseparable from how we feed ourselves and one another. Inversely, how we feed one another and ourselves is inseparable from how we relate morally to one another and ourselves.

LY: How do you see the relationship between Marx and the stories that characterize the Enlightenment tradition in which we think about the philosophy of history as a progressive move in a progressive direction, with history as the realization of human freedom. This picture led Enlightenment thinkers to adopt a particular way of understanding social development and social organization, for example, the four stages theories of history model that was very popular amongst Enlightenment thinkers and that Marx then appropriates and adapts. This model assumes progress from a nomadic stage to a hunter-gatherer stage to an agricultural stage, and then finally to a commercial society in which people come together to produce and distribute and exchange in a particular way. What was the distinctive contribution that Marx then gave to these debates? What is it that he adds to these theories that then gives Marxism its distinctive take on the world and generates its distinctive critique of liberalism and capitalism?

MH: The first thing to say is that for Marx, as for Hegel, the commitment to freedom and equality as universal principles is a historical achievement, which can only be realized and sustained by us. As Hegel emphasizes, the idea of freedom cannot be disembodied but must be embodied in our material practices. It must be embodied in how we reproduce our lives materially and how we recognize one another in the forms of our social institutions, because the idea of freedom is a *practice*, rather than an abstract idea. The decisive thing that Marx shows, however, is that the principles of freedom and equality are contradicted by the social form of wage labour that is the foundation of capitalism.

In the *Grundrisse*, Marx has an amazing argument about how the very idea of universal freedom and equality presupposes the advent of wage labour because wage labour is the first social form which recognizes that, in principle at least, everyone's time is inherently valuable and that everyone ought to be able to lead a free life. However, capitalism is unable to fulfil this promise of freedom and equality, which is why Marx pursues an immanent critique of the whole modern Enlightenment tradition. It's important to underline that there is no *causal* form of necessity that will lead to the overcoming of the contradictions of capitalism (as people often think in relation to Marx). Rather, Marx's point is that there is a *rational* necessity to overcome capitalism if we are committed to freedom and equality. Freedom and equality can only become actual – can only be actually embodied in our material and social practices – if we overcome capitalism. I take this to be the normative horizon of Marx's critique of capitalism.

LY: There are two things I'm really curious about: the first one is how you think about what we might call the institutionalization of freedom and equality. Are you in the more radical Hegelian tradition that says that we don't really know what freedom and equality are until we have those institutions that articulate them in a particular way, i.e., that give individuals rights, freedoms, and so on? Or are you more in the Kantian tradition that says that we *always* have freedom and equality as these are transcendental features and properties, and that whether they get institutionalized or not is somehow socially and historically contingent?

MH: I'm definitely a Hegelian on this issue in the sense that I think we can only learn these things through historical experience – and I take this to be important to Marx too. We could not have sat down in ancient Greece and just figured out all the things that we've learned about ourselves through the capitalist mode of production and through our forms of historical experience. What we have learned about ourselves is inseparable from those modes of production and those forms of historical experience.

However, I think this insight is completely compatible with recognizing that we have a distinct kind of freedom from the beginning just by virtue of being the kind of animal we are. We are rational animals and rationality is never an abstract disembodied ideal but a living practice. Unlike for non-rational animals, it never is (and never was) *given* for us how we should reproduce our lives, who we should be, what we should do, and so on. From the beginning to the end of our lives, we are always faced with the question of what we ought to do and what we ought to believe. At the same time, there are always actual historical conditions that enable or disable our ability to recognize, develop, and take responsibility for our freedom and our mutual dependence on one another.

LY: But isn't it then the case that we always *know* what morality requires from us? If the idea is that we always, in some ways, have the freedom to choose between these relations, to choose which commitments we take up, then what is the further insight that we gain by saying that we only really know which choice to make once history has unfolded?

MH: I think it's important to distinguish between what Jensen Suther has called constitutive freedom and historical freedom. On the one hand, we are constitutively free because we are inherently animated by the question of what to believe and what to do. Those questions cannot go away as long as we are agents – they are the irreducible questions of freedom that are built into the first-person agential standpoint of any rational animal. On the other hand, the question of *historical* freedom has to do with the conditions for embodying a form of life that can fully own up to and actualize our constitutive freedom. And this is not simply a process of making explicit something that is already there – it is a developmental process and what it requires of us can only be learned through historical experience.

In other words, we cannot simply derive the rational *content* of historical freedom from our constitutive freedom. Rather, constitutive freedom is the *form* of the fundamental questions of who we ought to be, what we ought to do, and so on. The form and the content are inseparable but distinguishable, in a dynamic interdependence that renders intelligible how our notion of freedom can change historically – both for better and for worse. Any contentful conception of freedom can only emerge and develop through historical experience, through our ways of recognizing and misrecognizing one another. We can only learn what freedom requires of us by trying and failing to lead a free life, by trying and failing to sustain a mutually satisfying form of life. This is the dynamic of Hegelian historical experience, which opens up the *possibility* of an emancipated form of life: the *possibility* of learning what actual freedom is, what actual mutual recognition is. But the achievement of an emancipated form of life is never guaranteed and never given once and for all. Even if we achieve it, an emancipated form of life will never have the form of a given fact; it will always require an embodied form of practice and practical judgement. To be our form of life, it will always have to be sustained by us: by our modes of production and our forms of social relations.

LY: I would like to turn now to the paradoxical nature of wage labour which is both liberating in one way and constraining in another: it is liberating, as Marx says, because it represents the first time that humans can decide what to do with their labour – to sell it, rather than just being driven to work the land, or to be slaves, with others deciding how you're going to use your labour. In some ways, then, the advent of capitalism is liberating because it is a departure from these other ways of organizing social relations, but it is also constraining because of the social relations and the market institutions that it establishes, which limits the workers' ability to display their full potential. Formally, wage labour signals a departure from slavery, but substantively it is actually in continuity with previous forms of domination.

MH: Marx seeks to show that the production of value under capitalism is at odds with the principles of freedom and equality that are made possible by the capitalist mode of production itself. In contrast to societies that require slavery or serfdom to function, wage labour under capitalism is historically the first social form which in principle recognizes that each one of us "owns" the time of our lives. Moreover, our lifetime is socially recognized as inherently "valuable", insofar as we are compensated with a wage for the "cost" of our labour time, which is supposed to serve as a *means* for us to achieve the *end* of leading a free life. When you have something like a generalized form of wage labour, this is supposed to establish that no caste, race, and so on, establishes one person as superior to another, or as having the right to dominate another. But the forms of domination instead come to be defined by economic relations. So forms of domination are justified differently – and that matters – but they still persist.

LY: The other thing we should start getting into is this notion of value, which is connected to the issue of wage labour and the way in which the capitalist system is able to sustain itself. How do you think about value under capitalism, where do you see the main problems with regard to value, and why it is that because of the particular form that value creation takes in a capitalist system, you consider only some options of liberation to be promising and plausible and sustainable in the long-term?

MH: The first thing to note is that in the form of wage labour, there is a formal recognition that labour that is merely done as a means to an end is a negative cost. Implicit in this is the recognition that the positive measure of value is the time that you can devote to activities that you recognize as intrinsically meaningful. The reasons I can count something as a cost to me, and therefore as something for which I should be compensated, is because I am positively committed to having time to lead my life, to engage with the question of what is worth doing, to do what I take to be worth doing as an end in itself. But this recognition of the time of every person as an end in itself is necessarily contradicted by how we measure the value of our time under capitalism. Under capitalism, our time does not have any value in itself except insofar as it serves as a means for the end of accumulating value in the form of capital.

LY: One of the really interesting things that you say about the difference between socialism and capitalism relates to this question of the meaningfulness of what we do. One of the things that you suggest is that because what we do is basically necessary just to reproduce ourselves in a way which does not liberate us but which keeps us bound to these material circumstances that make us respond to them in a particular way, capitalist society doesn't really enable us to engage with our activities in a meaningful way. Our engagement with our lives is always mediated by money, by value creation, by the particular capitalist social relations that we enter into, and so on. A Marxist response would be that once you overcome wage labour, once you overcome this particular way of thinking and creating value, then you enter the true realm of freedom.

But why do you think that people are not pursuing meaningful lives under capitalism if they are convinced that the lives they are pursuing are in fact meaningful? There may be someone here who is an investment banker and who draws a lot of satisfaction out of that activity and who finds that activity very meaningful – they've chosen it, they've studied to become it, they've put a lot of effort into it, it responds to a particular way of planning their lives and thinking about their desires and what they want to achieve. Surely they would be entitled to say something like: "Who do you think you are? Why do you think that my life is not meaningful? Why are you telling me that unless I overcome the particular way that I enter into these social relations, my life is not really meaningful and I am actually as much a slave as anyone else, including the workers I'm exploiting?"

The workers might see that they're oppressed and they're unfree because sometimes they need to get to the end of the month and they don't have the money and they have to pay rent and they're constrained, but the Marxian critique wants to go further than that because it questions the *whole* way of life, the whole system of value creation.

MH: It is very important not to reduce this to an individual psychological point about whether people take themselves to be free. Rather, the point is to recognize the forms of social domination and unfreedom that are intrinsic to capitalism as a form of life. Most fundamentally, our unfreedom under capitalism stems from how the purpose of our economy – the purpose of our life-sustaining activities – is already decided. The purpose is to generate profit because the question of what's profitable takes precedence over all questions of what is meaningful or useful. As a capitalist producer, I *must* try to make a profit, regardless of what I believe would be valuable to produce for the sake of the social good. Likewise, as a worker, I *must* subject myself to a job that allows me to earn a living wage, regardless of which forms of labour I believe would contribute to the social good. Whether we are capitalists or workers, the cultivation of our abilities and the satisfaction of our needs have no inherent value; what matters is whether our abilities and needs can be exploited for the sake of profit.

LY: How are we to think about capitalism, about the overcoming of capitalism, and a world beyond capitalism?

MH: In very broad strokes, *This Life* is trying to do two things with regard to these questions. On the one hand, the book tries to give the most rigorous account possible of what the structural contradictions of capitalism are and why they are irreducible regardless of which reforms are undertaken. On the other hand, the book also aims to give a rigorous account of the general and concrete principles of an emancipated form of life, which would overcome capitalism in favour of what Marx called communism and I call democratic socialism. But this shift from the first issue to the second raises the question of the transitional stage, and I don't aim to answer the question of what this transitional stage may involve so much as to make this question as urgent as possible and to give the reader as rigorous tools as possible to think about it. That said, on the level of strategy, I think it is important not to choose between reform and revolution, as while it is the case that reformism is to be criticized for not seeing the internal contradictions of reforms, it is also important to see that, strategically conceived, reforms can be a means towards the end of that larger transformation. That's as far as the book goes.

LY: Who are the agents in charge of this transformation? Is it citizens at large? Is it vulnerable people? Is it a particular class of agents who are particularly affected by these relations of oppression? Or is it everybody who has a conscience and who realizes that there's something wrong with capitalism and who has the ability and will to think about these contradictions?

MH: Marx was right to argue that the overcoming of capitalism requires an international alliance of the working classes, self-consciously and resolutely organized with the aim of achieving a revolutionary transformation of our global form of life. It is crucial to remember, however, that for Marx the revolution in question must be different in its very form than all previous revolutions in history. Unlike revolutions where one class seeks to take power over another, the proletarian revolution is ultimately about *universal* emancipation and the self-abolition of the proletariat. Even though our historical conditions have changed so dramatically and so devastatingly since the time of Marx, and even though the political horizon that informs his writings barely seems conceivable anymore, there is no actual hope for the future without the historical memory of that possibility. To keep that memory and that horizon alive, I seek to demonstrate, as rigorously as I can, why only the overcoming of capitalism can achieve actual freedom and equality. Given the power relations of capitalism under which we live, the achievement of democratic socialism can only be the result of a sustained and difficult political class struggle. An indispensable part of the struggle, however, is to clarify to ourselves what is wrong with our current form of life and where we are committed to going. I am under no illusion that my account of democratic socialism is *sufficient* to secure that it will be achieved, but I hold the account to be *necessary* to orient our struggle for freedom and grasp the meaning of a truly emancipatory social revolution.

FURTHER RESOURCES

Martin Hägglund and Lea Ypi, "Freedom at the end of history". A video recording of a second conversation between Hägglund and Ypi. https://www.youtube.com/watch?v=dZl2bbfCCAo

Martin Hägglund, *This Life: Why Mortality Makes Us Free*. London: Profile, 2019.

Frederic Neuhouser, Lea Ypi and Jensen Suther, "Time and timelessness: responses to Martin Hägglund's *This Life*". *The Philosopher* 107:4 (2019).

Lea Ypi, *Free: Coming of Age at the End of History*. London: Allen Lane, 2021.

20

Derrick Bell and racial realism

Timothy Golden in conversation with Darren Chetty

Part of what it means to live in the end times is to realize that some things will never change. For Derrick Bell, we must acknowledge both that anti-Black racism in America is permanent, and that we all have a moral obligation to resist it. This paradoxical formulation lies at the heart of his influential and controversial thesis of "racial realism". This conversation looks at Bell's thesis in the context of a supposedly post-racial America heralded by the election of Barack Obama as president. Critically engaging with the racial progress narrative, Golden argues that racism has in fact worsened since Obama's presidency, simmering away until unleashed by the Trump administration. As Timothy Golden concludes, the letter of the law may have changed in some domains, but there have not been corresponding changes to the hearts and minds of people.

TIMOTHY GOLDEN is Professor of Philosophy at Walla Walla University, Washington, USA. His areas of scholarly research include African American philosophy and critical race theory.

DARREN CHETTY is a teacher, doctoral researcher and writer with research interests in education, philosophy, racism, children's literature and hip hop culture.

Darren Chetty (**DC**): Who was Derrick Bell and what did he mean by "racial realism"?

Timothy Golden (**TG**): Derrick Bell was a legal scholar, activist and public intellectual who lived from 1930 to 2011. The expanse of Bell's oeuvre is truly impressive, worthy of extensive scholarly treatment in law, philosophy, social and political theory, and theology. In the current political climate, Bell is probably best known for being one of the originators of critical race theory. He advanced a trenchant critique of liberalism, seeing it as a handmaiden in maintaining the structural and material conditions of white supremacy, such that white supremacy is made "legal" through abstract notions of "rights" removed from the concrete political realities of Black life in America.

Turning to his thesis of "racial realism", it can be summed up as follows: on the one hand, anti-Black racism in America is permanent, but, on the other hand, we all have a moral obligation to resist it. This is Bell's most controversial thesis – both during his lifetime and beyond. Bell's claim about the permanence of American anti-Black racism is an inductive, empirical claim. To substantiate it, Bell commits to a careful study of socio-economic data that show racism flourishing in ways that disadvantage Black people not only in legal institutions but also in education, healthcare, economics, and so on. For Bell, American anti-Black racism has, at its core, a remarkable resiliency and adaptability that enables it to conceal itself while flourishing beneath the surface. For Bell, the abstractions of American constitutional jurisprudence are especially complicit here, as they reinforce notions of colour-blind liberalism that ignore history in the interest of "getting beyond" racism, which has yet to happen.

It is important to understand that Bell was working within a much broader tradition of Black intellectual history in the United States. In fact, in the final revisions that he made to his 1970 magnum opus, *Race, Racism and American Law*, he credits many of his insights about the permanence of racism to the work of African American political theorist Ralph Bunche who had critiqued the idea that the legal system would be a way for African Americans to gain liberation from the legacy of slavery. Bunche argued that the Supreme Court engaged in such a level of abstraction that it completely ignored the concrete realities of Black life, upholding the denial of Black suffrage, not based on the concrete realities of Black life, but based on abstract legal reasoning that neglected and de-historicized the material and social conditions of Black people. So, Bell is inheriting this intellectual tradition (that in fact goes all the way back to the work of Martin Delany in the nineteenth century), and it is from this intellectual heritage, as well as his own scrupulous interrogation of contemporary available data, that he arrives at the first part of his thesis: American anti-Black racism is permanent, and American law and legal institutions ultimately perpetuate racism rather than eradicate it.

The second part of the thesis is that despite racism's permanence, we still have a moral obligation to fight against it. This is what left a lot of people scratching their heads! In one interview, Bell likened this approach to that of an alcoholic who is trying to maintain sobriety. The alcoholic, Bell points out, will always have to say that they will always be an alcoholic because if they did not acknowledge this fact, the likelihood of a relapse increases. Similarly, we will always have to say that America will be racist. And in making that claim, we are, in some sense, channelling a spirit of resistance that comes to us from myriad ordinary Black people who exhibited extraordinary fortitude. One such person whom Bell points to in his work was a poor Black woman from Mississippi named Biona McDonald. When Bell asked her where she got her energy to continue to resist, her reply was, "Derrick, I can't speak for the others, but as for me, I am an old woman. I lives to harass white folks". For Bell, she embodied a spirit of resistance to racism against overwhelming odds. And this sense of resistance is where the victory lies. Racism has won the battle the day that we decide to give up the struggle against it.

DC: In his famous essay "Racial Realism", Bell writes, "Black people will never gain full equality in this country. Even those Herculean efforts we hail as successful will produce no more than temporary 'peaks of progress,' short-lived victories that slide into irrelevance as racial patterns adapt in ways that maintain white dominance". He then goes on to say, "We must acknowledge it and move on to adopt policies based on what I call: 'Racial Realism.' This mind-set or philosophy requires us to acknowledge the permanence of our subordinate status. That acknowledgement enables us to avoid despair, and frees us to imagine and implement racial strategies that can bring fulfillment and even triumph". As I read this, the first question that comes to mind is: how does this view enable us to avoid despair?

TG: Unsurprisingly, Bell was often asked this question! We have already touched upon one of the answers Bell gave in comparing this situation to that of the alcoholic. If we believe that racism is a temporary phenomenon, one that can somehow be overcome, there is a real risk that we rush to come up with theories and solutions to help solve a problem that we have failed to engage. Consider the kind of engagement required by white people (especially in the United States) in this context: to engage racism in all of its complexity is to come to grips with the role that they have played in maintaining white supremacy. And most of them are not prepared for that intense level of self-examination. For Bell, to say that racism is temporary is really just a way to avoid responsibility. If we think that one day it is going to all be over, then we can just keep kicking the can down the road, whereas, if we embrace it and acknowledge its permanence, then, much like the alcoholic, we have to remain vigilant against it, we cannot rest. In many ways, I am echoing the French philosopher, Emmanuel Levinas, who speaks of what he calls "insomnia" – a condition characterized by an inability to rest, an incessant vigilance, a complete disruption of one's economy of enjoyment. But most white people have become so accustomed to this economy of enjoyment that the thought of sacrificing it for the greater good of living in a less racist world that demands a relinquishment of their racial privilege is just too much.

But the other way that I'd like to touch on now is grounded in an ongoing commitment to the struggle for freedom. I find the play *Two Trains Running* by August Wilson instructive here. In that play, there is a character named Hambone. Hambone is promised a ham if he paints a fence for a white butcher shop owner. Hambone then diligently paints the fence, but when he demands his ham after he had fulfilled his end of the bargain, the butcher shop owner offers him a chicken instead. Hambone has a mental disability, and he can only say two things: "I want my ham" and "He gonna give me my ham". That is all he says. I have always thought that August Wilson wrote Hambone into the script to be a microcosm of the African American experience, which is to be on the receiving end of a broken promise. To be promised the ham of freedom, but to be given the chicken of despair (so to speak). Hambone becomes a hero in the story, because although he dies without ever getting his ham, his courage and persistence in demanding his ham every day for nearly a decade is where his real heroism lies. I call for – and I believe Bell does too – a Hambone-like commitment in the struggle for freedom in America, because, like Bell, I submit that the day we cease to struggle is the day we lose the battle. Hambone never stopped struggling, and neither should we. The resonance with the Judeo-Christian tradition is significant here, as Hambone is a literary representation, along with the widow in Jesus' parable of the unjust judge (Luke 18:1–8), of a spirit of importunity that Bell views as indispensable in the Black struggle for justice in America.

DC: I thought we could now turn to Bell's theory of "interest convergence". I take this idea to mean something like: what we take to be racial progress for African Americans would not have actually happened were it not for the fact that there are coexisting interests for white people at the heart of the changes that are made. You have written about how the election of Barack Obama was an example of interest convergence. You note that he was elected in the fallout from the 2008 financial crash, and that Obama was considered more competent than his opponents to handle the financial crisis facing the United States. As you write (echoing Langston Hughes), "[T]he financial interests of upper-class and upper-middle-class whites coincidentally converged with the hopes and dreams of African Americans – hopes and dreams that were longstanding because they were long deferred". My question is simply: what is the problem with interest convergence? The way it is presented is that what we may have thought of as progress is in fact simply interest convergence. But I am wondering whether it can be seen as good diplomacy, even as good activist strategy, to find a way of framing a gain to oneself or one's own group as helpful to those with whom you are negotiating?

TG: In line with what you have just said, I don't think that interest convergence is necessarily a bad thing. But that is not the sort of thing that Derrick Bell is talking about here. Bell is talking about a very specific phenomenon in which whites tend to set the agenda in the United States. And if it happens to be the case that the hopes and dreams of Black people coincide with what white people are interested in addressing in that historical moment, then we get what many will naively call "racial progress". But the moment that it is no longer a priority for white people, they can cease putting their efforts behind this sort of initiative. This is why Bell refers to the emblems of so-called racial progress as mere racial "symbols", and why the election of President Barack Obama in 2008 is such a good example of Bell's theory of interest convergence: the moral wrongness of racism took a backseat to the financial interests of upper-class and upper-middle-class whites, and we elected the first Black president while pushing the false narrative that his election signalled the beginning of a "post-racial" America.

And yet nothing could be further from the truth. Far from ending American anti-Black racism, Obama's election seemed to embolden it. From the seemingly endless police killings of unarmed Black men and women during the Obama presidency and their continuation during the Trump administration, to the white backlash against critical race theory, Black Americans are painfully reminded that racism has worsened since Obama's presidency, not improved. Obama's election, then, is a mere racial symbol resulting from interest convergence: it looks good from afar but ultimately rings hollow.

We could take other examples such as President Biden's declaration about Juneteenth. He declares Juneteenth a federal holiday and African Americans are pleased with that. But this is nothing but a racial symbol. Why? Because African Americans still don't have comprehensive legislation on police reform; because African Americans' right to vote, which has only been protected in federal law for 48 years in American history, is still vulnerable. Similarly, in 1983 when Ronald Reagan signed Martin Luther King Jr Day into law, he was at the same time espousing crippling criminal justice policies that have resulted in the phenomenon that legal scholar Michelle Alexander has referred to as "mass incarceration". Would you rather have a federal holiday or would you rather have federal legal protection of your most basic civil and constitutional rights? This is the kind of thing that Bell is talking about. He is targeting a very specific and devious kind of approach that whites use to placate Blacks in the United States when it comes to the idea of racial progress.

DC: What you say takes me back to the inscription at the front of *Faces at the Bottom of the Well* where Derrick Bell writes that "only by working together is escape possible". And yet he talks about how the poorest whites look down into the well at Black people. Over time, many reach out, but most simply watch mesmerized. They are prepared to condemn themselves simply in order to retain the self-esteem they gain by gazing down. Why have attempts for Black and white working-class interests to converge been so unsuccessful in the United States (and beyond the United States, of course)? Why is it that the working-class white American is satisfied with what W. E. B. Du Bois termed the "psychological wages of whiteness", rather than fair wages and good living conditions for all working-class people?

TG: What has tended to happen in recent American history is very similar to what you see happening today. In the wake of slavery, for example, there was an attempt to unify the interests of poor whites with those of poor Blacks. But wealthy slave owners convinced poor whites that, as you put it, the psychological wages of whiteness were worth more than any allegiance that they could ever hope to have with Black people. And I think that has become a political playbook, so to speak. In the case of President Trump, you have a wealthy white person who has convinced many poor whites, with whom he has very little in common, that any sort of solidarity or allegiance with Black people is somehow degrading or even outright evil. The consequence is that you have poor whites calling for the end of critical race theory, and so on. Wealthy whites have taken a page out of the post-reconstruction playbook and you see it play out with a terrifying accuracy today. Keeping Blacks and whites apart is a formula that wealthy whites use to maintain social and economic control. Racism has now gotten so deep that you have poor whites who would never imagine having any sort of alliance with Black people. And the consequences of this are playing out socially, politically, legally and economically. Obviously, chattel slavery has come to an end and there have been changes to American law that have prevented conditions like slavery. The letter of the law may have changed in some domains, but there have not been corresponding changes to the hearts and minds of people. And because of this, any perceived forms of racial progress are ephemeral at best.

FURTHER RESOURCES

Michelle Alexander, *The New Jim Crow: Mass Incarceration in the Age of Colorblindness*. New York: New Press, 2010.

Derrick Bell, *Faces at the Bottom of the Well*. New York: Basic Books, 1992.

Derrick Bell, "Racial realism". *Connecticut Law Review* 24(2) (1992): 363–79.

"Tommy Curry and the real critical race theory". The Philosopher and the News podcast, 15 June 2021. https://newsphilosopher. buzzsprout.com/1577503/8702397.

Timothy Golden (ed.), *Racism and Resistance: Essays on Derrick Bell's Racial Realism*. New York: SUNY Press, 2022.

21

Spinoza in the Anthropocene

Beth Lord in conversation with Chris Meyns

What can the enigmatic early modern philosopher Baruch Spinoza contribute to our thinking about the climate crisis, and specifically, our thinking about the emotions generated by it? In this conversation, Beth Lord argues that for Spinoza, that which increases human action and thinking is good, and deriving energy from fossil fuels has been a very great human good over the past 400 years. But we now understand our reliance on fossil fuels to be bad for our flourishing and that of other forms of life on earth. We can no longer rejoice in the consideration of collective human power; instead, we now fear its devastating predicted effects. What are the implications of this fear of our own power? What confusions does this fear emerge from? And how can we correct and clarify our emotional response to the climate crisis, especially the future-oriented emotions of hope and fear?

BETH LORD is a philosopher and professor in the School of Divinity, History and Philosophy at the University of Aberdeen. She specializes in the history of philosophy, especially the work and influence of Immanuel Kant and Baruch Spinoza, as well as contemporary continental philosophy.

CHRIS MEYNS is a poet, developer and architectural conservationist based in Uppsala, Sweden. They have published on the history of data, on Anton Wilhelm Amo's philosophy of mind, and the legacy of the philosophical canon.

Chris Meyns (**CM**): The climate emergency is very much alive to us right now. We are already noticing global heating, species going extinct, ice caps melting, floods and droughts. Spinoza, by contrast, lived in the seventeenth century, and didn't write about this catastrophic process. Maybe he did not foresee that anything like this might ever happen. What got you thinking about linking this seventeenth-century philosopher to this urgent contemporary topic?

Beth Lord (**BL**): The key idea that is relevant here is Spinoza's naturalism, as this really challenges how we think about the Anthropocene and the climate emergency. Spinoza is a monist, so he believes that all of being is one being, and this one being is called "God or Nature". Individual things like human beings and objects and animals and plants are not independent substances; rather we're the changing "modes", or ways of being, of "God or Nature". For Spinoza, everything is part of nature, and that means that we too are a part of nature. We are part of "God or Nature", which means that nature is not something over there that we do things to; rather, our actions are *expressions of nature*. And this complicates how we see climate change, because the transformations of the earth that are caused by human beings can now be understood as nature transforming itself. If we hold to Spinoza's naturalism, I am interested in how this changes the way we think and feel about the events of the Anthropocene and the climate.

CM: If the situation we find ourselves in – mass extinctions, the earth becoming uninhabitable, and the like – is just nature transforming, then is this really a *bad* thing? From Spinoza's point of view, can we call something good or bad, if it is just nature transforming itself?

BL: Spinoza thinks that we can take two different perspectives on events. We can take a human perspective, from which we think about things that have happened based on our own experience, our feelings, and our rational knowledge. From that human perspective, we evaluate things as being good or bad depending on what's useful for us and our survival and our flourishing, and what's less useful or actually destructive. From a strictly human perspective, actions that contribute to human knowledge and power are good, because they're good *for us*. The actions of the Anthropocene, such as extracting fossil fuels and depleting natural resources are actually good, from a human perspective – or, at least, they *have* been good – because they have enabled us to build up our knowledge and our science and our expertise and our power in order to survive and become healthier and more knowledgeable human beings.

The second perspective we can take is the perspective of "God or Nature" itself. And when we take that perspective, it's as if we try to take the point of view of eternity. Now, that's not a point of view that we take naturally. It's not normal for us to think from the perspective of eternity. But Spinoza thinks that as we understand more and more about ourselves and about our connectedness to the rest of nature, we increasingly take that perspective; what it is to become wise human beings is to take that eternal perspective. From that perspective, however, there are no values of good or bad. "God or Nature" is an infinite being that necessarily exists. Everything that happens – whether it's good or bad from *our* perspective – is just part of nature. It just is what it is. "God or Nature" can take on infinite configurations, and places no particular value on which configuration of nature it takes on at any given time. From the perspective of eternity, the Anthropocene and climate change are just minor blips; they're just different configurations of a nature that is in constant change.

CM: You suggested that, from the human perspective, it could be considered good to extract natural resources or to do other things that would damage the planet. How broad is that human perspective, for Spinoza? Does it just concern one person, during their lifespan? Or does it also involve, say, their friends, family, or past and future generations?

BL: Initially, every being for Spinoza is driven by the need or striving to persevere in its own being. It starts from just being about you, being about your own striving. But something that is very important to Spinoza is our relationship to others. He recognizes that our striving to go on being what we are is heavily interdetermined with the being of others and the being of the environment that we're in. It very quickly becomes a much bigger story. One of the key themes of his *Ethics* is that as we gain knowledge and become more rational, we understand more and more about what it is to be human. This means that we are able to come together with other human beings to work together, to understand together, and ultimately to be better human beings together. As I become more rational, I understand that what is good for me is actually about what's good for everybody.

To go back to the Anthropocene, it has seemed to us for the last 400 years that the actions of the Anthropocene (extracting fossil fuels, depleting natural resources, and so on) have been really good for human beings. They have enabled us to develop scientifically, technologically, industrially, economically, politically and medically. However, as our understanding of the natural world gets more and more advanced, we come to understand that the actions behind these developments are in fact really bad for human beings: it is bad for us to destroy ecosystems, to cut down the Amazon rainforest, to allow the ice caps to melt. Why is it bad? Well, it's not bad because it's bad *for nature*. As we've seen already, it's neither good nor bad from a natural perspective. It's bad because it's bad *for us*. If the ice caps melt, then huge numbers of human beings are going to be underwater. If the Amazon is burnt down, then the natural cooling system on the earth is going to collapse. We are going to see cascading disasters which will end human life everywhere.

CM: So, the human perspective is not condemned to short-term thinking as the only perspective from which we can view things?

BL: One way of thinking about it is in terms of a short-term perspective versus a long-term perspective. Another way of thinking about it is in terms of human knowledge developing over time. For example, we now have the benefit of much more complex scientific knowledge than was available in Spinoza's time. And, ironically, that's thanks to the Anthropocene! Without the activities of the Anthropocene, we wouldn't have the science to tell us what is going on. And as we develop this knowledge, we also develop our understanding of what is truly good for human beings, and that understanding changes. What was good for us in 1660 is not what's good for us now.

CM: I am interested in whether we can say which, if any, of these perspectives is *correct*. If we consider something from the perspective of "God or Nature" or eternity, is that always the correct perspective?

BL: From an absolute, God's-eye perspective, it is ultimately true that nothing is absolutely good or bad, because for God nothing is good or bad. But we shouldn't conclude from this that nothing is good or bad *for us*. What we judge to be good or bad for us is essential to being human – to how we live our lives and the decisions we make and the paths we take. It is not wrong to say that climate change is bad for us – it *is* bad for us! So, it is essential that we know which perspective we are taking when thinking about what is ultimately true.

CM: What might Spinoza say about how we handle conflicting approaches to the climate emergency? If we are all the same entity, then it may seem that any approach is just as natural or justifiable as the competing one?

BL: This is where Spinoza's rationalism really kicks in! People may not like this, but Spinoza thinks that there is a true, right answer to the question of what is good for us – and what is good for us as human beings is to figure out the answer to that question. But figuring out the answer to that question is not easy. It requires us to try to think as rationally as we can, to try to come together with others who think rationally, and to try to work this out. Spinoza thinks that disagreement is natural, even essential, because without it we won't figure out the truth of the matter. But there *is* a truth of the matter, and it can eventually be reached. In the current circumstances, however, we have very little time to deal with climate change and try to avert absolute catastrophe. What, then, do we do about differing opinions? We have to act very quickly. We may not have time to have those debates and those nice discussions about what's really best for us. And that makes things very difficult. We have to get together the most rational minds that we have, the people who have the best understanding of what's going on and what could work, and we need to direct our collective attention to those things.

CM: In your work you have focused on how Spinoza can help us think through our emotions and emotional responses. In that light, it may be natural to experience despair at the realization of the current emergency. To take Greta Thunberg as an example, one of the emotions that she brings in is panic. For example, in one speech she says, "My name is Greta Thunberg. I'm sixteen years old. I come from Sweden. And I want you to panic". She clarifies: "When your house is on fire and you want to keep your house from burning to the ground, then that does require a level of panic". Yet a second emotion that Thunberg often mentions is that of hope. In another speech, she responds to people from an older generation who say that her generation gives them so much hope: "Saying that everything will be all

right while continuing doing nothing at all is just not hopeful
to us. In fact, it's the opposite of hope. You can't just sit around
and wait for hope to come". What would Spinoza say about
these emotions of panic and hope?

BL: Spinoza has a lot to say about the emotions. All of part
three of the *Ethics* is dedicated to looking at what he calls "the
passions", which we would these days call emotions or feelings.
Spinoza thinks that emotions are inevitable – they're a part of
nature, they're a part of being human, they're a part of being
any kind of finite being. But he argues that emotions are tied to
what he calls "inadequate knowledge", i.e., the sort of haphaz-
ard knowledge that we get from experience, feelings, hearsay,
the bits and pieces that we pick up day-to-day. And, in general,
Spinoza thinks that emotions obstruct our rational thinking,
that they're not the right starting point for dealing with a problem. He considers negative emotions, such as sadness, despair,
or guilt, to be particularly bad, because they diminish our power
to act; they diminish our being so that we are unable to act or to
think.

To come to your examples, hope and fear (I'm taking panic
here to be a kind of fear) are particularly interesting emotions for Spinoza because they are both feelings of vacillation
about the future. When we don't know what is going to happen, we oscillate between feeling positive and negative about
the future. Or, as Spinoza puts it, we oscillate between feeling
hope and fear. And, in fact, for Spinoza, hope and fear are two
sides of the same coin. People who feel hopeful can be very easily made to feel fearful, and vice versa. Spinoza recognizes that
these emotions are very often used as political tools. To come
back to Greta Thunberg, I think that Spinoza would absolutely
understand the value of the *instrumental* use of hope and fear as
something needed in order to capitalize on peoples' feelings of
uncertainty about the future. And if we can use those feelings to
galvanize people to follow certain leaders or certain rules, then
hope and fear can be really useful in that sense. But ultimately,
he would say that they don't really help us to understand our
circumstances or to solve problems. For that, he thinks we need
to overcome our feelings and build up our rational knowledge.

CM: I am interested in how Spinoza's thoughts about the
emotions link to his idea that, because we are just transformations of nature, all of our actions are already determined. For

many people, this thought may evoke powerful emotions. For example, you might feel completely stuck if you think that you cannot really make a difference, given that everything is already determined. Or you might feel liberated, because you feel a burden of responsibility lifted from your shoulders. How might the idea of determinism or necessity fit in here?

BL: This is a really big theme in Spinoza's thought. Part of his belief that all of being is one being is the belief that being is fully determined, that what happens is fully necessitated to happen. One way into this topic is to think about the distinction between determinism and *pre*-determinism. Pre-determinism is the view that God has a plan for us, which is known in advance and which cannot be changed. It's like the ancient idea of fate. So, to take a famous example, Oedipus *will* kill his father no matter what he tries to do to change that outcome. Determinism, on the other hand, means that every event can be fully explained through natural causes. Most of us probably believe in determinism on that level. But, for Spinoza, what it means is that all events – all actions and all causes – are simply part of "God or Nature". This follows directly from his naturalism.

When Spinoza denies that we have free will, what he is denying is that there is a special part of the human mind that could act or make choices independently of that natural causation. What he is *not* denying is that we make choices or that we act. Of course, we decide what to choose and how to act. And, furthermore, we think of ourselves as free when we make those choices or act in those ways. In Spinoza's picture, such a belief is false – we're not really free. But it's perfectly natural and normal that we think of ourselves in that way. A nice metaphor for thinking about this is to conceive of our actions or decisions as being on the surface of a swirling mass of the infinite causal interactions of the universe. Our actions emerge from that swirling mass, but they're also part of that swirling mass, and they have effects on other actions and events. So, what happens to us depends on what is going on in that swirling mass and how we interact with it. And how we interact with it is partly determined by what we think and what we decide, which is in turn determined by other factors.

Returning to the question of how we should think about climate change and whether thinking deterministically could lead to despair or paralysis, Spinoza thinks that resigning ourselves to fate is one of the *worst* things we could do, because if we do that then we just stop thinking; we allow other forces of nature to determine our actions for us. Instead, what we need to do is to think carefully about how we're a part of nature, how we interact with other forces and actors in nature, and how we play a role in that swirling mass of events. We act most effectively for our own flourishing if we clearly understand our connections to other things.

CM: In terms of a way forward, where would Spinoza stand on the tension between legislation designed to encourage people to take the right action versus rebelliously challenging the legal status quo? The latter we might see, for example, in the protests carried out by Thunberg or by Extinction Rebellion.

BL: As we have seen, knowing what is good for us is really difficult! We need to have a lot of knowledge of ourselves and our position in the world. Spinoza thinks that we need to understand quite a lot about physics, metaphysics, and lots of other things besides. We need to rationally understand ourselves and our relations to other things as part of nature, so that we figure out what is truly good for human flourishing and what we should do in our lives. But that kind of rational understanding is really hard to achieve, and furthermore it is also unstable. It is not the case that if we achieve rational knowledge, we can permanently hang onto it. It is vulnerable to being taken apart. Rational knowledge is vulnerable to emotions, to being crowded out by erroneous beliefs, misleading narratives or bad leaders. Many people won't develop much rational understanding at all.

For Spinoza, the upshot of this precarious situation is that societies need laws. They need legislation that tells people how to behave and what is good for them. Ideally, laws would be based on sound reasoning. They would be based on what is truly good for us, and drawn up by a rational council of thinkers who truly understand human nature. But Spinoza is also realistic, and he knows that this is often not the case: laws are all too often based in superstition, in tradition, in the desire to repress others or to maintain a status quo that benefits the powerful. In these cases, we might think of ourselves as justified in breaking the law or challenging it, if we think that we have that rational understanding of what is good and we think we know better.

Spinoza is not in favour of outright rebellion against the law. But thinking about some of the things that Greta Thunberg and

Extinction Rebellion are doing, Spinoza would certainly recognize the power of performance, narrative, and storytelling in spurring people to think and act well. On the one hand, Spinoza thinks that real change rests with everybody thinking and discussing rationally, together with good leadership. But he also knows that emotions, stories, and performances are important in getting people to think in the right kinds of ways and to forge change. There would be room in his thinking for at least some of those kinds of actions.

CM: Do you have any final thoughts about how Spinoza's philosophy can be useful for understanding where we are at right now, and for looking toward the future?

BL: Spinoza is what is usually called a "parallelist" about the mind and the body. What that means is that mind and body are the same thing, understood in two different ways. We can think of the mind and the body as being identical to each other, we can think of them as being equal to each other, or we can think of them as being parallel to each other. But, in any case, there's no dualism here. Attached to this is the view that every body has an idea that is associated with it, and that idea can be understood as a mind. This comes very close to at least some versions of panpsychism, according to which consciousness is distributed everywhere in the universe: minds and consciousness are not just restricted to the human brain but are everywhere. On one reading, Spinoza thinks that all beings have minds of some kind. They don't all have minds that are as complex as the human mind, but every body that exists has some kind of mind attached to it.

In terms of whether this metaphysical picture can help us to develop a more ecological perspective, I think it can, as it goes along with increasing our understanding of ourselves and our place in the universe. Part of understanding ourselves and our connection to everything else is to understand that we are not as unique as we think we are. We are not, say, God-chosen beings who are the purpose of the universe. We are just one kind of being among others, and, importantly, those other beings are probably more like us than we think.

FURTHER RESOURCES

Beth Lord, "We are Nature". Aeon. https://aeon.co/essays/even-the-anthropocene-is-nature-at-work-transforming-itself.

Dan Taylor, "On damaged and regenerating life: Spinoza and the
  mentalities of climate catastrophe". *Crisis and Critique* 8(1) (2021).
Nancy Tuana, "Sensibilities". *The Philosopher* 110:1 (2022).

22

Animals, pandemics and climate change

Jeff Sebo in conversation with Lauren Van Patter

In 2020, Covid-19, the Australia bushfires, and other global threats served as vivid reminders that human and nonhuman fates are increasingly linked. Human use of nonhuman animals contributes to pandemics, climate change, and other global threats which, in turn, contribute to biodiversity loss, ecosystem collapse, and nonhuman suffering. This conversation coincided with the publication of Jeff Sebo's book, *Saving Animals, Saving Ourselves*. The conversation foregrounds the incalculable harms we inflict on non-human animals by causing or allowing countless of them to suffer and die for our own benefit and by driving many species to extinction and many ecosystems to collapse. In so doing, we are also serving to endanger our own future on this planet.

JEFF SEBO is Clinical Associate Professor of Environmental Studies, Affiliated Professor of Bioethics, Medical Ethics and Philosophy, and Director of the Animal Studies MA Program at New York University. His research interests include moral philosophy, legal philosophy and philosophy of mind; animal minds, ethics and policy; AI minds, ethics and policy.

LAUREN VAN PATTER is the Kim & Stu Lang Professor in Community and Shelter Medicine in the Department of Clinical Studies at the Ontario Veterinary College, University of Guelph. She is an interdisciplinary animal studies scholar whose research focuses most broadly on questions of "living well" in multispecies communities.

Lauren Van Patter (**LVP**): There is a widespread feeling that we can do much better than we are currently doing in our relationships with non-human animals. At the same time, however, many of us feel overwhelmed by the complexity involved in thinking about our responsibility to other animals. For example, when thinking about climate change, the situation is not so clear-cut that we can unequivocally say that climate change is bad for other species, while rewilding is good, both at the individual and the species level. How can we get past some of this paralysis around the immense complexity of these issues?

Jeff Sebo (**JS**): There are two things that I think are true, but holding both in our heads at the same time is really difficult, because it creates a lot of tension. One is to accept that we have a responsibility to address factory farming, deforestation, the wildlife trade, and so on. We have to significantly regulate or abolish these industries that are causing so much harm to humans, to other animals, and to the climate. We also have to address human-caused animal suffering by helping animals, including wild animals, to the degree that we can do so ethically and effectively. So, we have these vast responsibilities with respect to our global economy and ecology. But, on the other hand, we also have profound limitations with regard to how much we can do to address these problems ethically and effectively. Our economies and ecologies are so complicated, and we currently have so little knowledge about them, so little capacity and infrastructure for really predicting and controlling our impacts on them in a thoughtful way. We could use all these limitations and complications as an excuse for inaction, but I think there is a way to proceed.

If we just look at consuming animals as food, there are numerous questions that arise: If I reduce meat consumption in this region, is it going to cause meat consumption to increase in some other region in a way that neutralizes the benefits? If I help this animal, is that going to cause them to suffer later? Or will it cause some other animal to suffer, because it deprives them of a meal or turns them into a meal? We then also have to think about philosophical questions: Which animals matter? And how much do they matter? And if there are trade-offs between vertebrates and invertebrates, or between humans and other animals, how can we weigh those trade-offs in a just way? We also have to grapple with the reality that human activity is changing the world much faster than animals can adapt or evolve to keep up. So, as a general matter, I think we need to strike a balance between accepting our responsibilities and accepting our limitations. Ultimately, we need to do the best we can, and then learn from our mistakes and go from there.

LVP: Given these complexities, do you feel that operating with a single ethical framework would be insufficient to address the range of issues that you discuss?

JS: It can be easy to think of the various dominant ethical perspectives as diametrically opposed and adversarial, but when it comes to action in the real world each of these theories provides us with good reason to care about all of the other ones too, and they all converge on a general moral framework that we can use to create a better world for humans and other animals. To take as an example the question of what we owe to wild animals, if you think ethics is about maximizing happiness and minimizing suffering in the world, then you might think that we have a responsibility to intervene in wild animal suffering because wild animals are enduring massive amounts of suffering at scale due both to natural problems, like hunger, thirst, illness, injury, predators and parasites, and to human activity like deforestation, development, transportation, agriculture, pandemics and climate change. So, a consequentialist might have a very pro-interventionist stance. But then, if you think ethics is about respecting rights, then you might think that we have a responsibility *not* to intervene in wild animal suffering because that would interfere with the autonomy of wild animals, meddling in their affairs in a rather paternalistic way. On the face of it, then, these theories appear to offer conflicting guidance about assistance for wild animals.

But matters are much more complex in practice. On one hand, consequentialists need to take seriously the limitations of our current knowledge and power, the reality that we currently have very little ability to intervene in the lives of wild animals in a way that we can be confident is going to do more good than harm. We just do not know nearly enough about what their lives are like, how our activity will impact them, and what the long-term effects of our interventions will be. And, on the other hand, rights theorists need to accept the reality that human activity is increasingly complicit in wild animal suffering. Their suffering is no longer fully natural. Human activity is systematically transforming the world, so when wild animals are suffering, it will always now be an open question as to whether we had a hand in that. And to the degree that we *have* had a hand in what wild animals are now going through, we have a responsibility to help them because of our role in their plight.

Seen in this way, partial convergence becomes possible: the consequentialists want to help but they need to be careful, while the rights theorists may not want to help, but now acknowledge that they need to help at least a little bit because of our increasing complicity in these problems. They both converge on the idea that we should help – cautiously, humbly, selectively, strategically – when we can do so ethically and effectively, and without violating the rights of the animals in serious ways. I think this is a good place to start, because this is a pluralistic view around which we can build consensus, and we can then work together in order to take this approach, even if we disagree about which ethical theory is the right one. And even though my examples here focused on consequentialism and rights theory, I think that a similar general analysis can apply to other moral theories, like virtue theory and care theory on particular interpretations, as well.

LVP: Within these two opposing views that you point out – either as caretakers of other species or as needing to hold ourselves back from impacting an external sovereign nature – I worry that they both reinforce an understanding of humans as separate from nature. Is that a worry that you share?

JS: We are obviously a part of nature, so we need to complicate this nature-culture or natural-artificial divide that we often use in order to justify bad practices or a sense of human superiority. I also worry that humans are generally really bad at assessing how good or bad other lives are, what can improve other lives, and what can worsen other lives. So, not only is there a concern that we think of ourselves as separate from and above nature, but there is also a concern that even if we can correct for that mistake, we might still act on bad assumptions about what other animals need and what it would take to treat them well. At the same time, however, we have a lot of power over other animals, and we're exercising that power whether we like it or not. Furthermore, we're trapped in our human perspectives whether we like it or not. So, once again, we need to strike a balance here. We need to be mindful of our biases, mindful of our ignorance, mindful of our place as part of nature, but also mindful of the power that we're wielding, the unavoidability of wielding that power, and the need to do the best we can to reduce the harms that we're causing.

LVP: You have already highlighted the problem of human ignorance, but I am still interested in what your more radical visions for a just multi-species future might look like!

JS: In line with the human ignorance angle you picked up on, I don't think that we are in the position to think very concretely about what this just, multi-species, multi-national, multi-generational society will look like, but I do think that positive visions for the future can be motivating. So, in that spirit, I think first of all that we would end factory farming, deforestation, the wildlife trade, and other industries that exploit and exterminate animals for food, clothing, research, medicine, entertainment, and other purposes. We would adopt a plant-based global food system, scaling up plant-based alternatives, including (at least during the transition) plant-based meat and cell-based meat. In this way, we would feed the world healthy, sustainable, delicious, affordable food, while treating animals, global health, and the environment better.

We would also have a radically different kind of infrastructure designed from the ground up to accommodate everyone in our communities, both human and non-human. For example, we would add overpasses and underpasses and wildlife corridors to our transportation systems. We would also create new urban designs that provide habitats for animals where possible, use better glass for buildings to minimize collisions with birds, and minimize light pollution, noise pollution, and other sources of harm to animals.

Finally, animals would have legal and political status. They would be legal persons and political citizens. They would be parts of our communities, and we would accept that we have legal and political responsibilities to them. We would also have new systems of government that can represent the interests of everyone impacted by our behaviour – other nations, other generations and other species.

LVP: Please can you clarify what you mean by animals becoming citizens, or having citizenship rights as I don't think this is an idea that many people will be acquainted with?

JS: *Zoopolis* by Sue Donaldson and Will Kymlicka is a classic book that addresses what it would look like to extend existing categories of political membership, like citizenship or sovereignty, to non-human animals. To say that certain types of animals should be citizens is not necessarily to say that they should have *all* the rights that I, as a citizen, might have. But, as we know, even in the human case, citizenship rights are layered. I, as a citizen of the United States, have a right to participate in elections and run for public office. But I also have more basic rights like the right to have my interests represented by the political process. So, even if animals are not capable of running for public office or voting in elections, they are still capable of having their interests represented in the political process. All it means to refer to particular animals as citizens is to say that they should have those rights of citizenship that are appropriate to them, given their capacities, interests and needs.

LVP: Do you think that the kinds of changes you describe are possible in a capitalist system that is predicated on the exploitation of human and animal capital in all forms?

JS: If you favour liberal, democratic capitalism, there are significant things that can be done to improve our relationships with animals within those systems. For example, if animals become legal persons and political citizens with their own rights, then that would help enormously to improve their standing within liberal democratic systems. And if they are no longer considered property, but are rather considered individuals who can own property, then that would enormously improve their standing in capitalist systems.

We may think that we should go farther still, that we should be anti-capitalist, maybe even anti-liberal or anti-democratic. I am all for having those arguments and am very sympathetic with some of those arguments, but the main point that I want to stress now is that when we critically examine our basic legal, political and economic systems, we must include the interests and needs of members of other species, nations and generations in those conversations. Whatever systems we build in the future, we need to build them in ways that equitably consider the interests and needs of everyone affected by our behaviour, no matter what their national, generational, or biological categories are.

LVP: You write that we need pluralistic coalitions, and that helping animals requires addressing social, economic and environmental justice issues. But you also write about things like the need to persuade people that plant-based and cultivated meat products are consistent with personal, cultural and religious identities. I'm wondering what your thoughts are about the possible charge of cultural imperialism around other groups' relationships with animals.

JS: It is true that we need to build coalitions, and this means that to a very significant degree we must accept the choices and practices and traditions of other humans, even when we disagree with them. That is what it means to be in a liberal, pluralistic culture – and I think that is the kind of culture we should be seeking to build. But I do believe that non-human animals should be regarded as members of that culture as well. And even though we accept that we have personal, cultural and religious freedoms, we also accept that these freedoms can be limited. In particular, we have a responsibility not to exercise our freedoms in ways that violate the basic interests or rights of others unnecessarily. So when practices do violate the basic rights of non-human animals, I think that there can be justification for limiting those practices. But I also recognize that there is a long tradition of singling out marginalized or minoritized populations and their practices for censure or regulation, while allowing mainstream practices that are much more harmful in the aggregate to go unregulated.

The upshot is that we should advocate for better treatment of animals, but we should also be thoughtful about how we do that. For example, I have no need to go into cultures that are not authentically mine and tell people how they ought to understand their own beliefs and values. There are already plenty of people in each culture arguing for better treatment of animals with the authority to be making those arguments within that culture. Instead, I can create space for people to make those arguments. And where it would be possible or desirable, I can amplify the voices of people making those arguments, or help divert resources to them so they can do their work more productively. So, in general, we need to respect human cultures and religions and be mindful of our history of colonialism and imperialism, and we need to avoid repeating those mistakes. But we also need to not let toleration of human difference be a licence to happily continue killing trillions of non-human animals unnecessarily against their will. Accepting pluralism in our societies is compatible with, indeed benefits from, accepting non-human animals as members of our societies.

FURTHER RESOURCES

Alice Crary and Lori Gruen, *Animal Crisis: A New Critical Theory*.
    Cambridge: Polity, 2022.
Sue Donaldson and Will Kymlicka, *Zoopolis: A Political Theory of Animal
    Rights*. Oxford: Oxford University Press, 2011.
Jo-Anne McArthur, *Hidden: Animals in the Anthropocene*. Woodstock, NY:
    Lantern Publishing & Media, 2020.
Eva Meijer, *When Animals Speak: Toward an Interspecies Democracy*.
    New York: NYU Press, 2019.
Jeff Sebo, *Saving Animals, Saving Ourselves: Why Animals Matter for
    Pandemics, Climate Change, and other Catastrophes*. New York: Oxford
    University Press, 2022.
Jeff Sebo, "Animal". *The Philosopher* 110:1 (2022).
Lauren Van Patter, "Living well in the Anthropocene". *The Philosopher*
    109:2 (2021).

23

The task of thinking in the age of dumping

Michael Marder in conversation with Sofia Lemos

The earth, along with everything that lives and thinks on it, is at an advanced stage of being converted into a dump for industrial output and its by-products feeding consumerism and its excesses. So argues Michael Marder in his 2020 book, *Dump Philosophy*. In this conversation, Marder discusses the scope of his account of "dumpology"; the nihilistic, depressing affect that pervades the book and his wish to come up with a language for speaking about the sublime, uncanny and devastating transformation through which we are living; the possibility of emerging forms of solidarity between humans and non-human forms of life like animals and plants; and the irony of humans recognizing ourselves in the Anthropocene.

MICHAEL MARDER is Ikerbasque Research Professor in the Department of Philosophy at the University of the Basque Country. His work spans the fields of environmental philosophy and ecological thought, political theory and phenomenology.

SOFIA LEMOS is a curator and writer. She is Curator at TBA21 – Thyssen-Bornemisza Art Contemporary. Her writings on contemporary art and culture have featured in publications such as *Art Agenda*, *Document Journal*, *Spike* and *MOUSSE* as well as in several catalogues and monographs.

Sofia Lemos (**SL**): I am interested in the intersecting trajectories in your work. On the one hand, you have explored in depth the idea of plant thinking and being, of vegetality, but another strand of your work deals with ideas related to energy and entropy, dust and decay. Your work seems to create a delicate balance, or perhaps a generative friction, between decay and regeneration, hopefulness and nihilism. Would you agree with this statement, and where would your recent book *Dump Philosophy* fit within these trajectories?

Michael Marder (**MM**): *Dump Philosophy* is the other pole of vegetable thinking or plant thinking. In the dump, the very connection between growth and decay has been undone, and it is this that allows the dump to grow by accretion, because it is an accumulation of things that do not decay, decompose, or open the space and the time for future growth. Plants, of course, do the exact opposite: they are the very living bonds between growth and decay. There is no vegetable growth without decay, and there is no decay without vegetable growth. At the affective level, *Dump Philosophy* was written within a sense of an overall depression, a depressing mass of sheer facts and felt devastation. When you not only think about but see all around you the event of the sixth mass extinction, it cannot help but provoke these negative affective feelings – a depression which is no longer linkable to an event in one's personal life, but is really overarching. My more recent book on Saint Hildegard of Bingen, *Green Mass*, was in some sense written to try to cure myself (and maybe others) of this nihilistic, depressing affect. I think that Hildegard has a lot to tell us about how to live otherwise than by dumping and being dumped, even in an age as depressing as ours.

SL: *Dump Philosophy* open with this epigraph from Revelations 1:19: "Write, therefore, that which you see, and that which is, and that which will become after this". The subtitle of the book is *A Phenomenology of Devastation*, and you are trying to make legible a kind of violence that occurs gradually, that is out of sight a lot of times, that is dispersed across time and space. Is it fair to say that you are trying to find a new language to articulate the times that we're living?

MM: The epigraph from Revelations is a very apocalyptic injunction. In fact, it's the injunction to describe the apocalypse. And there is a sense in which the traditional language of philosophy – and by that I mean not only western philosophy, but also non-western traditions – is failing us, precisely because we are living through events that are quite singular and unique in the history not only of humanity but of the planet as well. As a result, I try to catch up with the physical, material events themselves at the level of discourse, even in relation to the so-called classical elements of water, fire, air and earth. These elements have by now received so much anthropogenic pollution that they have been transformed beyond recognition. When we think about water, we think about a pristine, clear and transparent substance, but even though it might not be visible to the naked eye without a microscope, what is called water is full of microplastics, heavy metals, and other sorts of pollutants. My proposal is that we call water a "hydrodump" (and, to take another example, air an "aerodump") in order that in our language, at the level of discourse, we try to approximate what is happening nowadays, not only at the environmental level, but also at the level of interpersonal relations, political realities, economic processes, and so on. I felt the need to come up with a language for speaking about what seems to be unspeakable: a sublime, uncanny, and devastating transformation through which we are living.

To my mind, "dump" is an appropriate word for thinking about the contemporary condition at all kinds of levels. Heidegger said that every epoch has its own word for being, and my idea was that "dump" – both as a verb and as a noun – could become that word for being in our twenty-first century.

SL: One of the phrases you use in the book that relates to this idea of dump and dumping is "shitting without giving a shit" – a form of transcendental indifference that you describe as a form of nihilism. Jean-Luc Nancy in fact described the book as a "great treatise on nihilism". Why do you think the "dump" is a capacious enough narrative figure to speak to our current times?

MM: Part of what I wanted to do was to understand the dynamics of what has now become widely known as the "Anthropocene", specifically the dynamics of creating a dump out of the planet itself. The traces of industrial activity that are now embedded in geological strata and in the atmosphere relate to a dumping not only of industrial waste, but the excrement of the human techno-body, a collective intergenerational techno-body that is marking the planet with its excremental waste. We do not only have our physiological bodies, we also have a collective techno-body – even if we are not the owners of this means of production. Everyone who is alive at the moment is participating in the collective techno-body of humanity – even people who are long dead have participated (which is why

I think of it as an *intergenerational* techno-body). It is this body that is reshaping the elements, that is leaving its waste embedded in the atmosphere and on the earth. That was why I chose the expression "shitting without giving a shit": dumping in its more vulgar and excremental sense involves large amounts of excrement that one expels, while to "not give a shit" suggests not caring, not having any concern whatsoever about something. For me, the two ideas really converge in the idea of the excremental Anthropocene.

The total indifference that is involved in transforming the whole planet and the elements into dumps is a very concrete expression of nihilism, of what Nietzsche already diagnosed as western nihilism. And, as both Nietzsche and Heidegger tell us, it is pointless to try and brush off nihilism, to try and separate oneself from it or protect oneself from it. Rather, the only hope for getting through it is by way of deepening the nihilistic mood, and then hopefully emerging on the other side in a process that might be very protracted (I think Nietzsche has several centuries in mind). However, in the twenty-first century we realize that we might not have as much time to go through the depths of western nihilism; that, in fact, our planet might be fully endangered and no longer inhabitable by the time this is worked out at the ideational and affective levels.

SL: An important caveat that people are increasingly noting when talking ecologically is to be clear about the "we" that we're speaking from. In your book, you make it very clear that it is not possible to avoid our complicity (on an individual, social, mental, economic, political level) in social relations of environmental harm. You talk about humanity's self-exclusion from the world – a "we" that is equated with this figure of humanity. But there is an important sense in which differential inheritances also produce differential responsibilities. Is this something that you would agree with?

MM: One of the performative gestures of *Dump Philosophy* was to write a philosophy not only about the dump, but also from the standpoint of the dump. Of course, in such an endeavour the risk is precisely seeing homogenization where things are heterogeneous, covering over of differences where there are real differences. And yet this is precisely the dynamic of the dump: in the dump, all differences melt away and evaporate. So, while there is a danger of overlooking differential responsibilities and different modes and degrees of victimization by the dynamics of the dump, at the same time I thought that such a strategy was justifiable. Even though the situation is not as homogeneous nowadays in terms of the felt effects of the dump, we can project ourselves into a not-so-distant future in which the toxic situation will become more generalized – more the rule than the exception.

Even though I did not explicitly mention it in the book, I was guided by a thesis from Herbert Marcuse that only the exaggeration is true. There is undeniably a hyperbolic element to what I call "dumpology": it is an exaggerated vision of the world or the un-world that we're living in. But it is an exaggeration that is justified by the historical tendency in which the world as a whole is moving – toward a general un-liveability as opposed to the more intense un-liveability experienced in certain parts of the world today.

Of course, those who have more privilege or wealth can try to look for those situations or locations where the effects of the dump are minimized. The super-rich, for example, can separate themselves from the doomed reality of the rest of the world in doomsday bunkers in New Zealand. But these are false solutions. Because when the very form of experience has been eviscerated, when the very possibility of experiencing the world and of living and of being in the world has been undercut, it is impossible to find exceptional places where experience would still be accessible or possible, given the destruction of the form of experience as such.

The "we" that emerges in the book is what I call "the dumped dumpers". So, even those who are the dumpers (the western upper-class humanity, as it were), those who say that they are speaking for the rest of humanity, who are in one way or another complicit with the industrial and post-industrial devastation that is going on – these dumpers are *themselves* the dumped dumpers. There is no way to have an active position of dumping without suffering the effects of the dump. I think that a "we" that is less differentiated, but nonetheless more general and even universal in a new sense, could emerge from the idea of the dumped dumpers – a "we" that is not only human, but that includes solidarity with, say, non-human forms of life like animals and plants that were industrially produced for the sake of being consumed and destroyed. The task is to take the position of the dump dumpers and to try to let a new form of solidarity emerge from it.

SL: That solidarity is also a kind of rewriting of knowledge. In the book, you argue that all forms of knowledge are no longer adequate, or at least that ecological realities are changing at a faster pace than the frameworks we have inherited for grasping them. I personally think that one of the greatest achievements in the book is how it presents masses of data, emissions, and non-decomposable products as epitomes of some of the most famous ideas in western philosophy: Plato's "ideas", Aristotle's "unmoved mover", Spinoza's "substance", Descartes' "split subject", and, of course, Kant's "thing in itself". How do you link these formidable achievements of western metaphysics to the dynamics of the dump?

MM: If we were to gather metaphysics under an overall heading (which also holds cross-culturally), then metaphysical being would be precisely the eternal being which does not undergo any changes, which does not perish, which is not generated, which does not decay. If this is the way in which we describe metaphysical being, then we can very easily see how it has been instantiated or concretely produced today in things like plastics that take hundreds of years to decompose or in nuclear waste takes thousands of years to degrade. The dump is a paradoxical generation of the un-generated. My idea is that the dream of eternal being, the *deranged* dream of metaphysics, has in fact now been realized here on earth – and its realization has shown what an absolute nightmare it is in environmental terms. What we have here on earth is something that is close to an eternally unchangeable being. Obviously, 500 years is not an eternity, nor 20,000 years nor even the 100,000 years that it may take certain nuclear materials to degrade, but from the standpoint of a human lifespan, or even of the lifespan of the human species compared to the half-lives of certain atomic elements, it is very close to eternity. Once the dimension of decay and decomposition is eliminated, or nearly eliminated from our world, an absolute nightmare ensues in environmental terms. My idea is to show that metaphysics is not just discourses, it is not just words, it is not just texts; rather, it is embedded and embodied in the concrete practices and things that surround us – and that may at this very moment make the world unliveable.

SL: You also write about how our corporeal, psychic interiority is equally toxic. You talk about a triad: "polluted sensorium", "venomous imagination" and "violent intellection", the latter of which is made up of toxic thoughts, toxic desires and toxic modes of reasoning. What happens when toxicity breaks down the metaphysical divide of the inner and outer?

MM: In the discussion of toxic interiority, I contrast toxic substances with poisons. A poisonous snake, for example, directs its venom toward a certain threatening other, and the bite from the snake can be lethal. But in attacking you, the animal *singularizes* you as a target – you are the one targeted, not anyone else in this particular instance. With toxicity, things do not work in such a manner, because toxic substances are so dispersed and so amorphously present that they do not target any singular entities. Instead, they affect everything that is in their path, regardless of species boundaries, regardless of kingdoms boundaries. A substance that is toxic for plants is likely to be toxic for your dog who goes and runs in the park, and in turn it is likely to be toxic to your child who strokes the dog. Toxicity is an undifferentiated form of harmfulness that I associate much more with the dump than the more singularized targeting by poison.

In recent years, the expression "toxic masculinity" has become very prevalent. It is a justifiable extension of the idea of toxicity into the ideational realm: whether it's a toxic substance that is physical or a toxic masculinity that is ideational, toxicity does not target this or that particular person or even group, but rather its effects are harmful in a dispersed way that targets everyone and everything in the path. Just as toxic masculinity is toxic not only for women but also for men, toxic substances are toxic for plants, animals, humans, even bacteria.

SL: This suggests that we need to reconstruct not only our epistemologies or knowledge-making practices, but even our sensorium, the ways we sense and experience the world.

MM: The approach I take in the book is rooted in phenomenology, and in phenomenology, starting with Husserl, consciousness is a directedness towards something. In this sense, consciousness is precisely a venomous animal that shoots its poison towards a certain target and singularizes it in that way. When I'm conscious of the screen in front of me, my consciousness is singularized by that toward which it is directed – there is a kind of mutual singularization of the targeting and the targeted. If this kind of singularization no longer works in the age of the dump, if the poison model has been substituted at an ontological level by the model of toxicity, then consciousness itself becomes dispersed like a toxic substance. It is no longer possible to just focus on one particular thing or target or being. That's why we find distraction to be the most prevalent form of attention in the dump. And it is true not only of the more abstract notion of consciousness, but also of our senses: we cannot seek purity in our sense of vision, or hearing, or taste, or even touch. Our senses are like garbage receptacles for the excessive stimuli that hit them. Take, for example, very bright lights or light pollution: you cannot see the subtler lights of the stars in a city where everything is flooded by light. Our senses are affected and deformed and de-shaped by these very events. There is no pure terrain, unaffected by the dump, either in our senses or anywhere else.

SL: You mention that purity may no longer be an option in the age of the dump, but is there anything you feel can be done with the idea of purity? Does it serve as an ideal, even if not an achievable one?

MM: I would say that purity as an ideal is in fact a very dangerous one. It is usually in the name of purity that the most polluting kinds of activities are undertaken. There are different levels at which purity can be dangerous. To take one important example, purity is really *the* metaphysical ideal, which presents the ideal of something that is pure and inviolable, that cannot be contaminated regardless of anything that happens in physical reality. Such an ideal can be a powerful and horrible justification for all kinds of violence.

To offer an example, for Emmanuel Levinas, *the* ethical philosopher of the twentieth century, the face of the other is the sight of purity that cannot be violated. I can do whatever I want to this person or to this being, but their purity, their inviolability will not be touched by whatever violence I unleash against them. No matter what I do to the other, whether I rape or kill or violate them, the face of the other remains untouchable. It cannot be violated. For me, this is the most metaphysical moment in all of Levinas. But what happens to the person who has been raped or killed or violated? It is no consolation that their face has been untouched and left in its purity. We are treading very dangerous terrain here, and even such an astute thinker as Levinas has fallen into the trap of purity.

The other danger of purity is at the level not of ideals but of ideas. So, as I said earlier, our idea of water includes the ideal of purity. But the being of the actual liquid substance we drink either from the tap or from a water bottle is very different from the idea which is shaped by the ideal. This gap between the actual reality and the idea or ideal is a dangerous thing, because we can overlook and neglect and ignore all kinds of contamin-ations – and very dangerous ones at that – in the name of the idea or ideal of purity.

SL: As a final question: Can one be human in the dump?

MM: Maybe the human, or what we call the human, *is* in fact a dumper, a being who dumps? The geological age that we live in has been called the Anthropocene which is derived from the Greek word for human, *Anthropos* (ἄνθρωπος). To offer an ironic reading of the Anthropocene, if the earth has been created or produced as a collection of techno-excrements, it is quite strange that we look into a sort of geological mirror made of shit – *and we recognize ourselves in it*! It becomes a kind of retro-active, self-definition of the human as a species that has been able to do this to the planet. Of course, there are many other species and kinds of beings that have had a planet-scale effect – from the first bacteria that created oxygen to plants themselves that have created a liveable world for other organic beings. In a sense, then, it is both a humanizing and a dehumanizing ges-ture to recognize oneself in the dump. If we look at the question in terms of whether we can revert to some kind of pre-dump way of being human, or whether we can start thinking again, feeling again, and sensing again in the age of the dump, my general response is that we cannot think or feel or experience outside of the dump; we have to learn to do so both with and against the dump. We have to hold this tense, ambivalent position of being with and against at the same time.

FURTHER RESOURCES

Nolen Gertz, *Nihilism*. Cambridge, MA: MIT Press, 2019.
Michael Marder, *Dump Philosophy: A Phenomenology of Devastation*. London: Bloomsbury, 2020.
Michael Marder, "Thinking from a void". *The Philosopher* 109:4 (2021).
Simone M. Müller, "Toxicity". *The Philosopher* 110:1 (2022).

24

Why misanthropy?

Ian James Kidd in conversation with Anthony Morgan

Misanthropy – the moral condemnation of humankind – is very topical these days. There are many inspirations for a sense of the collective awfulness of humankind, from the failures to act on the global environmental crisis to the rise of far-right ideologies to the avoidable mass suffering of billions of humans and animals. But philosophers rarely talk about misanthropy as a doctrine. When they do, it is usually narrowly defined as a hatred of human beings or coupled to extreme proposals. In this conversation, Ian James Kidd offers an overview of philosophical misanthropy, including his own definition ("the systematic condemnation of the moral character of humankind as it has come to be"), addresses some common misconceptions, considers the shortcomings of Rutger Bregman's "Homo puppy" brand of optimism, and clarifies how – and why – one may wish to be a misanthrope.

IAN JAMES KIDD is Assistant Professor of Philosophy at the University of Nottingham. He is interested in intellectual virtue and vice, the nature of a religious life, illness and mortality, misanthropy, and South and East Asian philosophies.

ANTHONY MORGAN has run out of new things to say about himself by this point.

Anthony Morgan (**AM**): Let's start with a simple question: why misanthropy?

Ian James Kidd (**IJK**): Misanthropy might not be an easy topic to get into, because the subject is of course intrinsically negative. I define misanthropy as the systematic condemnation of the moral character of humankind as it has come to be. For a misanthrope, humankind as it has come to be is morally atrocious.

For all sorts of philosophical and psychological reasons, that's not an attractive thesis for many people. I'm not temperamentally misanthropic myself. My engagement with the subject was through the work of my former Durham colleague, David Cooper. In 2018 he wrote a short book, *Animals and Misanthropy*, arguing that honest reflection on the exploitation and abuse of animals by humankind justifies a charge of misanthropy. Most people are familiar with misanthropy as a general concept or idea, but it has never been one that philosophers have really taken seriously. Moral philosophers might describe themselves as realists or sentimentalists or contractarians or utilitarians, but rarely as *misanthropes*. What was very interesting about David's claims in *Animals and Misanthropy* was, first, that he was talking philosophically about misanthropy, and I'm always attracted to new ideas. But he also made an extremely compelling case that reflection on how we treat animals as a culture, as a form of life, justifies a misanthropic verdict.

AM: I imagine that there must be many different ways into misanthropy beyond reflecting on our treatment of animals.

IJK: Different critics will want to emphasize different aspects of our awfulness: whether it is the way we treat animals, or nature, or marginalized groups, and so on. Historically, misanthropes focus on different things. For example, for medieval Christians the moral failings that really worried people were spiritual failings like impiety, lack of faith, and so on. As that example suggests, some of these failings might be relevant or intelligible to some of us, which suggests, interestingly, that there are varieties of misanthropy that cannot be taken seriously by those with different moral visions or worldviews. For many contemporary environmental activists, the salient failings are wastefulness, violence to nature, unsustainable and wasteful ways of life, and so on. The doctrine of misanthropy I am developing includes a whole range of different collective failings.

AM: In common parlance, misanthropy tends to mean one thing: a hatred, or at the very least a dislike, of all humans or humanity, possibly even extending towards life itself. What is the affective economy of misanthropy? Is hatred or strong dislike the primary affect that drives the misanthrope?

IJK: If you consult the very few philosophical discussions of misanthropy, they follow the dictionary definition in characterizing misanthropy as rooted in hatred. My dictionary says a misanthrope is someone who hates human beings or hates humanity. Philosophers like Judith Shklar, who have written about misanthropy, tend to follow that definition pretty closely. But when I began to look into the topic of misanthropy and at some candidate philosophical misanthropes, it seemed to me that characterizing it as hatred is far too narrow. Nobody's inner life is so simplistic that it is exhaustively characterized by one emotion – even a very strong one like hatred – and when you look at the attitudes of particular philosophical misanthropes, it is clear that there is a complex and dynamic interplay of different emotions, moods and feelings.

One of my candidate philosophical misanthropes is Confucius. If you read the *Analects*, there's a clear moral condemnation of humankind for its entrenched greediness, laziness, treacherousness, moral indifference, arrogance, dogmatism, and so on. But when you look at how Confucius responds to this, both as a philosopher and as a human being, he has a whole range of complex responses. There are moments of anger and frustration at the state of humanity, and then there are surges of optimism when he thinks we really could turn it around for the better, and then there are moments of quietist acceptance. Part of the difficulty of being a philosophical misanthrope is coping with this constant, painful oscillation between frustration, optimism, despair, resignation, pessimism and gloom.

AM: You are clearly trying to expand the scope of the concept of misanthropy beyond the narrow definition you mentioned. But why would you want to expand it into broader spheres of human life? What is the motivation?

IJK: One common argument given by misanthropes is that, depressing as it might seem, misanthropy does register a fundamental truth about humankind as it has come to be – a truth so central to humanity that we really have to face it in the course of any serious reckoning with the moral realities of human life. The German philosopher Arthur Schopenhauer, for instance, was a self-confessed misanthrope. But for him, what's really important about misanthropy is that it gives us a sobering perspective on the sheer scale of the moral challenges facing us. He was perfectly aware that there are good reasons to want to have a rosier, more optimistic vision of humankind. But he sees that as a temptation to look away from the realities of our moral failings. And, as with many areas of life, if you are not honest about the scale and extent of the problems, how can you ever hope to do something about them? I think that spirit runs through many philosophical misanthropes.

AM: At what level of analysis does philosophical misanthropy operate? I'm guessing that it can't be at the level of individual humans, as feeling hateful or negatively inclined towards all individual humans is surely a vice. Where do you operate in your analysis of the concept?

IJK: It is certainly correct that misanthropy is not an evaluation of individual human beings. For a misanthrope, one reason that you like certain individuals is that they may be admirably free of the vices and failings that characterize the world. It's very interesting that many philosophical misanthropes, like Michel de Montaigne, cling closely to friendship as the last and final guard against a slide into total misanthropy. Montaigne was misanthropic, but he considered his close friend Étienne de La Boétie to be a true person because he was free of those failings that characterize the mass of humankind. So, misanthropy is not a judgement on individuals, even if some individuals – like Donald Trump, perhaps – are especially exemplary of our moral failings.

But if misanthropy is not directed at individuals, what is the target? There seem to be two main answers: some misanthropes think that what is truly corrupt and vicious is our underlying nature. There are the older theological narratives, like Saint Augustine's idea that human nature is corrupted by original sin, which can only be overcome through divine grace. And then there are the modern riffs on this theme that we associate with certain evolutionary thinkers, for whom we have evolved to be intrinsically selfish.

But not all misanthropes think you need to tell a story about human nature. Take Jean-Jacques Rousseau: corruption of humanity can be largely traced to the influences of collectivized, civilized life. If so, our underlying nature is largely beside the point. The source of our moral corruption is the social world, the ways that institutions – private property, social hierarchies and stratification – scaffold vices like enviousness, greediness and aggression. Like Rousseau, David Cooper argues that a misanthrope can remain entirely silent about human nature. We don't have to make any suppositions at all about what we used to be like way back in the Pleistocene or the Garden of Eden, nor make claims about what we are like "deep down". What is being condemned is humankind as it has *come to be*, the particular and contingent ways we have of organizing and arranging our lives.

AM: Where does pessimism overlap or separate from misanthropy? I take someone like Schopenhauer, for example, to be both a pessimist and a misanthrope, and people tend to conflate the two quite easily. Do you think there are important distinctions to be drawn between those two attitudes toward life?

IJK: The pessimist and the misanthrope both agree that human existence is, in a very deep sense, awful. But while the pessimist focuses on deep features of reality or human existence that preclude the possibility of happiness or flourishing – features like alienation, suffering, the inevitability of death, the cosmic will, and so on – the focus of the misanthrope is on human vices and failings, our moral corruptions. You can think that human existence is fundamentally one of suffering and insatiable craving, driven by a cosmic will, without also needing a story about our moral corruptions. The world could be dreadful, even if we are good. Conversely, you might think that life is cosmically meaningful, even if most human beings are awful. Schopenhauer and his inspiration, the Buddha, think that, as it happens, the full story needs both pessimism and misanthropy.

AM: In *Straw Dogs* John Gray, a pessimist and misanthrope in a Schopenhauerian mould, refers to humanity as *Homo rapiens* – rapacious, greedy, destructive. More recently Rutger Bregman has referred to humanity as *Homo puppy* (cuddly, lovable, domesticated, etc.). Won't narratives like Bregman's encourage us to foreground our more puppy-like characteristics?

IJK: Bregman wants the idea that human beings are fundamentally *Homo puppies* to motivate an optimistic vision of our current moral performance and our moral possibilities going into the future. If human beings are by nature disposed to cooperativeness, playfulness, and other puppyish virtues, we can trust in our future moral progress. Bregman emphasizes that there's work to be done, and he favours broadly socialist policies. Certainly many find his vision of human beings very attractive. But attractiveness and accuracy are quite different things. An odd feature of his book is that Bregman often sounds like a misanthrope: he will talk at length about the violence, the competitiveness, the jealousy, the envy, the violence, the dogmatism of human life before saying, "But don't worry, because deep down we're really puppies". The obvious response to this is that deep down we *might* be puppies, but in our overt behaviour in our social communities we become wolves. *Homo homini lupus*, as the old Latin motto has it.

Let's consider one example from Bregman's book. He documents interesting data from military historians, indicating that in the majority of battles over the last 200 years, soldiers were in fact extremely reluctant to shoot at their enemies; rather, they would usually fire their guns upwards or not fire them at all. From this, Bregman draws the very optimistic conclusion that our resistance to killing our fellows is so strong as to validate the *Homo puppy* claim. But what he doesn't mention is that the history of military technology is *directed* at helping people to *overcome* that resistance. Examples include the development of ranged weapons like bows and rifles, the use of dehumanization techniques to present the enemy as violent or corrupt or as insects or vermin, and, more recently, the turn to drone technology for which you don't even have to be on the same continent as the people you kill. We may be reluctant to kill other human beings, but we're also very good at overcoming that reluctance and at dehumanizing our fellows.

As we have seen with his talk of our evolution in a puppy-like direction and what we are like *deep down*, Bregman is keen to ground his analysis in facts about our underlying nature. But I consider these facts to be irrelevant. The focus should be on how human beings live and behave within the actual arrangements of the contemporary world. The optimism of Bregman's narrative is achieved by playing down facts about the world or by encouraging us to think that change is just around the corner. Oddly for a socialist, Bregman also consistently ignores the structural constraints on human beings, all those temptations and pressures to be violent, divisive and greedy. Structures corrupt – that is a main theme of Rousseau's account of our moral history. Bregman, despite making Rousseau the hero of his story, tends to ignore this point by focusing on human nature.

But the problem, for a misanthrope, is not our nature but the corrupting realities of our world.

AM: It is interesting that Bregman tends to dismiss things like misanthropy and pessimism as clinical symptoms. Likewise, Steven Pinker has referred to certain pessimistic thinkers in clinical terms, like "psychopaths" or "sociopaths". What is your response to this tendency to psychologize or pathologize the misanthrope or the pessimist?

IJK: That was one of the more disappointing features of Bregman's book. He describes cynicism, pessimism and misanthropy as "clinical symptoms of a mean-world syndrome". But pathologizing one's critics means treating their rational judgements as signs of mental disorder or dysfunction, and that's dreadful. It's especially strange for Bregman to dismiss pessimism and cynicism as clinical symptoms of pathology, because elsewhere in the book he is very open about his socialist credentials. Would he tell feminist activists or the Black Lives Matters protestors that their pessimistic cynicism about the realities of a structurally racist patriarchal world was a symptom of some underlying pathology? I accept that some people's gloomy visions of the world might be partially pathological; some people clearly exult in doom-mongering visions. But to dismiss the variety of critical moral verdicts on humankind as signs of pathology is crude and distorting. It feeds a dogmatic optimism that sustains itself through derogation of its critics, a sort of tone-policing that only allows cheery and upbeat accounts of the human world. The American writer Barbara Ehrenreich calls this "bright-siding" in her splendid book *Smile or Die*.

Take, for instance, the fact that the experience of becoming a feminist and becoming initiated into the realities of patriarchy is likely to make you pessimistic and cynical. I take it that this outlook should be respected as a disclosure of important facts about this world, rather than dismissed in a pathologizing way. If people are genuinely serious about understanding the world, they should really start by listening to those people who have painful experience of the realities of that world, rather than just dismissing them as pathological, hysterical, or overwrought.

AM: Some people can exhibit a misanthropic strain in their thinking, but also hold onto a strong belief in new and enriched possibilities for humanity. By contrast, what we might call the "capital M" misanthrope tends to feel that we should not kid ourselves and nothing is really going to change. What do you make of these two misanthropic stances?

IJK: A person can have misanthropic attitudes and moods without being a full-blooded, card-carrying misanthrope. Schopenhauer is right when he says that people become misanthropes through "long, sad" experience of the world. If you have enough of these experiences, it can cultivate a certain mood that can eventually form itself into a doctrine of misanthropy. And I think that many people are really fighting against the tendencies of the misanthropic mood, so they then pull themselves back with more optimistic, bright-siding stories.

To take the pandemic as a case in point, there was a lot of talk of a forthcoming moral renaissance during the first lockdown in the UK. Commentators spoke of a newfound appreciation of the importance of neighbourliness, of compassion, of people pulling together. Personally, I am sceptical about that sort of moral rhetoric. I think that it is rarely the case that even dramatic events bring about this sort of fundamental moral change. I'm sure that many people genuinely enjoyed the sense of neighbourliness during the pandemic. Perhaps they chatted over the fence to their neighbours, pulled together as a street, and so on. But as soon as people feel safe again in their homes and can once again go out in the world, many of those things will simply fall away. If you really want to create positive moral changes that last, perhaps you have to fundamentally change people's habits and the structures of their life.

After all, we've heard these uplifting stories of moral transformation before. You can take any series of catastrophic events in human history and a constant refrain is, "Never again, never again". It was five years ago that the body of Alan Kurdi, a three-year-old Syrian refugee, washed up on a Mediterranean beach. The image of a young child dead, face-down in the ocean, was so appalling that even anti-immigrant newspapers said it must never happen again. But you read those same newspapers right now and they are demanding that the Royal Navy be deployed to turn away desperate refugees. A student of mine was once asked to sum up the concept "despair" in three words and her offering was "Things repeat, always".

AM: It seems to me that the "capital M" misanthrope is largely defined by their approach to action. They may either choose to dismiss or sneer at sentiments of the kind expressed by Bregman, Pinker, and the like. Or they may choose a form of quietism. But, either way, they would be extremely suspicious of any large-scale actions to bring about moral changes in humanity. What do you see as the consequences of misanthropy in terms of acting for change in the world?

IJK: There are different ways to be a misanthrope. I call these ways "misanthropic stances". The misanthropic stance that everyone tends to think of is what Kant calls "the Enemy of Mankind". The enemy is dominated by hatred or enmity, and their response is violence. They try to tear down the human world, to "unmake civilization", as some radical eco-misanthropes put it. But Kant also describes a second stance, "the fugitive from mankind", characterized by fear. They fear the violence human beings do, and they fear their becoming corrupted by the failings of humanity. As a result, their response is not violence, but flight – they pull away from the human world, retreating into monasteries or other isolated locations.

A misanthrope has other options than Enemy and Fugitive, however. Someone like Confucius is what I would call an "activist" misanthrope. He thinks that humankind as it has come to be is morally appalling, but also sees grounds for hope – there are things that can be done. For Confucius, this involves moral teaching, trying to influence rulers and initiate social reforms. Another stance is the "quietist", who thinks human beings are collectively morally appalling, but because there is really very little that can be done to change this a quietist will try to accommodate to the imperfections of the human world by living inconspicuously and keeping their head down. A quietist is still morally engaged – they perform small local acts of care and compassion, for instance – but resist pursuit of ambitious moral projects.

AM: What kind of sceptical response might the quietist have to, say, the activist misanthrope? Why would they be sceptical about the activist's faith in action, especially given that there is a long history of successful actions that have improved the human lot (morally and otherwise)?

IJK: There is a certain strain of argument that owes a lot to conservative political philosophy. It says that because the societies that we live in are organically developed over many, many generations and were not the products of systemic planning, there is always an inherent risk that moral projects might backfire. Big moral projects that aim at rapid and radical changes are dangerous – we cannot always anticipate their consequences, we don't have the time to go slowly and consider them in detail, and so on. You might sincerely think that making radical changes will do things for the best, but how do you know that? No one has an overall view of the hugely complex structures and operations of our social world, so there is a precautionary principle: keep the changes small, modest and local. A related worry shared by many quietists is that radical ambitious projects will supercharge our vices – our vainglory, hubris, reckless and self-righteousness. We often see this in conservative philosophers like Edmund Burke, but it's also there in the *suttas* of the Buddha. Monks should "keep to their own preserves", he says, and stay away from social and political participation. Trying to change the world encourages attachments and worldly ambitions – precisely the things a Buddhist should be trying to dissolve – and, anyway, being a social activist means being assertive and demanding, which is in obvious tension with the sorts of virtues a Buddhist should be cultivating, like quietude, equanimity and tranquillity.

AM: We often ask ourselves what future generations will judge us for. The assumption behind this thought is that future generations will be morally better, more enlightened people than us. What do you make of that kind of stance towards the future?

IJK: Belief in the improvability of humankind can take different forms. Is it something we're able to achieve through our collective rationality, or moral and spiritual practices, or would it require the support of Gods or the machinations of Fate? Does improvement mean overcoming our original sin, or purging ourselves of what Buddhists call the "unwholesome roots" (greed, hatred, delusion), or does it involve radical social reform, or some combination of these things? I suppose there's a pragmatic argument: if we believe that we can be improved, we're more likely to try and improve ourselves. And there's also a good worry about pessimistic self-fulfilling prophecies: if we think we can't get better, we're more inclined to acquiescence in our failings.

However, I think there are big dangers in lazy confidence

that moral progress is inevitable, that we just have to sit back and wait for it to happen. As a general rule, moral progress takes a *vast* amount of effort to realize in practice, and just as much effort to keep it in place. There seems to be some perverse law of social mechanics that moral progress takes a vast amount of energy to achieve, but very little energy to undo. Consider the fact that 80 years ago, it would have been inconceivable to the vast majority of people that National Socialism would ever return, whereas now, of course, we have open National Socialists and resurgent neo-Nazis in Europe and across the United States. It takes an enormous amount of constant moral work just to keep us where we are, and one worry I have about optimists like Bregman is that they make human progress seem much too *easy*. As the ancient Chinese philosopher, Xunzi, put it, goodness is "artificial" in the sense that it's not a natural or inevitable feature of the world. Goodness requires hard work and a disciplined transformation of our dispositions and natural inclinations.

AM: Even if misanthropy is true, should we broadcast the bad news about humanity? This question is partly inspired by Mary Midgley's critique of Richard Dawkins' "selfish gene" idea. She felt that this narrative of selfishness built in at a genetic level was just an extremely bad one to broadcast to humans, as it risks naturalizing, and thus deepening, our vices. In the case of spreading misanthropy as a narrative, it risks deepening, say, our despair, our indifference, our bitterness. What do you make of this kind of worry?

IJK: I think it would be crucial to ask two related questions. First, is a misanthropic verdict accurate? And, second, if it is accurate, is it useful to broadcast it to others? On the second question, misanthropes differ. Montaigne, for instance, clearly regards a misanthropic verdict as *true*, but he thinks it is unwise to broadcast it, except to certain select people. Other misanthropes take the line that if it's true you should broadcast it regardless of the consequences (maybe Schopenhauer falls into that category). But I think the majority of the misanthropes that I've studied are of the much more circumspect Montaignian view that even if it is true, you need to be extremely careful about whether you broadcast it. This is in part because of the reasons you give. It could licence our viciousness. It could be corrupting. It could give people a get-out-of-jail-free card to indulge the worst of their vices. It could cast us into unbearable and destructive despair.

I think that early Buddhism is highly misanthropic, and they give very good reasons for being fairly circumspective about this. These tend to be pragmatic reasons: for one thing, if people recognize that Buddhism is fundamentally a misanthropic appraisal of human beings, it is going to be very hard to recruit people to the Buddha's vision of life. This being the case, it may be wiser to open with happier things, like meditation, mindfulness and the cultivation of virtues. Once those practitioners are on board and psychologically and morally ready, they can then be presented with the truths of misanthropy. For the Buddha, misanthropy is not simply a paper doctrine; rather, it affects how we experience and engage with the world. It transforms how we live and think and feel. It is interesting that historical misanthropes, like the Buddha, have tended to be members of very small and intimate communities. They did not try to practise their misanthropy alone. I think one reason is that without friendship and collegiality and support people would find it difficult to bear emotionally the costs of misanthropy and would sink into a state of nihilism.

FURTHER RESOURCES

Andrew Gibson, *Misanthropy: The Critique of Humanity*. London: Bloomsbury, 2017.

Ian James Kidd, "Varieties of philosophical misanthropy". *Journal of Philosophical Research* 46 (2021): 27–44.

Mara van der Lugt, "Pessimism". *The Philosopher* 107:4 (2019).

Judith N. Shklar, *Ordinary Vices*. Cambridge, MA: Harvard University Press, 1985.

Index